WILLIAM LANGLAND

The probable author of *Piers Plowman*,
lived from *c*. 1332 to *c*. 1400.

WILLIAM LANGLAND

The Book Concerning Piers the Plowman

RENDERED INTO
MODERN ENGLISH BY
DONALD AND RACHEL ATTWATER

EDITED BY
RACHEL ATTWATER, M.A.

DENT: LONDON
EVERYMAN'S LIBRARY
DUTTON: NEW YORK

All rights reserved
Made in Great Britain
at the
Aldine Press · Letchworth · Herts
for
J. M. DENT & SONS LTD
Aldine House · Bedford Street · London
First included in Everyman's Library 1907
This translation first published in Everyman's Library 1957
Last reprinted 1967

NO. *571*

INTRODUCTION

THE POEM.   The work called compendiously *The Book concerning Piers the Plowman* (*Liber de Petro Plowman*) is known in forty-seven manuscripts, in which scholars have agreed to recognize three versions of the text, called respectively the A-text, written soon after 1362; the B-text, written about 1378; and the C-text, written in 1398 or 1399.   Each text contains two distinct parts (though they are not generally distinguished in the manuscripts), namely, The Vision of William concerning Piers the Plowman and the Vision of the same concerning Do-well, Do-better, and Do-best.   The standard editions of these texts are those of Dr W. W. Skeat, published by the Early English Text Society, in four volumes, in 1867–84, and by the Clarendon Press in two volumes, 1886.   The various known manuscripts are written in a mixture of the Midland and Southern dialects of Middle English, somewhat influenced by the Western dialect; but they vary considerably, both in dialect and text.   That on which Professor Skeat based his B-text is MS. Laud Misc. 581 in the Bodleian Library.

THE AUTHOR.   The authorship of this poem has been the subject of a wordy and involved dispute among literary historians and critics.   The traditional view, resting partly on external but mainly on internal evidence, was that the author's christening name was William, for he refers to himself as Will in several passages, and his name is given as William in most of the manuscripts; that his surname was Langland (which is given in two early manuscripts, one of which adds the information that he was son of one Stacy de Rokayle, who held land at Shipton-under-Wychwood); that he was born at Cleobury Mortimer about 1332 (according to a writer one hundred and fifty years later); that he was put to school, probably with the Benedictines at Great Malvern; that he became a clerk in minor orders and wrote *The Book concerning Piers Plowman* (A-text) shortly after he had gone to London, where he later re-wrote and enlarged the poem (B-text); and he lived for many years on Cornhill with his wife Kit and his daughter Kalote (that he married accounts for his not being further ordained); that he earned a precarious and poor living by such clerical means (in both senses) as he might, that he wore the clerical tonsure and dress, and that he was so tall as to be known familiarly as Long Will; that he again revised his poem (C-text), and died we know not when nor where.

With minor variations this account of the writer and the writing of the poem was accepted without question until the beginning of this century, when Professor J. M. Manly produced a theory, supported by textual evidence, that the poem was written not by one but by five persons: not, of course, in concert, but as independent editors and continuers. This provoked a very pretty battle of the kind in which literary historians and textual critics delight. Dr Furnivall and Dr Henry Bradley, with some hesitation, supported the conclusions of Professor Manly; and M. Jusserand led the single-author party, whose case was strengthened by the researches of Professor R. W. Chambers: articles, replies, pamphlets, rejoinders, letters and counter-letters were written and published; Langland was 'on trial for his life,' he was sentenced, hanged, drawn, quartered, and resuscitated— several times over.

But in spite of the difficulties raised by these learned men, it may be said with confidence that the balance of literary, textual, philological, and metrical evidence is still on the side of a single author; and that this author was William Langland has found fresh and valuable support in later investigations of a kind too little used in the solving of literary and historical puzzles, namely, research, inquiry, and observation in the neighbourhood concerned. It appears clear from the work of Mr Allan H. Bright (*New Light on 'Piers Plowman,'* Oxford, 1928) that we may continue to hold undisturbed the traditional account of Long Will, with two important modifications, namely, that he was born not at Cleobury in Cheshire but at Ledbury in Hereford-shire, and that he was the *illegitimate* son of Stacy de Rokayle.

THIS VERSION. Of the prologue and first seven *passus* of the B-text, for the version of which herein I alone am responsible, several translations into modern English have been made. My object in making another was simply and solely to produce a version with the minimum of alteration and verbal substitution of the Middle English text necessary for its understanding by an ordinary reader in the twentieth century. To do this, and at the same time always to retain the original alliterative metre, was impossible; nor did this grieve me overmuch: for Langland himself kept on breaking the metrical rules, either because he was more interested in the sense than the sound, or else because he did not think regularity necessary to make a good poem—he was no 'literary man,' and his academic fame to-day doubtless astonishes him. I paraphrased as little as possible, preferring a few obscurities to excessive messing about with the text. Those who wish for a straightforward version, in prose and with all things made clear, cannot do better than that of Miss Kate Warren (London, 1913); for a metrical version, with the poem sacrificed to the verse, there is that of Professor Skeat (London, 1905): I used both of these for reference purposes, especially Miss Warren's, which is an excellent piece of work.

Without the erudition and monumental labours of Professor Skeat this version would have been impossible, and I have to make acknowledgment to the Delegates of the Oxford University Press for their permission to use his B-text, the minor edition in the Clarendon Press Series, of which the ninth edition was published in 1906. I must also acknowledge my indebtedness for help and information to Mr Allan H. Bright.

THE THEME. Whatever may be the literary, philological, and historical importance of *The Book concerning Piers Plowman*, its interest to the ordinary reader is still the same as it was to its writer, namely, personal. I have said that Langland was not a 'literary man,' least of all in the self-conscious modern sense— perhaps the expression has no other sense: anyway, he was not primarily a man of art but a man of prudence, in fact, a moralist. And his poem is a tract. Therein is its interest to-day as in the fourteenth century; that is why it is republished in cheap editions and read by others beside professors and students. However much human nature may change superficially, men continue to have a bias towards inordinate behaviour in thought, word, and deed, and so long as we have that characteristic, whether the resulting disorder be regarded as 'sinful' or as simply 'anti-social,' so long will moralists, professional or amateur, rise up and endeavour to reduce us to the ways of virtue.

And the miserable sinners, however unwilling we may be to be cured of our distemper, are far from being uninterested in the attempts to do so; some even acquire considerable skill in criticism of the efforts; and this interest in our physicians is not an exhibition of diabolical cynicism. For we know that the moralist is really in the right of it; that the heart of man does tend to be desperately wicked—however you like to account for it; that left to ourselves we shall make a hell of this world and deserve the same in the next; that God is not mocked.

So Langland's poem is read, not indeed deliberately as an ascetical exercise, but because it is a good tract, a bit of moralist's work well done: the poem and the argument are one thing, and that thing gratifies our mind in general and satisfies our conscience in particular.

Those who have never read the book commonly suppose it to be an attack on the iniquities of those in places of power and advantage, especially of spiritual authority: that the author was a morning-star of the Reformation and a forerunner of what is called modern democracy. This is a complete misunderstanding. Langland was a faithful son of the medieval Church, and his politics were anything but 'radical': the State should be governed by a Prince, the personification but not the nominee or the tool of his people, whom he rules with the aid of Conscience and Reason. And his attack on wickedness and abuses was not by way of direct denouncement, of rhetoric (in its improper sense), or a playing on the feelings of a mob; but a logical explanation directed at common sense and right reason. 'This,' he said in effect, 'is how you behave, poor and rich, lowly as well as great. Of course it must follow that the world is in a mess and you are unhappy.' There is none of the demagoguery which flatters our self-esteem and tickles our lust for change, telling us what fine fellows we are and that it is our institutions that are at fault. On the contrary. He makes it clear enough to his contemporaries that their institutions were all right, but their human weakness and ill-will misused them or made them helpless. 'Christianity has been tried and has failed.' 'It has not failed because it has not been tried.' Langland's one remedy for the troubles of his day was religion: he was therefore not a social reformer in the classical sense.

The efforts of moralists, especially Christian moralists, are less effective than they should be, and bring down dislike and contempt on their makers, because the impression is so often given that the moralist views with jealousy, or is trying improperly to narrow the bounds of, lawful human enjoyment. The notion is quite wrong and quite understandable. The average professional moralist has only average insight, energy, enthusiasm, and spirituality, and so he takes the easiest line, concentrates on the more obviously disorderly actions and abuses of acts intrinsically good, and denounces and exhorts with a lamentable lack of discrimination and finesse, meeting exaggeration with exaggeration.

Not so Langland. 'Chastity without charity shall be chained in Hell,' he says, and has done. Charity, that is, not a vague benevolence, a 'universal embrace,' or even just refraining from adverse speech and being kind (especially to those one likes), but the habit or virtue which enables men to love God above all things for His own sake and for His sake to love all their fellow men; the *agape* of St Paul. It goes to the root of the matter, psychologically, theologically, and spiritually. He does not exhort his hearers to fantastic penances, to heroic renunciations, to revolutionary changes, to action against their proper state and personal nature: the rich are not abused for being rich, but told to have pity on the poor; the poor are to work and not over-reach their neighbours; the monk is not told to leave his cloister and get busy in the world, for prayer is work, and Christ ordained the contemplative life; those who will not work shall be coerced by Hunger, yet no beggar must be refused *quia incertum pro quo Deo magis placeas*; trade is not condemned, but merchants must try to be honest (Langland does not seem very hopeful about this); neither is the law condemned, but lawyers must observe equity; nothing shall be done out of measure. In a word, he preaches on the text of St Augustine: *Dilige et quod vis fac*, Love, and do what you will.

Joined with Charity as handmaidens of Truth (God the Father) is Reason. Charity is not personified in the poem, but Reason is, and the part he plays may be studied profitably both by those who have old-fashioned ideas about the 'ages of faith' and those who have new-fashioned and sub-human ideas about the worthlessness of intellectual processes. To Reason Conscience appeals against his projected wedding to Meed ('Graft'); with Conscience he is made the perpetual counsellor of the King; and his sermon moves the Deadly Sins to confess themselves to Repentance. Then, and not till then, towards the end of Passus V, does Piers himself appear on the scene, and he quickly develops from the hard-working, God-fearing yeoman farmer, taught by Truth through Conscience and Mother-Wit, into what is practically an incarnation of God the Son, embodying in himself Reason, Conscience, Mother-Wit, and the rest. Christ, as man, is the common man, Piers Plowman. To him God the Father entrusts the dispensing of a bull of pardon surpassing all others, that supreme indulgence which is man's Redemption and the price of which is good deeds, both spiritual and corporal.

DONALD ATTWATER.

1930.

The second part of the poem, *The Vision of Do-well, Do-better, and Do-best*, is a broadening and deepening of the theme. The strictures on the life of the world, and especially on the ways of church dignitaries in relation to that world, are still there in abundance. But Langland is primarily examining the fundamental principles on which his strictures rest. What is in fact 'the good life'? What is it to do well, to do better, and to do best? His illustrations and parallels are many and varied, but they are finally all taken up into the life of our Lord, and especially His death and resurrection. The poem, however, does not end on any such devotional climax. In Passus XIX Langland returns, or rather goes forward, to the church of to-day, as it were, working, suffering, fighting the arrayed forces of evil and betrayals from within not always with conspicuous success. Finally Conscience, in great distress, sets out to seek Piers the Plowman—Langland's continued symbol of integrity, from the man working in the field to Christ Himself. The pilgrimage has only just begun.

In making a version of the B-text of *The Vision of Do-well, Do-better, and Do-best* I have followed the same principles as those which directed the version of *The Vision of Piers Plowman*; that is, making changes only as it was necessary for clarification for the modern reader. It has been attempted to preserve the style of Langland, his own peculiar 'flavour,' which includes not only variety but a lack of academic care (if we do not call it carelessness) which makes such treatment not only possible but rewarding.

RACHEL ATTWATER.

1957.

SELECT BIBLIOGRAPHY

EDITIONS. W. W. Skeat: *The Vision of William concerning Piers the Plowman.* 2 vols. Oxford, 1886 (the standard edition of all three texts); *Publications of the Early English Text Society*, Nos. 28, 38, 54, 81 (separate editions of A, B, and C Texts, with notes and glosses).

TRANSLATIONS. W. W. Skeat: *The Vision of Piers Plowman*, London (1906); K. M. Warren: *The Vision of Piers the Plowman*, London (1913) (Prose. Prologue and Passus, B Text); H. W. Wells: *The Vision of Piers Plowman*, London (1935) (Verse. Whole poem); N. K. Coghill: *Visions from Piers Plowman*, London (1949) (Verse. Selections); J. F. Goodridge: *Piers the Ploughman*, Harmondsworth (1959) (Prose. Complete poem, B Text).

STUDIES. (*a*) *General*

D. Chadwick: *Social Life in the Days of Piers Plowman*, Cambridge (1922); R. W. Chambers: 'Long Will, Dante, and the Righteous Heathen,' *Essays and Studies*, 9; N. K. Coghill: 'The Character of Piers Plowman considered from the B Text,' in *Medium Aevum*, 2. 108–135, 1933; F. A. R. Carnegy: *The Relations between the Social and Divine Order in William Langland's Vision*, Breslau (1934); G. Hort: *Piers Plowman and Contemporary Religious Thought*, London (1938); R. W. Chambers: *Man's Unconquerable Mind*, chs. 4 and 5, London (1939); N. K. Coghill: *The Pardon of Piers Plowman*, London (1946).

(*b*) *Authorship, date, construction*

The Piers Plowman Controversy. Publications of the Early English Text Society, 139. Extra issue, 1910 (essays by Jusserand, Manly, Chambers, and Bradley); R. W. Chambers: 'Text of Piers Plowman: Critical Methods,' in *Modern Language Review* (Cambridge), *11*. 257–275 (1916); 'The Three Texts of Piers Plowman and their Grammatical Forms,' in *Modern Language Review*, *14*. 129–51 (1919); 'The Text of Piers Plowman' (with Grattan) in *Modern Language Review*, *26*. 1–51 (1926); A. H. Bright: *New Light on 'Piers Plowman*,' London (1928); J. A. W. Bennett: 'The Date of the B Text of Piers Plowman' in *Medium Aevum*, 11. 55–64 (1943); G. H. Gerould: 'The Structural Integrity of Piers Plowman' in *Studies in English Philology*, *45*. 60–75 (1948); J. R. Hulbert: 'Piers the Plowman after Forty Years' in *Modern Philology* (Chicago), *45*. 215–25 (1948); B. F. Huppé: 'Piers Plowman: the Date of the B Text Reconsidered' in *Studies in English Philology*, *46*. 6–13 (1949).

PUBLISHER'S NOTE

The Donald Attwater translation of *The Vision* is reproduced here by arrangement with Messrs Cassell & Co. Ltd.   *Do-well, Do-better and Do-best* is based on Dr Skeat's edition (1886) by permission of the Clarendon Press, Oxford.

CONTENTS

The poem is written in the traditional long alliterative line which is divided in two by a caesura, each part being linked by alliteration or 'initial rhyme.' In the present rendering this pause is indicated by a space.

INCIPIT LIBER
DE PETRO PLOWMAN

PROLOGUS

IN a summer season   when soft was the sun,
I clothed myself in a cloak   as I shepherd were,
Habit like a hermit's   unholy in works,
And went wide in the world   wonders to hear.
But on a May morning   on Malvern hills,
A marvel befell me   of fairy, methought.
I was weary with wandering   and went me to rest
Under a broad bank   by a brook's side,
And as I lay and leaned over   and looked into the waters
I fell into a sleep   for it sounded so merry.

Then began I to dream   a marvellous dream,
That I was in a wilderness   wist I not where.
As I looked to the east   right into the sun,
I saw a tower on a toft   worthily built;
A deep dale beneath   a dungeon therein,
With deep ditches and dark   and dreadful of sight.
A fair field full of folk   found I in between,
Of all manner of men   the rich and the poor,
Working and wandering   as the world asketh.
Some put them to plow   and played little enough,
At setting and sowing   they sweated right hard
And won that which wasters   by gluttony destroy.

Some put them to pride   and apparelled themselves so
In a display of clothing   they came disguised.

To prayer and penance   put themselves many,
All for love of our Lord   living hard lives,
In hope for to have   heavenly bliss.
Such as anchorites and hermits   that kept them in their cells,
And desired not the country   around to roam;
Nor with luxurious living   their body to please.

And some chose trade   they fared the better,
As it seemeth to our sight   that such men thrive.

And some to make mirth   as minstrels know how,
And get gold with their glees   guiltlessly, I hold.
But jesters and janglers   children of Judas,
Feigning their fancies   and making folk fools,
They have wit at will   to work, if they would;
Paul preacheth of them   I'll not prove it here—
Qui turpiloquium loquitur   is Lucifer's hind.

Tramps and beggars   went quickly about,
Their bellies and their bags   with bread well crammed:
Cadging for their food   fighting at ale;
In gluttony, God knows   going to bed,
And getting up with ribaldry   the thieving knaves!
Sleep and sorry sloth   ever pursue them.

Pilgrims and palmers   pledged them together
To seek Saint James   and saints in Rome.
They went forth on their way   with many wise tales,
And had leave to lie   all their life after—
I saw some that said   they had sought saints:
Yet in each tale that they told   their tongue turned to lies
More than to tell truth   it seemed by their speech.

Hermits, a heap of them   with hooked staves,
Were going to Walsingham   and their wenches too;
Big loafers and tall   that loth were to work,
Dressed up in capes   to be known from others;
And so clad as hermits   their ease to have.

I found there friars [1]   of all the four orders,
Preaching to the people   for profit to themselves,
Explaining the Gospel   just as they liked,
To get clothes for themselves   they construed it as they would.
Many of these master friars   may dress as they will,
For money and their preaching   both go together.
For since charity hath been chapman   and chief to shrive lords,
Many miracles have happened   within a few years.
Except Holy Church and they   agree better together,
Great mischief on earth   is mounting up fast.

There preached a pardoner [2]   as if he priest were:
He brought forth a brief   with bishops' seals thereon,
And said that himself might   absolve them all
From falseness in fasting   and of broken vows.
Laymen believed him   welcomed his words,

[1] See page 202.   [2] See page 202.

And came up on their knees   to kiss his seals;
He cozened them with his brevet   dimmed their eyes,
And with his parchment   got his rings and brooches:
Thus they gave their gold   gluttons to keep.
And lend it to such louts   as follow lechery.
If the bishop were holy   and worth both his ears,
His seal should not be sent   to deceive the people.
But a word 'gainst bishop   the knave never preacheth.
Parish priest and pardoner   share all the silver
That the parish poor would have   if he were not there.
    Parsons and parish priests   complained to the bishop
That their parishes were poor   since the pestilence time,
And asked leave and licence   in London to dwell
And sing *requiems* for stipends   for silver is sweet.
    Bishops and bachelors [1]   both masters and doctors,
That have charge under Christ   and the tonsure as token
And sign that they should   shrive their parishioners,
Preach and pray for them   and feed the poor,
These lodge in London in Lent   and at other times too.
Some serve the king   and his silver count
In Chequer and Chancery courts   making claim for his debts
Of wards and of wardmotes   waifs and estrays.
And some serve as servants   to lords and ladies,
And instead of stewards   sit in session to judge.
Their Mass and their matins   their canonical hours,
Are said undevoutly   I fear at the last
Lest Christ in his council   accurse will full many.
I perceived of the power   that Peter had to keep,
To bind and to unbind   as the Book telleth,
How he left it with love   as our Lord ordained,
Amongst four virtues   the best of all virtues,
That cardinal are called   for they hinge the gates
Where Christ is in glory   to close and to shut
And to open it to them   and show heavenly bliss.
But of cardinals at Rome   that received that name
And power presumed in them   a pope to make,
To have Peter's power   deny it I will not;
For to love and learning   that election belongeth,
Therefore I can, and yet cannot   of that court speak more.
    Then came there a king   with knighthood before him,

[1] See page 202.

The might of the commons   made him to reign;
Then came Mother-Wit   and he made wise clerks
For to counsel the king   and the commons save.
  The king and the knighthood   the clergy as well,
Planned that the commons   should provide for themselves.
  The commons contrived   of Mother-Wit, crafts,
And for profit of all   they plowmen ordained
To till and travail   as true life asketh.
The king and the commons   and Mother-Wit too
Cause by law and loyalty   each man to know his own.
  Then looked up a lunatic   a lean thing withal,
And kneeling before the king   well speaking said:
'Christ keep thee sir King   and thy kingdom,
And grant thee to rule the realm   so Loyalty may love thee,
And for thy rightful ruling   be rewarded in heaven.'
  Then in the air on high   an angel of heaven
Stooped and spoke in Latin   for simple men could not
Discuss nor judge   that which should justify them,
But should suffer and serve   therefore said the angel:
    '*Sum Rex, sum Princeps: neutram fortasse deinceps;*
      O qui jura regis Christi specialia regis, hoc quod agas melius justus es,
        esto pius!
      Nudum jus a te vestiri vult pietate; qualia vis metere talia grana sere.
      Si jus nudatur nudo de jure metatur; si seritur pietas de pietate metas.'
  Then an angry buffoon   a glutton of words,
To the angel on high   answered after:
    '*Dum rex a regere dicatur nomen habere,*
      Nomen habet sine re nisi studet jura tenere.'
  Then began all the commons   to cry out in Latin,
For counsel of the king   construe how-so he would:
    '*Praecepta regis sunt nobis vincula legis.*'
  [1] With that there ran a rout   of rats at once,
And small mice with them   more than a thousand,
And came to a council   for their common profit;
For a cat from the Court   came when he liked
And o'er leaped them lightly   and caught them at will,
Played with them perilously   and pushed them about.
'For dread of divers dangers   we dare not look about;
If we grumble at his game   he will attack us all,
Scratch us or clutch us   and in his claws hold us,

[1] See page 202.

So that we loathe life   ere he lets us go.
Could we with any wit   his will withstand
We might be lords above him   and live at our ease.'
  A rat of renown   most ready of tongue
Said, as a sovereign   help to himself:
'I have seen men,' quoth he   'in the city of London
Bearing bright necklaces   about their necks,
Some with collars of skilful work   uncoupled they wander
Both in warrens and wastes   wherever they like;
And otherwhile they are elsewhere   as I tell you.
Were there a bell on their collars   by Jesus, I think
Men might know where they went   and get out of their way!
And right so,' quoth that rat   'reason me showeth
To buy a brass bell   or one of bright silver
Make it fast to a collar   for our common profit,
And hang it on the cat's neck   then we may hear
When he romps or rests   or runneth to play.
And if he wants play   then we may look out
And appear in his presence   the while he play liketh,
And if he gets angry, beware   and shun all his paths.'
All this rout of rats   to this plan assented.
But though the bell was bought   and on the collar hanged,
There was not a rat in the rout   for all the realm of France
That dare bind on the bell   about the cat's neck,
Nor hang it round her ears   all England to win;
They held themselves not bold   and their counsel feeble,
Esteemed their labour as lost   and all their long plotting.
  A mouse that knew much more   as it seemed to me,
Ran forth determined   and stood before them all,
And to the rout of rats   rehearsed these words:
'Though we killed the cat   yet there would come another,
To scratch us and all our kind   though we creep under benches.
Therefore I counsel all the commons   to let the cat be,
And be we never so bold   to show to him the bell;
For I heard my sire say   now seven years ago,
"When the cat is a kitten   the Court is right wretched,"
As witnesseth Holy Writ   whoso will it read:
     "*Vae tibi, terra, cujus rex puer est.*"
No man can have rest there   for the rats by night;
While the cat catcheth conies   he covets not our carrion,
But feeds himself on venison   may we never defame him!

For better is a little loss   than a long sorrow;
He's the fear among us all   whereby we miss worse things.
For many men's malt   we mice would destroy,
And the riot of rats   would rend men's clothes,
Were it not for that Court cat   that can leap in among you;
For had ye rats your will   ye could not rule yourselves.
As for me,' quoth the mouse   'I see so much to come
That cat nor kitten never shall   by my counsel be harmed,
Nor carping of this collar   that cost me nothing.
Though it had cost me full dear   I would not own to it
But suffer him to live   and do just as he liketh:
Coupled and uncoupled   to catch what they can.
Therefore each wise wight I warn   to watch well his own.'
   What this dream meaneth   ye men that be merry,
Divine ye, for I never dare   by dear God in heaven!
   There hovered an hundred   in caps of silk,
Serjeants they seemed   who practised at Bar,
Pleading the law   for pennies and pounds,
And never for love of our Lord   unloosing their lips.
You might better measure the mist   on the Malvern hills,
Than get a sound out of their mouth   unless money were showed.
   Barons and burgesses   and bondmen also
I saw in this crowd   as you shall hear later.
Bakers and brewers   and butchers a-many,
Woollen-websters   and weavers of linen,
Tailors and tinkers   toll-takers in markets,
Masons and miners   and men of all crafts.
Of all kinds of labourers   there stood forth some;
Ditchers and diggers   that do their work ill
And spend all the day singing   '*Dieu vous sauve, dame Emme!*'
Cooks and their knaves   cried 'Pies, hot pies!
Good pork and good goose!   Come, dine!   Come, dine!'
   Taverners unto them   told the same tale:
'White wine of Alsace   red wine of Gascony,
Wine of the Rhine, of Rochelle   to help settle your meat!'
All this I saw sleeping   and seven times more.

PASSUS I

WHAT this mountain meaneth   and the dark dale
And the field full of folk   I fairly will show.
A lady, lovely of looks   in linen clothed,
Came down from a castle   and called me fairly
And said: 'Son, sleepest thou?   Seest thou this people,
How busy they be   about all the throng?
The most part of this people   that passeth on earth,
Have worship in this world   and wish for no better;
Of other heaven than here   they hold no account.'
  I was feared of her face   though she were so fair,
And said, 'Mercy, madam   what is this to mean?'
'The tower on the toft,' quoth she   'Truth is therein
And would have that ye do   as his word teacheth;
For he is Father of Faith   formed you all
Both with flesh and with face   and gave you fine wits
To worship him therewith   while that ye are here.
Therefore he hath bade the earth   to help you each one
With woollen, with linen   with food at your need,
In reasonable measure   to make you at ease.
  'And commanded of his courtesy   three things in common.
None are needful but those   and name them I will
And reckon them rightly   rehearse thou them after.
The first one is vesture   to save thee from chill;
And meat for meals   to save thee misease
And drink when thou art dry   but do naught out of reason
Lest thy worth be wanting   when thou shouldest work.
  'For Lot in his lifetime   for liking of drink
Did with his daughters   what the Devil liked.
He delighted in drink   as the Devil wished,
And Lechery was gainer   and lay with them both,
Putting blame on the wine   for that wicked deed:
> *Inebriamus eum vino, dormiamusque cum eo, ut servare possimus de*
> *patre nostro semen.*
Through wine and through women   there was Lot overcome,
Begetting in gluttony   boys that were blackguards.

7

Therefore dread delicious drink   and thou shalt do the better;
Measure is medicine   though thou yearn for much.
All is not good for the spirit   that the guts asketh,
Nor livelihood to thy body   that is life to the soul.
Believe not thy body   for him a liar teacheth:
That is, the wretched world   which would thee betray.
For the fiend and thy flesh   follow thee together;
This and that chaseth thy soul   and speak in thine heart;
That thou shouldest be ware   I teach thee the best.'
    'Madam, mercy,' quoth I   'I like well your words.
But the money of this earth   that men hold to so fast,
Tell me, madam, to whom   that treasure belongeth?'
    'Go to the Gospel,' quoth she   'that God spoke himself,
When the people posed him   with a penny in the Temple,
Whether they should therewith   worship king Caesar.
And God asked of them   of whom spake the writing
And likewise the image   that stood thereon?
"*Caesaris,*" they said   "Each one sees him well."
    "'*Reddite Caesari,*" quoth God   "that *Caesari* belongeth,
Et quae sunt Dei, Deo   or else ye do ill."
For rightful Reason   should rule you all,
And Mother-Wit be warden   your wealth to keep,
And tutor of your treasure   to give it you at need;
For husbandry and they   hold well together.'
Then I asked her plainly   by him that made her,
'That dungeon in the dale   that dreadful is to see,
What may it mean   *ma dame*, I beseech you?'
    'That is the castle of Care   whoso cometh therein
May curse he was born   in body or in soul.
Therein abideth a wight   that is called Wrong,
Father of Falsehood   who built it himself.
Adam and Eve   he egged on to ill;
Counselled Cain   to kill his brother;
Judas he jockeyed   with Jewish silver,
And then on an elder   hanged him after.
He is the letter of love   and lieth to all;
Those who trust in his treasure   betrayeth he soonest.'
    Then had I wonder in my wit   what woman it were
That such wise words   of Holy Writ showed,
And asked her in the high name   ere she thence went,
Who indeed she was   that taught me so fairly?

'Holy Church I am,' quoth she   'thou oughtest me to know.
I received thee first   and taught thee the faith,
And thou broughtest me sponsors   my bidding to fulfil
And to love me loyally   while thy life lasteth.'
    Then I fell on my knees   and cried of her grace,
And prayed her piteously   to pray for my sins,
And to teach me kindly   on Christ to believe,
That I might work his will   that made of me man.
'Show me no treasure   but tell me this only—
How may I save my soul   thou that holy art held?'
    'When all treasures are tried,' quoth she   'truth is the best;
I appeal to *Deus caritas*   to tell thee truth;
It is as dear a darling   as dear God himself.
    'Whoso is true of his tongue   and telleth none other,
And doth works therewith   and willeth no man ill:
He is a god, says the Gospel   on earth and in heaven,
And like to our Lord   by Saint Luke's own words.
The clergy that know this   should tell it about,
For Christian and heathen   alike claim the truth.
    'Kings and their knights all   should care for it rightly;
Ride to reach the oppressors   all round the realms,
And take *trangressores*   tying them tightly,
Till Truth had determined   the tale of their trespass.
That profession plainly   pertaineth to knights;
Not to fast on one Friday   in five score winters,
But hold with him and with her   that desireth all truth
And never leave them for love   nor for seizing of silver.
    'For David in his days   dubbed knights,
And swore them on their swords   to serve Truth ever;
And whoso passed that point   *apostata* was from the order.
    'But Christ, king of all kings   ten orders knighted,
Cherubim and Seraphim   seven such and one other,
And gave them might of his majesty   the merrier they thought it;
And over his common court   made them archangels,
Taught them by the Trinity   the truth to know
And to bow to his bidding   he bade them naught else.
    'Lucifer with his legions   learned it in Heaven,
But because he obeyed not   his bliss he did lose,
And fell from that fellowship   in a fiend's likeness
Into a deep dark hell   to dwell there for ever;
And more thousands with him   than man could number

Leapt out with Lucifer   in loathly form:
For they believed in him   that lied in this manner—
    Ponam pedem in aquilone, et similis ero altissimo.
    'And all that hoped it might be so   no Heaven might hold them;
They fell out in fiend's likeness   nine days together,
Till God of his goodness   steadied and stayed
Made the heavens to be shut   and stand so in quiet.
    'When these wicked went out   wonderwise they fell;
Some in air, some in earth   and some in deep hell;
But Lucifer lowest   lieth of them all.
For the pride he put on   his pain hath no end;
And all that work wrong   wander they shall
After their death day   and dwell with that wretch.
But those that work well   as holy writ telleth,
And end, as I have said   in truth, that is best,
May be sure that their soul   shall wend to Heaven,
Where Truth is in Trinity   and enthroneth them all.
Therefore I say, as I said   in sight of these texts,
When all treasures are tried   Truth is the best.
Learn these unlearned   for lettered men know it,
That Truth is treasure   the best tried on earth.'
    'Yet have I no natural knowing,'[1] quoth I   'ye must teach me better,
By what craft of my body   begins it, and where.'
    'Thou doting duffer,' quoth she   'dull are thy wits;
Too little Latin thou learnest   man, in thy youth;
    Heu mihi, quod sterilem duxi vitam juvenilem!
    'It is natural knowing,' quoth she   'that teacheth thine heart
For to love thy good Lord   liefer than thyself;
No deadly sin to do   die though thou shouldest:
This I trow to be Truth   who can teach thee better,
See you suffer him to say   and then teach it after.
For thus witnesseth his words   work thou thereafter;
For Truth telleth that Love   is the remedy of Heaven;
No sin may be seen in him   that useth that sort,
And all his works he wrought   with Love as he listed;
And taught it Moses for the best thing   and most like to Heaven
With the plant of peace   most precious of virtues.
    'For Heaven might not hold it   so heavy of itself,
Till it had of the earth   eaten its fill.
    'And when it had of this fold   flesh and blood taken,

[1] See page 202.

Never was leaf upon linden   lighter thereafter,
And pricking and piercing   as the point of a needle,
That no armour might stay it   nor any high walls.
     'Therefore is Love leader   of the Lord's folk of Heaven,
And a mean, as the mayor is   between king and commons;
Right so is Love a leader   and the law shapeth,
Upon man for his misdeeds   he fixeth the fine.
And for to know it by nature   it springeth in might,
In the heart is its head   and there its well-spring.
     'For in natural knowing   there might beginneth
That comes from the Father   that formed us all,
Looked on us with love   and let his Son die
Meekly for our misdeeds   to amend us all;
And yet would he them no woe   that wrought him that pain,
But meekly with his mouth   mercy he besought
To have pity of that people   that pained him to death.
     'Here might thou see examples   in himself alone,
That he was mightful and meek   and mercy did grant
To them that hanged him on high   and pierced his heart.
     'Therefore I rede you rich   to have pity on the poor;
Though ye be mighty at law   be meek in your works.
     'For the same measures that ye mete   amiss or aright,
Ye shall be weighed therewith   when ye wend hence;
          Eadem mensura qua mensi fueritis, remetietur vobis.
     'For though ye be true of your tongue   and honestly earn,
And as chaste as a child   that weepeth in church,
Unless ye love loyally   and give to the poor,
Such goods as God sends you   to them gladly giving,
Ye have no more merit   in Mass or in hours
Than Malkin of her maidenhood   that no man desireth.
     'For James the gentle   judged in his books
That faith without deed   is right nothing worth
And as dead as a door-post   unless actions follow;
          Fides sine operibus mortua est, etc.
     'Therefore chastity without charity   shall be chained in hell;
It is lacking as a lamp   that no light is in.
Many churchmen are chaste   but their charity is away;
Are no men more avaricious   when they be advanced:
Unkind to their kin   and to all Christian folk,
They chew up their charity   and chide after more.
Such chastity without charity   shall be chained in hell.

'Many pastors keep themselves   clean in their bodies
But are cumbered with covetousness   they can not drive it from them
So hardly hath avarice   hasped them together.
And that is no truth of the Trinity   but treachery of hell,
Lessoning the unlearned   to withhold their alms.
    'Therefore these words   are written in the Gospel,
Date et dabitur vobis   for I give to you all.
And that is the lock of Love   that letteth out my grace
To comfort the care-full   encumbered with sin.
    'Love is leech of life   and next our Lord's self,
And also the right road   that runneth unto Heaven;
Therefore I say as I said   before by the texts,
When all treasures be tried   Truth is the best.
Now have I told thee what Truth is   that no treasure is better;
I may linger no longer thee with   now look on thee our Lord!'

PASSUS II

YET I knelt on my knees   and cried of her grace,
And said: 'Mercy, Madame   for Mary's love of Heaven,
That bore that blissful Child   that bought us on the rood,
Teach me by some skilled way   Falsehood to know.'

  'Look upon thy left side   and lo! where he standeth,
Both Falsehood and Flattery   and their many fellows!'

  I looked on my left side   as the lady taught me,
And was ware of a woman   worthily clothed,
With fringes of fur   the finest on earth,
Crowned with a crown   the king hath no better
Featly her fingers   were framed with gold wire,
And thereon red rubies   as red as any coal,
And diamonds of dearest price   and two kinds of sapphires,
Orientals and beryls   poison banes to destroy.

  Her robe was full rich   of red scarlet dyed,
With ribands of red gold   and of richest stones;
Her array me ravished   such riches saw I never;
I had wonder what she was   and whose wife she were.

  'What is this woman,' quoth I   'so worthily attired?'
'That is Meed [1] the Maid,' quoth she   'who hath vexed me full oft,
And lied of my lover   that Loyalty is called,
And slandered him to lords   that have to guard laws;
In the pope's palace   familiar as myself,
Though truth would not so   for she is a bastard.

  'For Flattery was her father   that had a fickle tongue
And never said sooth   since he came to earth.
And Meed is mannered after him   right as nature requireth;
     Qualis pater, talis filius bona arbor bonum fructum facit.

  'I ought to be higher than she   my birth is the better.
My father the great God is   and ground of all graces,
One infinite God   and I his good daughter;
And he gave me Mercy   to marry with myself.
And what man be merciful   and loyally me love
Shall be my lord, I his lover   in highest Heaven.

  'And what man taketh Meed   mine head dare I lay
That he shall lose for her love   a lot of *caritatis.*
How construeth David the king   of men that take Meed

[1] See page 202.

13

And of men of this mould   that maintaineth Truth
And how ye shall save yourselves   the Psalter beareth witness:
    Domine, quis habitabit in tabernaculo tuo, etc.
  'And now will Meed be married   all to a cursed wretch,
To one False-Fickle-Tongue   offspring of a fiend.
Flattery through his fair speech   hath this folk enchanted,
And all is Liar's leading   that she is thus wedded.
  'To-morrow will be made   the maiden's bridal,
And there might thou know if thou wilt   which they be all
That belong to that lordship   the less and the more.
Know them there if thou canst   and keep thy tongue still,
Blame them not, but let be   till Loyalty be judge
And have power to punish them   then put forth thy plaint.
  'I commend thee to Christ,' quoth she   'and his clean mother,
And may no conscience cumber thee   for coveting of Meed.'
  Thus left me that lady   there lying asleep.
And how Meed was married   meseemed in a dream
That all the rich retinue   that with Falsehood reign
Were bidden to the bridal   on both the two sides
Of all manner of men   the mean and the rich.
To marry this maiden   was many man assembled,
As of knights and of clerks   and other common people,
Assessors and summoners [1]   sheriffs and their clerks,
Beadles and bailiffs   and brokers of wares,
Couriers and victuallers   advocates of the Arches—
I cannot reckon the rout   that ran about Meed.
  But Simony and Civil Law   and assessors of courts
Were most privy with Meed   of any man, methought.
But Flattery was the first   that fetched her out of bower,
And like a broker brought her   to be with Falsehood joined.
When Simony and Civil Law   saw the will of them both,
They assented, for silver   to say as both would.
Then leapt Liar forth and said   'Lo here! a charter
That Guile with his great oaths   gave them together,'
And prayed Civil Law see   and Simony read it.
Then Simony and Civil Law   stand they forth both
And unfold the enfeoffment   that Falsehood hath made,
And thus being these fellows   to read out full loud:
    '*Sciant praesentes et futuri, etc.*
  'Wit ye and witness ye   that wander on this earth,

      [1] See page 202.

That Meed is married   more for her goods
Than for any virtue or fairness   or generous nature.
Falseness is fain of her   for he knows her riches;
And Flattery with fickle speech   invests them by charter
To be princes in pride   poverty to despise,
To backbite and to boast   and false witness to bear,
To scorn and to scold   and slander to make,
Disobedient, and bold   to break the Ten Laws.
   'And the earldom of Envy   and of Wrath together,
With the stronghold of Strife   and Chattering-out-of-Reason,
The county of Covetousness   and its coasts about,
That is, Usury and Avarice   all them I grant,
With bargains and brokerage   and the borough of Theft.
   'All the lordship of Lechery   in length and in breadth,
As in works and in wards   and watching with eyes,
And in clothes and in wishings   and with idle thoughts
Where the will gladly would   but the power is weak.'
   Gluttony he gave also   and great oaths together,
And all day to drink   at divers taverns,
There to jangle and jape   and judge their fellow Christians.
And on fast days to feed   before the full time
And then sit and sup   till sleep them assail,
And to breed like town swine   and repose at their ease,
Till sloth and sleep   make sleek their sides;
And Despair to awaken them so   with no will to amend;
They believe themselves lost   this is their last end.
   And they to have and to hold   and their heirs after,
Dwelling with the Devil   and damned be for ever,
With all that pertaining to purgatory   in the pain of hell.
Yielding for this thing   at one year's end
Their souls to Satan   to suffer with him pains
And with him to wander with woe   while God is in heaven.
   In witness of which thing   Wrong was the first,
And Piers the pardoner   of the Pauline order,
Bart the beadle   of Buckinghamshire,
Reynold the reeve   of Rutland soke,
Mund the miller   and many more other.
'On the date of the Devil   this deed I enseal,
In sight of Sir Simony   and by Civil Law's leave.'
   Then Theology was vexed   when this tale he heard,
And said to Civil Law   "Now sorrow mayest thou have,

Such weddings to wangle   to work against Truth;
And ere this wedding be wrought   woe thee betide!
  'For Meed is a woman   of Amends engendered,
And God granted to give   this Meed to Truth;
Thou hast given her a beguiler   now God give thee sorrow!
Thy text telleth thee not so   Truth knows the sooth,
For *dignus est operarius*   his hire to have;
Thou hast fastened her to Falsehood   fie on thy law!
For all by lying thou livest   and lecherous works;
Simony and thyself   shame Holy Church;
The notaries and thee   annoy the people.
Ye shall atone for it both   by God that me made!
Well wot ye, ye liars   unless your wit fails,
That Falsehood is faithless   and false in his works,
And was a bastard born   of Beelzebub's kin.
And Meed is a mistress   a maiden of wealth,
And might kiss the king   as his cousin, if she would.
  'Therefore, work ye by wisdom   and by wit also,
And lead her to London   there law is declared,
If any law will allow   of their lying together.
And though justices judge her   to be joined with Falsehood,
Yet beware of their wedding   for a wise one is Truth
And Conscience is of his council   and knoweth you each one;
And if he find you in default   and with Falsehood hold,
It shall beset your souls   full sour at the last!'
  Hereto assented Civil Law   but Simony would not
Till he had silver for his service   and also the notaries.
  Then fetched Flattery forth   florins enough,
And bade Guile to give   gold all about,
And notably to the notaries   that them none might fail,
And fee False-Witness   with florins enough:
'For he can manage Meed   and make her assent.'
  When this gold was given   great was the thanking
To Falsehood and Flattery   for their fair gifts;
And they came to comfort   from care this Falsehood
And said: 'Certes, sir   cease shall we never
Till Meed be thy wedded wife   through the wits of us all.
For we have Meed managed   with our merry speech,
That she granteth to go   with a very good will
To London to look   if that the law would
Adjudge you jointly   in joy for ever.'

　　Then was Falseness fain　　and Flattery as blithe,
And caused all men to be summoned　　from the shires about,
And bade them be bound　　beggars and others,
To wend with them to Westminster　　to witness this deed.
　　But then looked they for horses　　to carry them thither,
And Flattery fetched forth then　　foals enough,
And set Meed on a sheriff　　all newly shod;
Falsehood sat on an assessor　　that softly trotted;
Flattery on a flatterer　　finely attired.
　　Then had notaries none　　annoyed they were
That Simony and Civil Law　　should on their feet go.
　　But then swore Simony　　and Civil Law both
That summoners should be saddled　　and serve them each one,
And had provisors apparelled　　in palfrey wise.
'Sir Simony himself　　shall sit their backs.
　　'Deans and subdeans　　draw you together,
Archdeacons and officials　　and all your registrars,
Saddle them with silver　　our sin to sanction,
As adultery and divorces　　and secret usury,
To bear bishops about　　on visitations.
　　'Partisans of the Paulines [1]　　for plaints in consistory
Shall serve myself　　that Civil Law is called;
And cart-saddle the commissary　　our cart shall he draw
And fetch forth our victuals　　from fornicators' fines.
　　'And make of Liar a long cart　　to draw all these others,
Such as friars and false fellows　　that on their feet run.'
And thus Falsehood and Flattery　　fared forth together,
And Meed in the midst　　and all these men after.
I have no time to tell　　the tail that them followed,
Of many manner of men　　that on this mould live;
But Guile was foregoer　　and guided them all.
　　Truth saw them well　　and said but a little,
But pricked his palfrey　　and passed them all,
And came to the king's court　　and Conscience it told.
And Conscience to the king　　rehearsed it after.
'Now by Christ!' quoth the king　　'if I might catch
Falsehood or Flattery　　or any of his fellows,
I would wreak on those wretches　　that work so ill,
Make them hang by the neck　　and all that maintain them!
Shall no man on this mould　　go bail for the least,

[1] See page 202.

C 57¹

But right as law shall allow   let it fall on them all.'
   And commanded a constable   the first one that came,
To, 'Arrest those tyrants   at any cost, I bid;
And fetter Falsehood fast   in spite of any gifts
And get off Guile's head   and let him go not.
And if ye light on Liar   let him not escape
Ere he be put in pillory   for any prayer, I bid;
And bring ye Meed to me   in spite of them all.'
   Dread at the door stood   and the doom heard,
And how the king commanded   constables and serjeants
Falseness and his fellowship   to fetter and to bind.
Then Dread went quickly   and warned Falsehood
And bade him flee for fear   and his fellows all.
   Falsehood for fear then   fled to the friars.
And Guile started to go   aghast for to die.
But merchants met with him   and made him abide
And shut him in their shops   to show their wares,
And apparelled him as a prentice   the people to serve.
   Lightly then Liar   leaped away,
Lurking through lanes   lugged about by many.
He was nowhere welcome   for his many tales,
Everywhere hooted   and hustled away;
Till pardoners had pity   and pulled him indoors.
They washed him and wiped him   and wound him in clouts;
And sent him with seals   on Sundays to churches,
To give pardons [1] for pence   by pounds at a time.
Then looked at him leeches   and letter they sent
That he should live with them   and look at men's water.
Spicers spoke with him   to inspect their wares,
For he kenned their craft   and knew many gums.
But minstrels and messengers   met with him once
And held him an half-year   and eleven days.
   Friars with fair speech   fetched him thence,
And lest others should know him   dressed him as a friar.
But he hath leave to leap out   as oft as him liketh,
And is welcome when he will   to stay with them oft.
   All fled for fear   and were hiding in holes;
Save Meed the Maid   no man durst abide.
But truly to tell   she trembled for dread,
Her hands wrung, and wept   when she was arrested.

                [1] See page 202.

PASSUS III

Now is Meed the Maid   and no more of them all,
With beadles and bailiffs   brought before the king.
The king called a clerk   (I know not his name)
To take Meed the Maid   and make her at ease.
'I shall try her myself   and truly inquire
What man of this earth   is dearest to her.
And if she works by my wisdom   and my will follows
I will forgive her this guilt   so me God help!'
    Courteously the clerk then   as the king ordered,
Took Meed by the middle   and brought her indoors,
And there was mirth and minstrelsy   Maid Meed to please.
They that harboured in Westminster   honoured her all;
And gently with joy   of the justices some,
Betook them to the bower   where the bride dwelled
To comfort her kindly   with Learning's leave;
And said: 'Mourn not thou Meed   nor make no sorrow,
For we will counsel the king   and thy way shape
To be wedded at thy will   and where thy love liketh,
For all Conscience's care   or craft, as I trow.'
    Mildly Meed then   thanked them all
For their great goodness   and gave them each one
Cups of clean gold   and cups of silver,
Rings also with rubies   and rich things many,
The least men of her train   money of gold.
Then took they their leave   these lords, of Meed.
    With that came clerks   to comfort her too
And bade her be blithe   'for we be thine own
For to work thy will   so long as thou last.'
Prettily she then   promised them the same,
To 'love you loyally   and lords to make,
And in consistory of the court   to call out your names;
Lack of wit shall not hinder   the man that I love
That he be well advanced   for I am known
Where learned clerks`   shall be left behind.'
    Then came there a confessor   clothed as a friar;
To Meed the Maid   he muttered these words
And said full softly   in shrift as it were:

19

'Though ignorant men and learned   had lain by thee both
And Falseness had followed thee   these fifty winters,
I shall absolve thee myself   for a horse-load of wheat,
Also be thy bedesman   and bear well thy message
Amongst knights and clerks   Conscience to turn.'

Then Meed for her misdeeds   to that man kneeled,
And shrove her of her sinfulness   shamelessly, I trow,
Told him a tale   and tendered a noble
For to be her bedesman   and her broker too.

Then soon he absolved her   and afterwards said:
'We have a window a-making   will mulct us in much;
Wouldst thou glaze that gable   and grave on it thy name,
Surer should thy soul be   heaven to have.'

'Wist I that,' quoth that woman   'I would not spare
For to be your friend, friar   and fail you never
All the while you love lords   that lechery haunt
And blame not the ladies   that love well the same.
'Tis but frailty of flesh   you find it in books—
In the course of nature   whereof we all come;
If you scandal escape   scathe is soon mended;
It's the sin of the seven   soonest forgiven.

'Have you mercy,' quoth Meed   'on men that it haunt
And I shall cover your church   and your cloister make,
Your walls well whiten   and their windows glaze,
Do painting and picturing   and pay for the making,
That all seeing it shall say   'of your house I'm a sister.'

But God to all good folk   such graving forbiddeth,
To write so in windows   of their worthy deeds,
Lest pride be painted there   and pomp of the world.
For Christ knoweth thy conscience   thy inmost intention,
The cost and thy covetousness   and whose was the wealth.

Therefore I advise you, lords   leave ye such works,
To write up in windows   of your worthy deeds
Or call for God's men   when ye deal out doles,
Lest ye have your reward here   and your Heaven also.

Nesciat sinistra quid faciat dextra.

Let not thy left half   later or sooner,
Know what thou workest   with thy right side;
For thus bids the Gospel   good men to do alms.

Mayors and mace-bearers   the means are between
The king and the commons   to see the law kept,

To punish on pillories   and punishment stools
Brewers and bakers   butchers and cooks,
For these are this world's men   that work the most harm
To the poor people that   must buy piece-meal.
　For they poison the people   privily and oft,
Get rich by retailing   and buy themselves rents
With what the poor people   should put in their bellies;
For traded they truly   they'd have built not so high,
Nor bought any ground-rents   be full certain of that!
　But now Meed the Maid   the mayor hath besought
Of all such sellers   silver to take,
Or presents without pence   as goblets of silver,
Rings or other riches   trade's frauds to maintain.
　'For my love,' quoth that lady   'love them each one,
And suffer them to sell   somewhat against reason.'
　Solomon the sage   a sermon he made
For to amend mayors   and men that guard laws,
And told them this theme   that I think to tell:
　　Ignis devorabit tabernacula eorum qui libenter accipiunt munera, etc.
　Among lettered men   this Latin is to mean
That fire shall fall and burn   all to blue ashes
The houses and the homes   of them that desire
Presents or briberies   because of their office.
　The king from council came   and called after Meed,
And sent for her quickly   with serjeants many,
That brought her to bower   with bliss and with joy.
　Courteously the king then   commenced to talk
To Meed the Maiden   speaking these words:
'Unwisely, woman   wrought hast thou oft;
But worse wroughtest thou never   than when Falsehood you took.
But I forgive thee that guilt   and grant thee my grace;
Hence on, to thy death day   do so no more!
　'I have a knight, Conscience   come of late from beyond.
If he willeth thee to wife   wilt thou him have?'
'Yea, lord,' quoth that lady   'the Lord forbid else!
If I be not wholly at your hest   let me hang soon!'
　And then was Conscience called   to come and appear
Before king and council   the clerks and the others.
Kneeling, then Conscience   to the king louted
To learn what his will were   and what he should do.
　'Wilt thou wed this woman,' quoth the king   'if I will assent?

For she is fain of my fellowship   for to be thy mate.'
    Quoth Conscience to the king   'Christ it me forbid!
Ere I wed such a wife   woe me betide!
For she is frail of her faith   fickle of her speech,
And maketh men misdo   many score times,
Trust in her treasure   betrayeth full many.
To wives and widows   wantonness she teacheth,
And learneth them lechery   that love her gifts.
Your father she felled   through her false behest,
And hath poisoned popes   and impaired Holy Church.
There is no better bawd   by him that me made!
Though me search through the earth   between heaven and hell.
For she is lecherous in her looks   and loose in her tongue,
Common as a cart-road   to each knave that walks,
To monks and to minstrels   and lepers in hedges.
Assessors and summoners   such men her praise;
Sheriffs of shires were ruined   if she were not.
For she makes men to lose   their land and life both.
She letteth pass prisoners   and pays for them often,
Giveth gold to gaolers   and great groats as well
To unfetter the false   to flee where they like;
And taketh the true man by the top-knot   and tieth him fast
And hangeth him for hatred   that harm never did.
To be cursed by a council   she counts not a rush,
For she clotheth the commissory   and covers his clerks;
She's absolved as soon   as herself liketh,
And may nigh as much do   in one single month
As your secret seal   in six score of days.
For she is privy with the pope   provisors it know
For Sir Simony and herself   seal all their bulls.
    'She blesseth the bishops   though they be unlearned
Provideth for parsons   and priests enableth
To have lemans and lovers   all through their lives
And beget them babies   though the law forbids.
Where she is well with the king   woe is the realm,
For she favoureth the false   and fouleth truth oft.
    'By Jesus! with her jewels   your judges she shames,
Lieth against Law   and gets in his way
That Faith may not pass by   her florins are so thick.
She leadeth the law as she list   and law-days maketh,
And makes men lose through her love   that the law may win;

A poor person's perplexed   though he plead for ever.
Law is so lordly   and loth to make end;
Without presents or pence   she pleaseth full few.
   'Barons and burghers she   brings into sorrows,
And the commons to care   that would live in truth;
For clerkship and coveting   she coupleth together.
This is the life of that lady   the Lord give her sorrow!
And all that maintaineth her men   mischance them betide!
For poor men have no power   to complain, though they smart,
Such a master is Meed   among men of wealth.'
   Then mourned Meed   and moaned to the king
To have space to speak   succeed if she might.
   The king granted her grace   with a good will:
'Excuse thee if thou canst   I can no more say,
For Conscience accuseth thee   to cast thee off for ever.'
   'Nay, lord,' quoth that lady   'believe him the less,
When ye understand truly   where the wrong lieth.
Where that mischief is great   Maid Meed may help.
And thou knowest, Conscience   I came not to chide
Nor deprave thy person   with a proud heart.
Well thou knowest, liar   unless thou wilt be,
How thou hast been with me   eleven times,
And griped at my gold   to give where thee liked;
And why thou art wrathful now   a wonder methinketh.
Yet I may, if I might   make to thee gifts
And maintain thy manhood   more than thou knowest.
   'But thou hast famed me foully   before the king here.
For killed I never no king   nor counselled thereafter
Nor did as thou deemest   I appeal to the king!
   'In Normandy was he not   annoyed for my sake.
But thou thyself soothly   shamedst him oft;
Crept into a cabin   for cold of thy nails,
Weening that winter   would have lasted for ever,
And didst dread to be dead   because of the downpour
And hiedest thou homeward   for hunger of guts.
   'Without pity, pillager   poor men thou didst spoil
And bore their brass on thy back   to Calais to sell.
While I lingered with my lord   his life for to save;
I made his men merry   and mended their mourning
I patted their backs and   emboldened their hearts
And made them hop for hope of   my help at their will.

Had I been marshal of his men   by Mary of heaven!
I durst have laid my life   and no less a pledge,
He should have been lord of that land   in length and in breadth,
And also bring of that country   his kin for to help—
The least brat of his blood   the peer of a baron.
    'Cowardly thou, Conscience   counselled him thence
To leave all his lordship   for a little silver,
And that the richest realm   that rain hovereth over.
    'It becometh a king   that keepeth a realm
To give meed to men   that meekly him serve,
To aliens and to all men   to honour them with gifts.
Meed maketh him loved   and for a man holden.
Emperors and earls   and all manner of lords
For gifts have young men   to run and to ride.
The pope and all prelates   presents accept
And fee men themselves   to maintain their laws.
Servants for their service   we see well the sooth,
Take meed of their masters   as they may agree.
Beggars for their begging   beg of men meed;
And minstrels for their mirth   meed do they ask.
The king hath meed of his men   to make peace in the land;
Men that teach children   crave of them meed.
Priests that preach to the people   for goodness, ask meed,
And mass-pence and their meat   at their meal times.
All kinds of craftsmen   crave meed for their prentice;
Merchants and meed   must needs go together.
No wight, as I ween   without me, Meed, may live.'
    Quoth the king to Conscience   'By Christ! as methinketh
Meed is well worthy   the mastery to have.'
    'Nay,' quoth Conscience to the king   and kneeled to the earth,
'There are two manner of meeds   my lord, with your leave.
The one, God of his grace   granteth, in his bliss,
To those that do good deeds   the while they are here.
The prophet preacheth thereof   and put it in the Psalter:
        Domine, quis habitabit in tabernaculo tuo?
"Lord, who shall dwell in thy dwellings   and with thy holy saints,
Or rest on thine holy hills?"   this asked David.
    'And David answered himself   as the Psalter telleth:
        Qui ingreditur sine macula, & operatur justitiam.
"Those spotless that enter   and all of one will,
And have wrought their works   with right and with reason;

And he that useth not   the life of usury,
And instructeth poor men   and pursueth truth;

> *Qui pecuniam suam non dedit ad usuram, et munera super innocentem,*
> *etc.*

And all that helpeth the innocent   and hold with the rightful,
And without meed do them good   and the truth helpeth."
Such manner of men, lord   shall have this first meed
Of God, at their great need   when they go hence.

'There is another meed, measureless   that masters desire.
To maintain misdoers   meed they do take;
And thereof saith the psalter   at a psalm's end,

> *In quorum manibus iniquitates sunt, dextra eorum repleta est mun-*
> *eribus;*

And he that graspeth her gold   so me God help!
Shall abide it bitterly   or the Book lieth!

'Priests and parsons   that pleasure desire
And take meed and money   for the masses they sing,
Receive their meed here   as Matthew us teacheth:

> *Amen, amen, receperunt mercedem suam.*

That which labourers and low folk   take of their masters
Is in no manner meed   but a moderate hire.

'In merchandise is no meed   I may well it avow:
It is clearly exchange   one pennyworth for another.

'But readest thou never *Regum* [1]   thou recreant Meed,
Why the vengeance fell   on Saul and his children?
God sent to Saul   by Samuel the prophet
That Agag of Amalek   and all his people after
Should die for a deed   that their elders had done.
"So," said Samuel to Saul   "God himself biddeth
Thee be true at his bidding   his will to fulfil.
Wend to Amalek with thine host   and what thou findest there, slay it;
Both men and their beasts   burn them to death;
Widows and wives   women and children,
Chattels and fixtures   and all that thou findest,
Burn, and bear not away   be it never so rich,
For meed nor for money   look thou destroy it,
Spill it and spare it not   thou shalt speed the better."

'Because he coveted cattle   and the king spared,
Spared both him and his beasts   the Bible witnesseth,
Otherwise than he was   warned by the prophet,

[1] See page 203.

God said then to Samuel that Saul should die,
And his seed for that sin shamefully end.
Such a mischief Meed made King Saul to have
That God hated him for ever and all his heirs after.
The conclusion of this case I care not to show;
For fear that it vex men no end will I make.
For so is this world's way with them that have power,
That whoso saith sooth is the soonest blamed.
 'I, Conscience, know this Mother-Wit me it taught,
That Reason shall reign and the realms govern.
As it happened to Agag shall happen to others.
Samuel shall slay him and Saul shall be blamed,
And David shall be diademed and subdue them all;
And one Christian king shall care for them all.
 'Meed shall no more be master as she is now,
But Love and Lowliness and Loyalty together,
These shall be masters on earth Truth to save.
 'And who trespasseth against Truth or traverseth his will,
Loyalty shall judge him no living man else.
Shall no serjeant for service wear a silk hood
And no fur on his cloak for pleading at bar.
Meed of many misdoers maketh more lords,
And over the lords' laws ruleth the realms.
 'But man's Love shall come yet and Conscience together,
And make Law a labourer such love shall arise
And such peace among the people and a perfect truth
That Jews shall ween in their wits and wax wondrous glad,
That Moses or Messiah be come into this earth,
And have wonder in their hearts that men be so true.
 'All that bear a dagger broad sword or lance,
An axe or an hatchet or any weapon else
Shall be doomed to the death if he have it not smithed
Into sickle or scythe into plow-share or coulter.
  Conflabunt gladios suos in vomeres, etc.
Each man to play with a plow a pick-axe or spade,
Spin, or spread dung or perish in sloth.
 'All priests and parsons shall hunt with *placebo* [1]
And cry upon David each day until eve.
Hunting or hawking if any of them use,
The boast of his benefice shall be taken from him.
       [1] See page 203.

Shall neither king nor knight   constable nor mayor,
Oppress the commons   nor summon to court
Not empanel them on juries   to make them plight truth
But according to the deed done   one judgment shall reward,
Mercy or no mercy   as Truth shall accord.

'King's court and common court   consistory and chapter,
All shall be but one court   and one baron judge:
Namely True-Tongue, a tidy man   that troubled me never.
Battles shall not be   nor no man bear weapon,
And what smith that any maketh   be smitten therewith to death,

> *Non levabit gens contra gentem gladium, etc.*

'And ere this fortune fall   men shall find the worst,
By six suns and a ship [1]   and an half sheaf of arrows;
And the full of the moon   shall turn Jews to the Faith,
And Saracens at that sight   shall sing *Gloria in excelsis, etc.*,
For Mahomet and Meed   shall mishap at that time;

> *For melius est bonum nomen quam divitiae multa.*'

As wroth as the wind then   waxed Meed in a while.
'I know no Latin,' quoth she   'but clerks know the truth.
See what Solomon saith   in Wisdom book,
That they that giveth gifts   the victory win
And much worship have therewith   as holy writ telleth:

> *Honorem adquiret qui dat numera, etc.*'

'I well believe, lady,' quoth Conscience   'that thy Latin be true;
But thou art like a lady   that once read a lesson:
It was, *Omnia probate*   and that pleased her heart
For that line was no longer   being at the leaf's end.
Had she looked the other side   and turned the leaf over,
She would have found many words   following thereafter:
Quod bonum est tenete.   Truth made that text!
And so fared ye, madam!   Ye couldst no more find,
Though ye looked on Wisdom   sitting in your study.
This text that ye have told   were good for the lords
But you lacked a cunning clerk   that could the leaf turn!
And if ye seek Wisdom again   find shall ye that followeth
A full troublesome text   to them that take meed;
And that is, *animam autem auferet accipientium, etc.*
That is the tail of the text   of that that ye shewed:
That, though we win worship   and with meed have victory,
The soul that bribes taketh   is by so much in bonds.'

[1] See page 203.

'CEASE now!' saith the king   'I suffer you no longer,
Ye shall agree, forsooth   and then serve me both.
Kiss her,' quoth the king   'Conscience, I bid thee.'
    'Nay, by Christ!' quoth Conscience   'dismiss me for ever!
Unless Reason rede me thereto   rather will I die.'
    'And I command thee,' quoth the king   to Conscience then,
'Be ready to ride   and Reason thou fetch;
Command him that he come   my counsel to hear.
For he shall rule my realm   and rede me the best,
And account with thee, Conscience   so me Christ help!
How thou lessonest the people   the learned and unlearned.'
    'I am glad of that charge'   said the man then,
And rode right to Reason   rehearsed in his ear,
And said as the king bade   and soon took his leave.
    'I shall array me to ride,' quoth Reason   'rest thee awhile;'
And called Cato his knave   courteous of speech,
And also Tom-true-tongue-   tell-me-no-tales-
Nor-lies-for-to-laugh-at-   for-I-loved-them-never;
'And set saddle upon Suffer-   till-I-see-my-time,
And girdle it well   with Wise-Word's girths,
Hang on the heavy bridle   to hold his head low,
For he will neigh more than once   ere that he be there.'
    Then Conscience on his courser   fareth forth fast
And Reason with him rode   rehearsing together
What masteries Meed   maketh on this earth.
    One Warren Wisdom   and Witty his fellow
Followed them fast   they had business to do,
In Exchequer and at Chancery   to be discharged:
And rode fast, for Reason   should advise them best
For to save them, for silver   from shame and from harm.
    And Conscience knew them well   they loved covetousness,
And bade Reason ride fast   and reck of them neither.
'There are wiles in their words   and with Meed they dwell;
Where wrath is and wrangling   there win they silver;
But where loyalty and love is   they will not come near.
    Contritia & in felicitas in viis eorum, etc.

They will give naught for God   not even one goose wing,
    Non est timor Dei ante oculos eorum.
For, God knows, they would do more   for a dozen chickens
Or as many capons   or for a sack of oats,
Than for the love of our Lord   or all his loyal saints.
Therefore, Reason, let those rich ones   ride by themselves,
For Conscience knows them not   nor does Christ, as I think.'
And then Reason rode fast   on the right highway,
As Conscience advised   till they came to the king.

    Courteously the king then   came to meet Reason,
And between himself and his son   set him on a bench,
And they talked most wisely   a great while together.

    Then came Peace into parliament   and put forth a bill—
How Wrong against his will   had his wife taken,
How he had ravished Rose   Reginald's love,
And Margaret her maidenhood   not minding her kicks.
Both my poultry and pigs   his purveyors fetch;
I dare not for fear of him   fight or complain.
He borrowed my bay horse   and brought him home never,
Nor no farthing there for   for aught I could plead.
He maintaineth his men   to murder my menials,
Fighteth in my markets   and forestalleth my fairs,
Breaketh up my barn door   beareth off my wheat,
And for ten quarters of oats   tenders a tally;
He beats me also   and lies with my maid—
I am not brave enough   to give him a look.'
The king knew he said sooth   for Conscience him told
Wrong was a wicked wretch   who wrought much sorrow.

    Wrong was afeared then   and Wisdom he sought
To make peace with his pence   and proffered him many,
And said: 'Had I the king's love   little would I reck,
Though Peace and his power   complained for ever.'

    Then went Wisdom   and Sir Warren the witty,
For that Wrong had wrought   so wicked a deed,
And warned Wrong then   with this wise tale:
'Whoso worketh wilfully   wrath maketh oft;
I say it of thyself   thou shalt it well find.
Except Meed it mend   thy mischief is certain,
For both thy life and thy land   lie in his grace.'

    Then wooed Wrong   Wisdom full hard
To make peace with his pence   paid out on the sly.

Wisdom and Wit then   went they together
And took Meed along with them   mercy to win.
    Peace put forth his head   and his bloody pate:
'Without guilt, God knoweth   got I this harm;
Conscience and the Commons   know I speak sooth.'
    But Wisdom and Wit   worked away fast
To come over the king   with money, if they might.
    The king swore, by Christ   and by his crown both,
That Wrong for his works   should woe endure,
And commanded a constable   to cast him in irons,
'And let him not in seven years   see his feet once.'
    'God knows,' quoth Wisdom   'that were not the best;
If he make amends   let Surety have him
And be bail for his baseness   and buy his well-being,
So amend what is misdone   and evermore be better.'
Wit accorded therewith   and said the same:
'Better it is that good   evil down bring,
Than evil be beaten   and good never the better.'
    Then began Meed to moan   and mercy besought,
And proffered Peace a present   all of pure gold.
'Have this, man, of me,' quoth she   'to amend thy scathe,
For I will wager for Wrong   he will do so no more.'
    Piteously Peace then   prayed to the king
To have mercy on that man   that misdid him so oft;
'For he hath pledged me well   as Wisdom him taught,
And I forgive him that guilt   with a good will,
So that the king assent   I can say no better,
For Meed hath made me amends   and I may no more ask.'
    'Nay,' quoth the king then   'so me Christ help!
Wrong mendeth not so away   first will I know more;
For if let off so lightly   laugh loud he would,
And afterwards bolder be   to beat my subjects.
Unless Reason have ruth on him   he shall rest in my stocks,
And that as long as he liveth   except Lowliness him bail.'
    Some men prompted Reason   to have pity on that wretch,
And counselled the king   and Conscience after;
And that Meed might be surety   Reason besought.
    'Tell me not,' quoth Reason   'pity to have,
Till lords and ladies   all love truth
And hate all wickedness   to hear it or speak it;
Till Pernel puts her pretty things   away in her drawer;

And cherishing of children   be by chastening with rods;
And holiness of rascals   be held not a marvel;
Till covetousness of clerks   the poor clothes and feeds;
And roaming religious sing   *Recordare* [1] in cloister,
As Saint Benet them bade   Bernard and Francis;
And till preachers' preaching   be proved on themselves;
And till the king's counsel   be common profit;
Till bishops' bay mares   buy shelter for beggars,
Their hawks and their hounds   help for poor religious.

  'And till Saint James be sought   where the poor sick be,
So none go to Galicia   but to stay there for ever;
And all the Rome-runners   to robbers beyond
Bear no silver over sea   that shows the king's sign,
Neither graven nor ungraven   golden nor silver,
Upon forfeiture of that fee   whoso finds him at Dover,
Except he be merchant or his man   or messenger with letters,
Provisor or priest   or penitent for his sins.
And yet,' quoth Reason, 'by the Rood   I shall no ruth have
While Meed hath the mastery   in this moot-hall.
But I may shew examples   as I see otherwiles.
I say for myself,' quoth he   'and it so were
That I were king with a crown   to care for a realm,
Should never wrong in this world   that I might know,
Be unpunished in my power   on peril of my soul!
Nor get my grace for gifts   so me God save!
Nor for no Meed have mercy   except she be meek.

  'For *nullum malum* the men   met with *impunitatem*
And bade *nullum bonum*   be *irremuneratum*.

  'Let your confessor, sir king   construe this without gloss;
And if ye put it to test   I pledge both my ears
That Law shall turn labourer   and spread dung afield,
And Love lead thy land   as thou likest best!'

  Clerks that were confessors   coupled them together
All to construe this clause   and for the king's profit,
Nor for comfort of the commons   nor for the king's soul.

  For I saw Meed in the moot-hall   on men of law wink,
And they laughing leaned to her   and many left Reason.

  Warren Wisdom   winked upon Meed
And said: 'Madam, I am your man   whatever my mouth say;
I fall in with florins,' quoth that fellow   'and then my speech fails.'

                    [1] See page 203.

All the righteous recorded   that Reason told truth,
Wit accorded therewith   and commended his words,
And most people in the hall   and many of the great
Held Meekness the master   and Meed a vile shrew.

Love held her lightly   and Loyalty still less,
And said it so loudly   that all the hall heard:
'Whoso wants her for wife   for the wealth of her goods,
If he be not a cuckold   then cut off my nose.'

Meed mourned then   and made heavy cheer,
For the commons in that court   called her an whore.
But a sizer and a summoner   pursued her fast,
And a sheriff's clerk   cursed all the rout,
'For often have I,' quoth he   'helped you at bar
And yet gave ye me never   the worth of a rush.'

The king called Conscience   and afterwards Reason
And recorded that Reason   had rightfully shown;
And moodily upon Meed   with might the king looked,
Waxed wroth with Law   Meed almost had fouled it,
And said: 'Through your law   I lose many escheats;
Meed over-mastereth Law   and Truth mightily hinders.
Reason shall reckon with you   if I reign any while,
And judge you, by this day   as you have deserved.
Meed shall not bail you   by Mary of heaven!
I will have loyalty in law   and stop all your jangling,
And as most folk witness well   Wrong shall be sentenced.'

Quoth Conscience to the king   'If the commons assent not
'Tis full hard, by mine head   thereto to bring it,
All of your liege-men   to lead thus aright.'

'By him racked on the wood'   quoth Reason to the king,
'If I rule not your realm   rend out my ribs!
If ye order Obedience   to be on my side.'

'And I assent,' saith the king   'by Saint Mary my lady!
When my council comes   of clerks and of earls.
But readily, Reason   thou shalt not ride from me,
For as long as I live   I will not let thee go.'

'I am ready,' quoth Reason   'to rest with you ever;
If Conscience will be of our council   I care for no better.
'And I grant,' quoth the king   'God forbid that it fail!
As long as our life lasteth   live we together.'

PASSUS V

THE king and his knights   to the church went
To hear matins of the day   and the Mass after.
Then waked I of my winking   and was woeful withal
That I had not slept sounder   and so seen more.
But ere I fared a furlong   faintness me seized,
I might not go further a foot   for want of my sleep;
And sat softly adown   and said my Creed
And as I babbled on my beads   they brought me asleep.

   And then saw I much more   than I before told:
For I saw the field full of folk   that I before spoke of,
And how Reason got ready   to preach to the realm,
And with a cross before the king   began thus to teach.

   He proved that these pestilences [1]   were purely for sin,
And the south-west wind   on Saturday at even
Was plainly for pure pride   and for no point else.
Pear-trees and plum-trees   were puffed to the earth
For example, ye men   that ye should do better.
Beeches and broad oaks   were blown to the ground,
Turned upwards their tails   in token of dread
That deadly sin at doomsday   shall undo them all.

   Of this matter I might   mumble full long,
But I will say as I saw   so God me help!
How plainly before the people   Reason began to preach.

   He bade Waster go work   at what he best could
And win back his wasting   with some manner of craft.

   And prayed Pernel put off   her costly array
And keep it in her box   for money at her need.

   Tow Stowe he taught   to take two staves
And from women's punishment [2]   bring Phyllis home.

   He warned Wat   his wife was to blame,
That her hat was worth half a mark   his hood cost not a groat.
And bade Batt cut down   a bough or even two
And beat Betty therewith   unless she should work.
And then he charged chapmen   to chasten their children:

[1] See page 203.   [2] See page 203.

'Let no wish for wealth spoil them　　while they be young,
Nor for power of the pestilence　　please them out of reason.
　　My sire said so to me　　and so did my dame,
That the more loved the child　　the more teaching it needs,
And Solomon said the same　　that Wisdom made,
　　　　Qui parcit virgae, odit filium.
The English of this Latin is　　whoso will it know,
Whoso spareth the sprig　　spoileth the children.'
　　And then he prayed prelates　　and priests together,
'What ye preach to the people　　prove it on yourselves
And do it in deeds　　it shall draw you to good;
If ye live as ye teach us　　we'll believe you the better.'
　　And then he counselled religious　　their rule to uphold,
'Lest the king and his council　　your commons curtail
And be stewards of your steads　　till ye be better ruled.'
　　Then he counselled the king　　the commons to love,
'They're thy treasure in treason　　and help at thy need.'
And then he prayed the pope　　to pity Holy Church,
And ere he give any grace　　to govern first himself.
　　'And ye that have laws to guard　　let truth be your desire
More than gold or other gifts　　if ye will God please;
For whoso contrarieth truth　　he telleth in the gospel,
That God knoweth him not　　nor doth no saint in Heaven:
　　　　Amen dico vobis, nescio vos.
　　'And ye that seek Saint James　　and the Saints of Rome,
Seek ye Saint Truth　　for he may save you all,
Qui cum Patre & Filio　　may fair them befall
That list to my sermon'　　And thus said Reason.
Then ran Repentance　　and rehearsed his theme
And made Will to weep　　water with his eyes.

SUPERBIA

　　Pernel Proud-heart　　leaned her to the earth
And lay long ere she looked　　and 'Lord, mercy!' cried,
And vowed to him　　that us all made
She should unsew her shift　　and wear a hairshirt
To enfeeble her flesh　　that fierce was to sin.
'Shall never high heart have me　　but hold myself lowly
And suffer myself slighted　　and so did I never.
But now will I be meek　　and mercy beseech,
For all this I have　　hated in mine heart.'

LUXURIA

Then Lecher said: 'Alas!' and on our Lady he cried,
To make mercy for his misdeeds between God and his soul,
If he should every Saturday for seven year thereafter
Drink but with the duck and dine only once.

INVIDIA

Envy with heavy heart asked them for shrift,
And sadly *mea culpa* began to repeat.
He was pale as a stone in a palsy he seemed,
And clothed in coarse cloth which I could not describe;
In a kilt and a coat and a knife by his side;
Of a friar's frock were the fore-sleeves.
Like a leek that had lain too long in the sun,
So looked he with lean cheeks lowering foully.
 His body bursting with wrath so that he bit his lips,
And went wringing with his fists to wreak himself he thought
With works or with words when he saw his time.
Each sentence he said was of an adder's tongue,
Chiding and challenge was his chief livelihood
With backbiting and blackguarding and bearing false witness
This was all his courtesy wherever he showed him.
 'I'd be shriven,' quoth this wretch 'and I for shame dare not;
I'd be gladder, by God that Gib had mischance
Than if I'd this week won weight of Essex cheese.
I've a neighbour nigh me whom I've annoyed oft,
And lied on him to lords to make him lose his silver,
And made his friends be his foes through my false tongue;
His grace and his good haps grieve me full sore.
Between family and family I make debate oft,
That both life and limb is lost through my speech.
And when I meet him in market that I most hate,
I hail him heartily as I his friend were;
For he is braver than I and I dare do no other;
But had I mastery and might God wot my will!
 'And when I come to the church and should kneel to the rood
And pray for the people as the priest teacheth,
For pilgrims and palmers and for all people after,
Then I cry on my knees that Christ give them sorrow
Who bare away my bowl and my ragged sheet.

'Away from the altar then   turn I mine eyes,
And behold how Helen   hath a new coat:
I wish then it were mine   and all the webb as well.
At men's losses I laugh   that liketh mine heart.
For their winnings I weep   and wail all the time;
Deem that they do ill   where I do far worse;
Whoso chides me therefore   I hate him deadly after.
I would that each wight   were mine own knave,
For whoso hath more than I   angereth me sore.
And thus I live loveless   like a lousy dog,
So that my body bursts   for bitterness of my gall.
I might not eat many years   as a man ought,
For envy and ill will   is bad to digest.
Can no sugar nor sweet thing   assuage my swelling,
Nor no *diapenidion* [1]   drive it from mine heart,
Nor neither shrift nor sham   if my maw be not scraped?'
     'Yes, readily,' quoth Repentance   and ruled him from the best.
'Sorrow for sins   is salvation of souls.'
     'I am sorry,' quoth the man   'I am but seldom other,
And that maketh me thus meagre   for I cannot revenge.
Among burgesses have I been   dwelling at London,
And got Backbiting by a broker   to blame men's wares.
When one sold and I not   then was I ready
To lie and lower on my neighbour   and slander his goods.
I will amend this if I may   by the Almighty's might.'

IRA

Now awaketh Wrath   with two white eyes
And snivelling at the nose   and his neck hanging.
     'I am Wrath,' quoth he   'I was some time a friar
And the convent's gardener   for to graft shoots.
On limiters and lectors [2]   lyings I grafted,
Till they bare leaves of lowly speech   the lords to please;
And then they blossomed abroad   in bowers to hear shrifts.
And now is fallen a fruit   that folk much prefer
To show their sins to them   than be shriven by their parsons.
     'And now parsons have perceived   that they must share with friars,
The beneficed ones preach   and the friars defame;
The friars find them at fault   as folk bear witness,

----

¹ See page 203.   ² See page 203.

That when they preach to the people   in any place about
I, Wrath, walk with them   and guide them from my looks.
Thus they speak of the spirit   but either despiseth other
Till they be both beggars   and by my ministering live,
Or else all are rich   and ride horses about.
I, Wrath, rest never   but that I must follow
This wicked folk   for such is my grace.

'I have an aunt a nun   and an abbess as well;
Her were liefer swoon or die   than suffer pain.

'I've been cook in her kitchen   in the convent served
Many months with them   and with monks as well.
I was prioresses' pottager   and for other poor ladies,
And made them pottage of prattling   that Dame Joan was a bastard;
Dame Clarice a knight's daughter   and a cuckold her sire;
And Dame Pernel a priest's wench   prioress to be never,
For she childed in cherry-time   as the whole chapter knew.

'Of wicked words, I, Wrath   their salads made,
Till "Thou liest!" and "Thou liest!"   leaped out at once
And either hit other   under the cheek;
Had they had knives, by Christ   each had killed other.

'Saint Gregory was a good pope   and had good forewit,
That no prioress should be priest [1]   so he ordained.
They had else incurred infamy   the very first day
That they took up their office   they're so ill to keep counsel.

'Among monks I might be   but oft times I shun them,
For there be many strict ones   mine affairs to espy,
Both prior and subprior   and our *pater abbas*.
If I tell any tales   they counsel together
And make me fast Fridays   on bread and water;
I'm charged in the chapter-house   as if I a child were
And beaten on my backside   no breeches between,
So have I no liking   with those men to dwell.
I eat there stale stockfish   and feeble ale drink.
At other time, when wine cometh   when I drink wine at eve
I have a flux of a foul mouth   a good five days after.
All the wickedness I know of   by any of our brethren,
I tell it in the cloister   till the whole convent knows.'

'Now repent ye,' quoth Repentance   'and rehearse thou never
Counsel that thou knowest   by favour or by right.
And drink not over delicately   nor too deep neither,

[1] See page 203.

Lest thy will because thereof　　to wrath might be turned.
Esto sobrius,' he said　　and absolved me after
And bade me wish to weep　　my wickedness to amend.

AVARICIA

And then came Covetousness　　I can him not describe,
So hungry and hollow　　Sir Harvey him looked.
He was beetle-browed　　and blubber-lipped too,
With two bleared eyes　　as a blind hog;
And as a leather purse　　lolled his cheeks
Yet lower than his chin　　trembling with age;
And as a bondman's with bacon　　his beard was bedraggled.
With an hood on his head　　a lousy hat above,
And in a tawny tabard　　of twelve winters' age,
All tattered and dirty　　and full of lice creeping—
But if a louse could not　　have leaped with the best
She could not have walked there　　so threadbare the stuff.
　'I have been covetous,' quoth this caitiff　　'I acknowledge it here.
For some time I served　　Sim-at-the-stile
And was his prentice pledged　　his profit to serve.
First I learned to lie　　for a leaf or two;
Wickedly to weigh　　was my first lesson.
To Weyhill and Winchester　　I went to the fair,
With many manner of merchandise　　as my master me bade;
And had not grace of Guile　　gone in with my wares
They had been unsold this seven years　　so help me God!
　'Then tarried I amongst drapers　　my grammar to learn;
To draw the selvedge along　　the longer it seemed;
Among the rich ranged cloths　　I rendered a lesson,
To pierce them with a pack-needle　　and plait them together,
Put them in a press　　and pin them therein
Till ten yards or twelve　　had tolled out to thirteen.
　'My wife was a weaver　　and woollen cloth made.
She spoke to the spinsters　　to spin it all out,
But the pound that she paid by　　poised a quartern more
Than did mine own balance　　whoso weighed true.
　'I bought her barley malt　　she brewed it to sell.
Penny-ale and pudding-ale　　she poured together
For labourers and for low folk　　that was kept by itself.
　'The best ale lay in my bower　　or in my bedchamber,

And whoso tasted thereof   bought it thereafter
A gallon for a groat   no less, God knows:
And 'twas measure in cupfuls   this craft my wife used.
Rose the Retailer   was her right name;
She hath holden huckstering   all through her lifetime.
    'But I swear now, may I thrive!   that sin will I stop,
And never wickedly weigh   nor wicked chaffer use,
But wend to Walsingham   and my wife also
And pray the Rood of Bromholm [1]   bring me out of debt.'
    'Repentedest thou ever,' quoth Repentance   'or restitution madest?'
    'Yes, once I was harboured   with an heap of chapmen;
I rose when they were at rest   and rifled their bags.'
    'That was no restitution   but a robber's theft.
Thou haddest be better worthy   to be hanged there for
Than for all that   that thou hast here showed.'
    'I weened rifling were restitution   for I've not learned in books
And I know no French, i'faith   but of furthest end of Norfolk.'
    'Usedest thou every usury   in all thy life-time?'
    'Nay, soothly,' he said   'save in my youth.
I learned a lesson   among Jews and Lombards,
To weigh pence with a weight   and pare down the heaviest;
And lend it for love of the Cross   for a pledge, to be lost;
Such deeds I did write   lest he due day miss.
I have more money through arrears   than through *miseretur et commodat.*
I have lent lords   and ladies my goods,
And been their broker after   and bought it myself.
Exchanges and contracts   with much chaffer I deal;
Lend to folk that will lose   of every noble a part.
And with Lombard's letters   I lend gold to Rome,
Here took it by tally   and told it there less.'
    'Lentest ever to lords   for love of protection?'
    'Yea, I have lent to lords   who loved me never after,
And have made many a knight   both mercer and draper
That paid for his prenticehood   not a pair of gloves even.'
    'Hast thou pity on poor men   that must needs borrow?'
    'I have as much pity of poor men   as hath pedlar of cats
He would kill if he could   for the sake of their skins.'
    'Art thou generous to thy neighbours   with thy meat and drink?'
    'I am holden as kind   as a hound in the kitchen;
Among my neighbours especially   I have such a name.'

[1] See page 203.

'Now God never grant thee   but thou soon repent,
His grace on this ground   thy goods well to bestow,
Nor thine heirs after thee   to have joy of thy winnings,
Nor executors spend well   the silver thou leavest;
That which by wrong was won   by wicked men to be spent.
For were I friar of that house   where is good faith and charity,
I'd not clothe us with thy cash   nor our church amend,
Nor have for our pittance   a penn'orth of thine
For the best book in our house   though bright gold were leaves,
If I knew indeed   thou wert such as thou tellest,
Or if I could know it   in any sure way.

> *Servus es alterius cum fercula pinguia quaeris,*
> *Pane tuo potius vescere, liber eris.*

'Thou art an unkindly creature   I cannot absolve thee
Till thou make restitution   reckon up with them all;
And till Reason enrol   in the register of Heaven
That thou hast made each man good   I may not absolve thee—

> *Non dimittitur peccatum, donec restituatur oblatum, etc.*

'For all that have aught of thy goods   so God have my truth!
Will be held at the high Day of Doom   to help thee to restore.
And whoso believeth not this   let him look in the Psalter,
In *Miserere mei Deus*   whether I speak truth;

> *Ecce enim veritatem dilexisti, etc.*

'Shall never workman in this world   thrive with what thou winnest;
Cum sancto sanctus eris   construe me that in English.'
Then drooped the scamp in despair   and would have himself hanged,
Had not Repentance the rather   recomforted him in this manner,
'Have mercy in thy mind   and with thy mouth ask it,
For God his mercy is more   than all his other works;

> *Misericordia ejus super omnia opera ejus, etc.*

'And all the wickedness in this world   that man might work or think
Is no more to the mercy of God   than a live coal in the sea;

> *Omnis iniquitas quantum ad misericordiam Dei, est quasi scintilla in*
> *medio maris.*

'Therefore have mercy in mind   and in merchandise, trust it:
For thou hast no good ground   to get thee a cake with,
Unless it were with thy tongue   or else with thy two hands.
For the goods thou hast gotten   began all with falsehood,
And whilst thou livest therewith   thou payest not, but borrowest.
And if thou know never to which   nor to whom to restore,
Bear it to the bishop   and bid him of his grace

Bestow it himself   as is best for thy soul.
For for thee shall be answer   at the high Day of Doom;
For thee and many more   shall that man give a reckoning
What he taught you in Lent   believe thou none other,
What he gave of our Lord's goods   to lead you from sin.'

GULA

Now beginneth Glutton   for to go to shrift
And carries him to kirk-ward   his fault there to show.
But Betty the brewster   bade him good-morrow
And asked of him with that   whitherward he would.
'To holy church,' quoth he   'for to hear Mass,
And after will be shriven   and then sin no more.'
'Gossip, I've good ale,' quoth she   'Glutton, wilt thou try it?'
'Hast thou aught in thy bag?   Any hot spices?'
'I have pepper and peony   and a pound too of garlic,
And a farthing's worth of fennel-seed   for fasting days.'
Then goeth Glutton in   and great oaths come after.
Cis the shoe-seller   sat on the bench,
Wat the game-keeper   and his wife too,
Tim the tinker   and two of his prentices,
Hick the horsedealer   and Hugh the needle-seller,
Clarice of Cock lane   and the clerk of the church,
Davy the ditcher   and a dozen other;
Sir Piers the priest   and Pernel of Flanders,
A fiddler, a rat-catcher   the street sweeper of Cheapside,
A roper, a riding-man   and Rose the dish-seller,
Godfrey of Garlickhithe   and Griffith the Welshman,
And old-clothesmen a heap   early in the morning
Give Glutton with glad cheer   good ale for himself.
Clement the cobbler   cast off his cloak
And named it for sale   at the 'new fair' game.[1]
Hick the horse dealer   heaved his hood after
And bade Bart the butcher   be on his side.
There were chapmen chosen   the goods to appraise;
Whoso hath the hood   should have amends for the cloak.
Two rose up quickly   and whispered together
And priced these pennyworths   apart by themselves.
They could not in their conscience   agree on a value,

[1] See page 203.

Till Robin the roper   arose for the truth
And named himself umpire   to avoid a debate
And to settle this business   betwixt them three.
   Hickey the hostler   he had the cloak,
In covenant that Clement   should the cup fill
And have Hick hostler's hood   and hold himself served;
And whoso sooner repented   should arise after
And give to Sir Glutton   a gallon of ale.
   There was laughing and lowering   and 'Let go the cup!'
They sat so till evensong   singing now and then,
Till Glutton had gulped down   a gallon and a gill.
His guts 'gan to grumble   like two greedy sows;
He pissed a pot-full   in a paternoster-while;
And blew with the bugle   at his backbone's end,
That all hearing that horn   held their nose after
And wished it were stopped up   with a wisp of furze.
   He could neither step nor stand   before he had his staff;
Then began he to go   like a gleeman's bitch,
Sometimes aside   sometimes astern
As whoso layeth lines   for to snare fowl.
   And when he drew to the door   then dimmed his eyes;
He stumbled on threshold   and fell to the earth.
Clement the cobbler   caught him by the middle
For to lift him aloft   and laid him on his knees;
Glutton was a great lout   and lumpish to lift
And coughed up a caudle   in Clement's lap:
No hound is so hungry   in Hertfordshire
Dare lap up those leavings   so unlovely they smelt.
   With all the woe of this world   his wife and his wench
Bare him home to his bed   and brought him therein.
And after all his excess   he had such a head
He slept Saturday and Sunday   till the sun went to rest.
Then waked he of his winking   and wiped his eyes;
The first word that he said   was: 'Where is the bowl?'
His wife began to reproach him   for how wickedly he lived,
And Repentance right so   rebuked him that time:
'As thou with words and works   hast wrought evil in thy life,
Shrive thee and be shamed therefore   and show it with thy mouth.'
   'I, Glutton,' quoth the wretch   'confess me guilty,
That I have trespassed with my tongue   I can not tell how oft:
Sworn "by God's soul" and   "so help me, God and his saints,"

Where there was no need   over nine hundred times.
And surfeited me at supper   and sometimes at noon,
That I, Glutton, threw it up   ere I'd gone a mile
And spilt what might be spared   and spent on some hungry one.
Over-delicately on fasting-days   drunken and eaten,
And sometimes sat so long I   slept and ate together.
For love of tales dined I   in taverns to drink more,
And hurried to meat ere noon   when fasting-days were.'
    'This shewing of shrift,' quoth Repentance   'shall merit to thee.'
    Began Glutton to cry   and great dole to make
For his evil life   that he had so lived;
And vowed to fast   'for hunger as for thirst
Shall never fish on Friday   digest in my womb,
Till Abstinence mine aunt   hath given me leave;
And yet have I hated her   all my life long.'

ACCIDIA

    Then came Sloth all beslobbered   with two slimy eyes.
'I must sit,' said the fellow   'or else should I nap.
I cannot stand nor stoop   nor without a stool kneel.
But were I put to bed   unless my tail made me,
Should no ringing make me rise   ere I were ripe to dine.'
He began *Benedicite* [1] with a belch   and knocked on his breast
And stretched and snored   and slumbered at last.
'Awake, wretch!' quoth Repentance   'and run thee to shrift.'
'Should I die on this day   I'd not trouble to look.
I know not *Paternoster*   as the priest it singeth,
But I know rhymes of Robin Hood   and Earl Randolph of Chester,
But of our Lord or our Lady   not the least ever made.
I have made forty vows   and forgot them at morning;
I performed never penance   as the priest me bade,
Nor right sorry for my sins   yet was I never.
If I pray any prayers   except it be in wrath,
What I tell with my tongue   is two miles from mine heart.
I am occupied each day   holidays and other,
With idle tales in the alehouse   and sometimes in churches.
God's pain and his passion   seldom think I thereon.
I visited never feeble men   nor fettered folk in jail;
I had liefer hear an harlotry   or cobbler's summer games,

[1] See page 203.

Or lyings to laugh at   and belying my neighbour,
Than all that ever Mark made   Matthew, John and Luke.
And vigils and fasting days   all these I let pass,
And lie abed in Lent   my wench in my arms,
Till matins and Mass be done   then I go to the friars;
Come I to *Ite, missa est*   I hold myself served.
I'm not shriven for a long time   unless sickness make me,
Not twice in two years   and then confession is a guess.

'I have been priest and a parson   passing thirty winters,
Yet can I not sing *sol-fa*   nor read the saints' lives;
But I can find in a field   or a furrow an hare,
Better than in *Beatus vir*   or *Beati omnes*
Construe one clause well   and teach my parishioners.
I can hold love-days [1]   and hear a reeve's reckoning,
But in the canon or decretals   I can not read a line.
If I buy on tick   unless it be tallied
I forget it as soon   and if men me it ask,
Six times or seven   I deny it with oaths,
And thus trouble I true men   ten hundred times.

'And my servants' salary   a long time is behind;
Rueful is the reckoning   when we render account.
So with wicked will and wrath   my workmen I pay.

'If man doth me a benefit   or helpeth me at need,
I am unkind to his courtesy   and can not understand it;
For I have, and have had   something of a hawk's manner:
I am not lured with love   unless there lie aught under the thumb.

'Kindness my fellow Christians   accorded me formerly,
Sixty times I, Sloth   have forgot it since.
In speech, and in sparing speech   I waste many a time
Both flesh and fish   and much other victual;
Both bread and ale   butter, milk and cheese,
I spoiled in my service   so it might serve no man.

'I ran about in my youth   nor set me to learn,
And ever since have been beggared   for my foul sloth:

    Heu mihi, quod sterilem vitam duxi juvenilem.'

'Repentest thou not?' quoth Repentance   and right with that he
                                   swooned,

Till *Vigilate* the vigilant   fetched water from his eyes
And flooded his face   and fast on him cried
And said, 'Beware of Despair   who would thee betray.

                    [1] See page 203.

"I am sorry for my sins,"   say so to thyself,
Beat thyself on the breast   and beseech of him grace:
For is no guilt there so great   that his goodness is not more.'
    Then sat Sloth up   and crossed himself
And made a vow to God   'gainst his foul sloth:
'Shall no Sunday be for seven year   unless sickness me stop,
That I go not before dawn   to the dear church
And matins hear and Mass   as though I were a monk.
No ale after meat   shall hold me thence
Till evensong I've heard   I vow it to the rood.
Moreover will I pay back   if I it have,
All I've wickedly won   since I had wit.
    'Though I lack livelihood   stop will I not
Till each man shall have his   ere that I go hence;
And with the residue and remnant   by the Rood of Chester!
I shall seek Truth first   before I see Rome.'
    Robert the Robber   on *Reddite* looked;
He'd naught to pay with   and wept full sore.
But yet the sinful wretch   said to himself,
'Christ, that on Calvary   upon the cross died,
When Dismas [1] my brother   besought you of grace,
Thou haddest mercy on that man   for *memento's* sake
Have pity on this robber   that cannot repay
And may never hope to win   with work what I owe.
But for thy much mercy   mitigation I beseech;
Damn me not at doomsday   for that I did ill.'
    What fell to this felon   I can not fairly show;
Well I wot he wept water   fast with both eyes,
And acknowledged his guilt   right soon after to Christ,
That his pike of penitence   he should polish anew
And use it on pilgrimage   all his life-time,
For he had lain with *Latro*   Lucifer's aunt.
    Then had Repentance ruth   and bade them all kneel:
'For I shall beseech for all sinners   our Saviour of grace
To amend us of misdeeds   and do mercy to all.
    'Now God,' quoth he, 'that of thy goodness   didst the world make
And of naught madest aught   and man most like to thyself,
And since suffered him to sin   a sickness to us all,
Yet for the best—as I hold   whatever the Book telleth,
    O felix culpa! O necessarium peccatum Adae! etc.

[1] See page 203.

'For through that sin thy son   sent was to this earth,
And became man of a maid   mankind to save,
And thyself with thy son   was made like to us sinners:
>   *Faciamus hominen ad imaginem et similitudinem nostram;*
>   *Et alibi:*
>   *Qui manet in caritate, in Dea manet, & Deus in eo.*

'And then with thy Son's self   in our suit [1] died
On Good Friday for man's sake   at full time of day,
Where thyself nor thy Son   no sorrow felt in death,
But in ourselves was the sorrow   and thy Son it led—
>   *Captivam duxit captivitatem.*

'The sun thereof for sorrow   lost sight for a time
About midday, when most light is   the meal time of saints,
When thou didst feed with thy fresh blood   our forefathers in darkness:
>   *Populus qui ambulabat in tenebris, vidit lucem magnam;*
Through the light that leaped from thee   Lucifer was blinded,
And all thy Blessed blown   into Paradise bliss.
The third day after   thou goest in our guise;
A sinful Mary saw thee   before Saint Mary thy mother,
And all to solace the sinful   thou sufferedest it so:
>   *Non veni vocare justos, sed peccatores ad poenitentiam.*

'And all that Mark hath written   Matthew, John and Luke,
Of thy doughtiest deeds   were done beneath our arms:
>   *Verbum caro factum est, et habitavit in nobis.*

'And by so much, meseemeth   the more surely we may
Pray and beseech   if it be thy will,
That art our father and brother   to be merciful to us;
And to have pity on those ribalds   that repent them here sore
That they wrathed thee in this world   in word, thought or deeds.'

Then grasped Hope an horn   of *Deus, tu conversus vivificabis nos,*
And blew it with *Beati quorum   remissae sunt iniquitates,*
So that all saints in Heaven   sang loudly together:
>   *Homines & jumenta salvabis, quemadmodum multiplicasti miseri-*
>   *cordiam tuam, Deus, etc.*

A thousand men then   came thronging together,
Who cried upward to Christ   and to his clean Mother
To have grace to go with them   Truth for to seek.

But there was no wight so wise   that he knew the way thither
But blundered like beasts   over banks and on hills
A long time, till 'twas late   that they a man met

---

[1] See page 203.

Apparelled as a Paynim   in a pilgrim's wise.
He bare a staff bound   with a broad strip
In bindweed wise   wound about.
A bowl and a bag   he bare by his side;
An hundred ampullas   on his hat set,
Signs of Sinai   and shells of Galicia,
Many a cross on his cloak   keys also of Rome
And the vernicle in front   so that men should know
And see by his signs   what shrines he had sought.[1]
   This folk asked him first   from whence he did come.
   'From Sinai,' he said   'and from our Lord's sepulchre;
Bethlehem and Babylon   I have been in both;
In Armenia, in Alexandria   and many other places.
Ye may see by my signs   that sit on my hat
That I've walked full wide   in wet and in dry,
And have sought good saints   for my soul's health.'
   'Knowest thou aught of a saint   that men call Truth?
Could'st thou show us the way   where that wight dwelleth?'
   'Nay, so help me God!'   said the man then,
'I saw never palmer   with pike nor with scrip
Ask after him, till   now in this place.'
   'Peter!' quoth a plowman   and put forth his head,
'I know him as well   as a clerk doth his books.
Conscience and Mother-Wit   made known his place
And made me swear surely   to serve him for ever
Both in sowing and setting   so long as I work.
I have been his follower   all these fifty winters,
Both sown his seed   and driven his beasts,
And watched over his profit   within and without.
I dike and I delve   and do what Truth biddeth:
Sometimes I sow   and sometimes I thresh;
In tailor's and tinker's craft   what Truth can devise;
I weave and I wind   and do what Truth biddeth.
For though I say it myself   I serve him to his pleasure;
I have good hire of him   and oftentimes more.
He is the readiest payer   that a poor man knoweth;
He withholds not his hire   from his servants at even.
He is lowly as a lamb   and lovely of speech,
And if ye are wishful to know   where that he dwelleth,
I shall show you surely   the way to his place.'

[1] See page 203.

'Yea, dear Piers,' quoth these pilgrims   and proffered him hire
For to wend with them   to Truth's dwelling-place.
'Nay, by my soul's health!' quoth Piers   and began for to swear,
'I would not take a farthing   for Saint Thomas's shrine!
Truth would love me the less   a long time thereafter!
'But if ye will to wend well   this is the way thither,
That I shall say to you   and set you in the path.
Ye must go through Meekness   both men and their wives,
Till ye come into Conscience   let Christ know the truth
That ye love our lord God   the best of all things;
And then your neighbours next   in no wise use
Otherwise than thou wouldest   be wrought to thyself.
'And so bend round by a brook   Be-humble-of-speech,
Till ye find a ford called   Honour-your-fathers:
    Honora patrem et matrem, etc.
Wade in that water   and wash you well there,
And you shall leap the lighter   all your lifetime.
And so shalt thou see Swear-not-   but-it-be-for-need-
Especially-not-idly-   by-God-Almighty's-name.
'Then shalt thou come by a croft   but come not therein;
That croft is called Covet-not-   men's-cattle-nor-their-wives-
Nor-none-of-their-servants-   that-might-them-annoy.
Look ye break no boughs there   unless it be your own.
'Two stocks there standeth   but stay ye not there;
They're called Steal-not and Slay-not   strike forth by both
And leave them on thy left hand   and look not thereafter
But hold well thine holiday   holy till even.
'Then shalt thou turn at a tump   Bear-no-false-witness
He is fenced with florins   and other fees many;
Look that thou pluck no plant there   for peril of thy soul;
'Then shall ye see Say-sooth-   as-it-is-to-be-done-
And-in-no-manner-else-   for-any-man's-bidding.
'Then shalt thou come to a court   as clear as the sun;
The moat is of Mercy   the manor about,
And its walls are of Wit   to hold the Will out,
Crenellated with Christendom   mankind to save,
Buttressed with Believe-so-   or-thou-beest-not-saved.
And all the houses are covered   the halls and the chambers,
With no lead but with Love   and Low-speech-of-brethren.
The bridge is of Pray-well-   the-better-mayest-thou-speed;
Each pillar is of Penance   and of Prayers to saints;

Of alms-deeds are the hooks   whereon the gates hang.
   'Grace is the gateward   a good man forsooth;
His man is Amend-you   many men him know:
Tell him this token   that Truth may know sooth:
"I performed the penance   the priest me enjoined,
And full sorry for my sins   and so shall be ever
When I think thereon   though I were a pope."
   'Bid Amend-you full meekly   his master to ask
To draw up the wicket   that the woman shut
When Adam and Eve   ate apples unroasted:
   Per Evam cunctis clausa est, & per Mariam virginem iterum patefacta est.
For he hath key and catch   though the king sleep.
   'And if Grace grant thee   to go in this wise,
Thou shalt see in thyself   Truth sit in thine heart
In a chain of charity   as thou a child were
To suffer him and say naught   against thy Sire's will.
   'But beware then of Wrath-thee   that is a wicked wretch;
He hath envy for him   that in thine heart sitteth,
And putteth forth Pride   for praise of thyself.
Boldness of thy benefactions   then maketh thee blind
And thou'lt be driven out as dew   and the door closed,
Keyed and clamped up   to keep thee without;
And hundred winters haply   ere ever thou enter.
So thus might thou lose his love   by uplifting thyself,
And never enter haply again   unless thou have grace.
   'But there are seven sisters   that ever serve Truth
And are porters of the posterns   that belong to the place;
One is called Abstinence   and Humility another;
Charity and Chastity   be his chief maidens;
Patience and Peace   much people they help;
The lady Largesse   hath let in full many:
She hath helped thousands out   from the Devil's pinfold.
He who is kin to this seven   so help me God!
He is wondrously welcome   and fairly received;
And unless ye be kin   to some of these seven,
'Tis full hard, by my head!   for any of you all
To get in at any gate   unless grace be given.'
   'Now, by Christ!' quoth a cutpurse   'I have no kin here!'
'Nor I,' quoth an apeward   'for aught that I know!'
'God knows,' quoth a waferer [1]   'knew I this for sooth

                              [1] See page 204.

E 57[1]

I'd go no foot further   for any friar's preaching.'
    'Yes,' quoth Piers the Plowman   and pushed them towards good,
'Mercy is a maiden there   hath might over all;
She is cousin to all sinners   and her Son also;
Through help of them two   (hope not in none other)
Thou might get grace there   if thou go betimes.'
    'By Saint Paul,' quoth a pardoner   'perchance I'm not known there.
I'll fetch my box with my briefs   bishop's letters and a bull!' [1]
'By Christ!' quoth a common woman   'thy company I'll follow,
Thou shalt say I'm thy sister   I know not where they've gone!'

[1] See page 204.

PASSUS VI

'THIS were a wicked way   unless we had a guide
That would show us each step'   thus these folk complained.
Quoth Perkin the plowman   'By Saint Peter of Rome!
I've an half acre to plow   hard by the highway.
Had I plowed this half acre   and sown it after,
I would wend then with you   and show you the way.'
    'This were long delay'   quoth a dame in a veil,
'What should we women   work at meanwhile?'
    'Some shall sew sacks,' quoth Piers   'for sheltering the wheat;
And ye, lovely ladies   with your long fingers,
Have silk and sendal   to sew, while there's time,
Chasubles for chaplains   churches to honour.
Wives and widows   wool and flax spin;
Make cloth, I counsel you   and so teach your daughters.
The needy and naked   take heed how they lie
And contrive for them clothes   for so commands Truth.
I shall get them livelihood   unless the land fails,
Flesh and bread both   to rich and to poor,
As long as I live   for the Lord's love of Heaven.
And all manner of men   that by meat and drink live,
Help ye them to work well   that win you your food.'
    'By Christ!' quoth a knight then   'he teaches the best;
But on this theme truly   taught was I never.
Teach me,' quoth the knight   'and, by Christ, I will try!'
    'By Saint Paul!' quoth Perkin   'ye proffer so fairly
That I'll swink and sweat   and sow for us both,
And other labours do for thy love   all my lifetime,
In covenant that thou keep   Holy Church and myself
From wasters and wicked men   that this world destroy.
And go and hunt hardily   for hares and for foxes,
For boars and for badgers   that break down mine hedges;
And go train thy falcons   wildfowl to kill,
For such come to my croft   and crop off my wheat.'
    Courteously the knight then   answered these words:
'By my powers, Piers,' quoth he   'I plight thee my troth
51

That pact to fulfil   though for it I fight;
As long as I live   I shall thee maintain.'
    'Yea; yet one point,' quoth Piers   'I pray of you more.
Look ye sue no tenant   unless Truth assent.
Though he may amerce them   let Mercy be taxer
And Meekness thy master   in spite of Meed's checks.
And though poor men proffer you   presents and gifts,
Take it not; for perchance   ye may not deserve it,
And then must repay it   again at a year's end
In a full perilous place   purgatory called.
Mishandle not bondmen   the better may thou speed.
Though he be underling here   well may happen in heaven
That he'll be worthier set   more blissful than thou,
Unless thou do better   and live as thou shouldest:
    Amice, ascende superius.
    'In the charnel at church   churls are hard to pick out,
Or a knight from a knave   know this in thine heart.
See thou'rt true of thy tongue   and tales that thou hate,
Unless they have wisdom   to chasten thy workmen.
Hold with no rascals   and hear not their tales,
Especially at meat   such men eschew;
They're the devil's minstrels   I bid thee to know.'
    'I assent, by St James!'   said the knight then,
'For to work by thy words   while my life endures.'
    'And I shall apparel me,' quoth Perkyn   'in pilgrim's wise,
And wend with you I will   till we find Truth;
Put on me my clothes   patched-up and ragged,
My leggings and mittens   'gainst cold of my nails,
Hang my seed basket at my neck   instead of a scrip,
And a bushel of breadcorn   bring me therein;
For I will sow it myself   and then will I wend
To pilgrimage as palmers do   pardon for to have.
Who will help me to plow   or to sow ere I wend
Shall have leave, by our Lord!   to glean here in harvest
And with it make himself merry   spite of who may begrudge it.
And all kinds of craftsmen   who will honestly live,
I shall find them food   that faithfully work.
Save Jack the juggler   and Janet of the stews,
Daniel the dicer   and Denot the bawd,
All lying friars   and folk of their order,
And Robin the ribald   for his smutty words——

Truth told me once and　　bade me repeat it:
Deleantur de libro viventium　　I'll not deal with them,
For Holy Church of their like　　is told no tithe to take:
　　Qui cum justis non scribantur;
By good luck they've escaped　　now God them amend!'
　　Dame Work-while-time-is　　Pier's wife was called;
His daughter, Do-right-so-　　or-thy-dame-shall-thee-beat;
His son, Suffer-thy-sovereigns-　　to-have-their-will-
Judge-them-not-for-if-thou-dost-　　thou-shalt-it-dearly-rue.
'May God be with all　　for so his word teacheth.
For now I am hoary and old　　and have goods of mine own
To penance and pilgrimage　　I will pass with these others.
Wherefore ere I wend　　I'll write out my bequest.
　　'*In Dei nomine. Amen*　　I make it myself.
He shall have my soul　　that best hath deserved it
And if from the fiend will defend　　for so I believe,
Till I come to his account　　as my *Credo* me telleth,
To have release and remission　　on that rental, I hope.
The church shall have my corpse　　and keep all my bones,
For of my corn and cattle　　she gathered the tithe.
I paid parson promptly　　for peril of my soul;
So is he holden, I hope　　to name me in his mass
And make a *memento* [1]　　among other Christians.
　　'My wife shall have my　　honest gains and no more,
To share with my daughters　　and my dear children.
For should I today die　　all my debts are quit;
I bore back what I borrowed　　ere I to bed went.
And with the residue and remnant　　by the Rood of Lucca!
I will worship therewith　　Truth, while I live,
And be his pilgrim at plow　　for all poor men's sake.
My plow-foot shall be my pike-staff　　and pick apart the roots
And help my coulter to carve　　and clean up the furrows.'
　　Now is Perkin and his pilgrims　　to the plow gone;
To plow his half acre　　helped him many.
Ditchers and delvers　　digged up the balks;
Therewith Perkin was pleased　　and praised them soon.
Other workmen there were　　that worked eagerly;
Each man in his manner　　made himself busy,
And some to please Perkin　　piked up the weeds.
　　At high prime-tide Piers　　let the plow stand,

---

[1] See page 204.

To oversee them himself   and whoso worked best
Should be hired thereafter   when harvest time came.
   Then sat down some   and sang over the ale
And helped plow his half acre   with 'Ho, trollo-lolli!'
   'On peril of my soul!' quoth Piers   out of pure anger,
'Unless ye rise swiftly   and speed you to work,
Shall no grain that groweth   gladden you at need,
And though ye die for dole   devil take him who cares.'
   The false fellows were afeared   and feigned themselves blind;
Some laid their legs awry   in the way such louts know,
And made their moan to Piers   and prayed of him grace;
'For we have no limbs to labour with   Lord, thanked be thee!
But we pray for you, Piers   and for your plow too,
That God of his grace   your grain multiply
And yield to you for your alms   that ye give us here;
For we can not swink nor sweat   such sickness us aileth.'
   'If it be sooth,' quoth Piers, 'that ye say   I shall soon it espy.
Ye be wasters, I wot well   and Truth wots the sooth!
I am his old hind   and am bidden by him to warn
Those in this world   who have harmed his workmen.
Ye waste what men win   with travail and trouble,
But Truth shall teach you   his plow-team to drive,
Or ye shall eat barley bread   and of the brook drink.
But if one be blind, broken-legged   or bolted with irons,
He shall eat wheat bread   and drink with myself,
Till God of his goodness   amendment him send.
But ye might travail as Truth wills   and take meat and hire
To keep kine in the field   the corn from the beasts,
To dike or to delve   or thresh out the sheaves,
Or help to make mortar   or bear muck afield.
In lechery and in lying   ye live, and in sloth,
And it is on sufferance   that vengeance is not taken.
But anchorites and hermits   that eat not but at noon,
And no more ere the morrow   mine alms shall they have,
And my goods shall clothe those   that have cloisters and churches.
But Robert the runabout   shall have naught of mine,
Nor friars; unless they preach well   and have leave of the bishop—
These shall have bread and pottage   and make themselves at ease:
'Tis an unreasonable religion [1]   hath right naught to depend on.'
Then a waster was wrath   and so would have fought,

[1] See page 204.

And to Piers the Plowman   he proffered his glove.
A Breton, a braggart   at Piers boasted too;
Bade him piss with his plow   for a starveling wretch!
'Willy or nilly   we will have our will;
Of thy flour and thy flesh   fetch when us like
And make merry therewith   despite thy accounts.'
    Then Piers the Plowman   complained to the knight
To keep him, as covenant was   from cursed wretches
And from these wolfish wasters   that do the world harm:
'For they waste and win naught   and meanwhile there'll be
No plenty for the people   while my plow be idle.'
    Courteously the knight then   as his nature was,
Warned the waster   and told him to mend:
'Or, by the order I bear   thou shalt suffer the law!'
    'I was not wont to work,' quoth Waster   'and now will not begin'—
And made light of the law   and less of the knight,
Set Piers and his plow   at the price of a pea
And menaced Pier's men   if they met again soon.
    'Now by peril of my soul   I shall punish you all!'
Piers whooped after Hunger   who heard him at once.
'Avenge me,' quoth he, 'on these wasters   who worry the world!'
    Hunger in haste then   seized Waste by the maw
And wrung him so by the belly   that both his eyes watered;
The Breton he buffeted   about the cheeks
That he looked lantern-jawed   all his life after.
He beat them so both   that he near burst their ribs;
Had not Piers with a pease-loaf   prayed Hunger to cease
They had been buried both   believe thou none other!
'Suffer them to live,' he said   'let them eat with the hogs
Or else beans and bran   baked up together,
Or else milk and mean ale'   thus prayed Piers for them.
    Loungers for fear thereof   fled into barns
And flapped on with flails   from morning till eve,
So that Hunger less hardily   looked upon them,
For a potful of pease   that Piers had made.
A heap of hermits   hung on to spades
And cut up their capes   to make themselves coats,
And went out as workmen   with spades and with shovels
To dig and to delve   to drive away hunger.
    The blind and bedridden   were bettered by thousands;
Those that sat to beg silver   soon were they healed;

For what was baked for a horse　　was a boon for the hungry,
And many a beggar for beans　　glad was to sweat,
And each poor man was well pleased　　to have pease for his hire;
And what Piers prayed them to do　　they did swift as a sparhawk.
Thereof was Piers proud　　and put them to work,
Gave them meat as he might　　and a moderate hire.

　Then had Piers pity　　and prayed Hunger to wend
Home into his own place　　and holden him there.
'For I am well avenged now　　of wasters, through thy might.
But I pray thee, ere thou pass'　　quoth Piers to Hunger,
'With beggars and bidders　　what's best to be done?
For I wot well, when thou'rt gone　　they will work full ill;
For misfortune makes them　　to be so meek now
And for default of their food　　this folk is at my will.
They're my brethren by blood　　for God bought us all.
Truth taught me once　　to love them each one
And to help them in all things　　always, as they need.
And now would I know of thee　　what were the best,
How I might master them　　and make them to work.'

　'Hear now,' quoth Hunger　　'and hold it for wisdom:
Bold beggars and big　　that might earn bread by work,
With hounds' bread and horse bread　　hold up their hearts,
Abate them with beans　　to keep down their bellies;
And if grumblers grouse　　bid them go work,
And they shall sup sweeter　　when they've it deserved.

　'And if thou find any fellow　　that any false man
Or fortune hath injured　　find how such to know!
Comfort him with thy goods　　for Christ's love of Heaven,
Love them and lend to them　　so God's law teacheth:
　　Alter alterius onera portate.
And all manner of man　　that thou mayest espy
That be needy and have naught　　help them with thy goods;
Love them and loathe them not　　let God take the vengeance;
If they've done thee evil　　let thou God alone;
　　Mihi vindicta, & ego retribuam.
If thou wilt be gracious before God　　do as the gospel teacheth,
And be loved among lowly men　　so shalt thou have grace,
　　Facite vobis amicos de mamona iniquitatis.'

　'I would not grieve God　　for all the goods on ground.
Might I do as thou sayest and be sinless?'　　said Piers then.
　'Yea, I promise thee,' quoth Hunger　　'or else the Bible lieth.

Go to Genesis the giant   engenderer of us all:
"*In sudore* and swink   thou shalt earn thy meat
And labour for livelihood"   and so our Lord bade.
And Wisdom saith the same   I saw it in the Bible:
"*Piger prae frigore*   no field would till,
Therefore shall he beg and bid   and no man cure his hunger."
  'Matthew-with-man's-face   mouthed these words,
That *servus nequam* had a coin   and as he would not chaffer
Had rebuke of his master   for evermore after;
Who because he would work not   took away his coin
And gave that coin to him   that ten others had;
And with that he said so   that Holy Church heard:
"He that hath shall have   and be helped when he needeth,
And he that naught hath shall naught have   and no man him help;
And of that he weeneth to have   I will him bereave."
  'Mother-Wit wisheth   that each wight should work
In diking or in delving   or travailing in prayers;
At contemplative or active life   Christ would that men work,
The psalter saith in the psalm   of *Beati omnes*,
He that feedeth himself   with his faithful labour
He is blessed by the Book   in body and in soul:
     Labores manuum tuarum, etc.'
  'Yet I pray you,' quoth Piers   '*par charité*, if ye know
Any line of leechcraft   teach it me, my dear.
For some of my servants   and myself also
For all a week work not   so our belly acheth.'
  'I wot well,' quoth Hunger   'what sickness you aileth;
You have munched overmuch   and that maketh you groan.
But I bid thee,' quoth Hunger   'as thou thine health willest,
That thou drink not each day   ere thou dine somewhat.
Eat naught, I command thee   ere hunger thee take
And send thee of his sauce   to savour thy lips;
And keep some till supper-time   and sit not too long,
Rise up ere appetite   have eaten his fill.
Let not Sir Surfeit   sit at thy board;
Listen not, for he is lecherous   and lickerish of tongue,
After many manner of meats   his maw is anhungered.
  'And if thou diet thee thus   I dare lay mine ears
That Physic his furred hoods   for his food shall sell,
And his Calabrian cloak   with the knots of gold,
And be fain, by my faith   his physic to leave

And learn to labour on land   for livelihood's sweet.
For murderers are many leeches   the Lord them amend!
Making men die through their drinks   ere destiny wills.'
     'By St Paul,' quoth Piers   'these are profitable words!
Wend thou, Hunger, when thou wilt   and well be thou ever.
For this lovely lesson   may the Lord requite thee.'
     'I swear to God,' quoth Hunger   'hence will I not wend
Till I have dined this day   and drunken also.'
     'I have no penny,' quoth Piers   'pullets for to buy,
Nor neither geese nor pigs   but two green cheeses,
A few curds and cream   and an oaten cake,
And two loaves of beans and bran   baked for my youngsters.
And yet I say, by my soul   I have no salt bacon;
Nor no hen's eggs, by Christ   collops [1] for to make.
But I have parsley and leeks   with many cabbages,
And a cow and a calf   a cart-mare also
To draw dung afield   while the drought lasteth.
With this for our living we must live   until Lammas time come,
And by that I hope I have   harvest in my croft;
Then may I make thee thy dinner   as I'd like to dearly.'
All the poor people then   their peascods fetched,
Beans and baked apples   they brought in their laps,
Onions and chervils   and many ripe cherries,
And proffered Piers this present   wherewith to please Hunger.
   Hunger ate all in haste   and asked after more.
Then poor folk for fear   fed Hunger quickly;
With green leeks and pease   to poison him they sought.
By that it nighed near harvest   new corn came to market;
Then were folk fain   and fed Hunger with the best,
With good ale, as Glutton taught   and made Hunger go sleep.
   Then would Waster not work   but wandered about,
Nor no beggar eat bread   that had beans therein
But asked for the best   white, made of clean wheat;
Nor none halfpenny ale   in no wise would drink,
But of the best and the brownest   for sale in the borough.
   Labourers that have no land   to live on but their hands
Deigned not to dine at day   on worts a night old.
May no penny ale please them   nor no piece of bacon,
Only fresh flesh or fish   fried, roast, or baked,
And that *chaud* or *plus chaud*   'gainst chilling their maw.

[1] See page 204.

He must be hired at a high rate   else will he chide,
And wail at the time   when he was workman made;
And against Cato's counsel   begins he to rail:
    Paupertatis onus patienter ferre memento.
He has grievances against God   and grumbles against Reason;
Then curseth he the king   and all his counsel after
For licensing laws that   labourers grieve.
But while Hunger was their master   then would none of them chide
Nor strive against his statute   so sternly he looked.
But I warn you, workmen   earn while ye may,
For Hunger hitherward   hasteth him fast,
He shall awake with water   wasters to chasten.
Ere five years be fulfilled   such famine shall arise,
Through floods and foul weather   all fruits shall fail.
So said planet Saturn [1]   and sent to warn you:
When ye see the sun gone amiss   and heads of two monks,
And a Maid have the mastery   and multiply by eight,
Then shall Death withdraw him   and Dearth be the judge,
And Davy the ditcher   shall die of hunger,
Unless God of his goodness   do grant us a truce.

<hr>

[1] See page 204.

PASSUS VII

TRUTH hereof heard tell   and to Piers he sent,
To take him his team   and to till the earth;
And provided a pardon   *a poena et a culpa* [1]
For him, and for his heirs   for evermore after.
And bade him hold him at home   and plow up his fields,
And all that helped him to plow   to set or to sow,
Or any other work   that might Piers avail,
Pardon with Piers Plowman   Truth them hath granted.
   Kings and knights   that keep Holy Church
And rightfully in realms   rule over the people
Have pardon through purgatory   to pass full lightly,
With patriarchs and prophets   in paradise to be fellows.
   Bishops most blessed   if they be as they should,
Legists of both the laws   to preach to the lawless,
And inasmuch as they may   amend all sinners,
Are peers with the apostles   (this pardon Piers showeth),
And at the day of doom   at the high dais to sit.
   Merchants to the good   had many years,
But none *a poena et a culpa*   would the pope them grant,
For they hold not her holy days   as Holy Church teacheth,
And they swear 'by their souls'   and 'so God must them help'
Clean against conscience   merchandise to sell.
   But under his secret seal   Truth sent them a letter
That they should buy boldly   what they liked best,
And afterwards sell again   and save their profits
Therewith to amend *maisons Dieu*   and miserable folk help;
To repair rotten roads   where plainly required;
And to build up bridges   that were broken down;
Help maidens to marry   or make of them nuns;
Poor people and prisoners   to find them their food;
And set scholars to school   or to some other craft;
Relieve poor religious   and lower their rents—
'And I shall send you myself   Michael mine archangel,
That no devil shall you daunt   nor fright you at death,

[1] See page 204.

And keep you from despair   if ye will thus work,
And send your souls safely   to my saints in joy.'
   Then were merchants merry   many wept for joy,
And praised Piers the Plowman   that provided this bull.
Men of law less pardon had   that pleaded for Meed;
For the psalter saveth not them   such as taketh gifts,
And especially from innocents   that no evil know:
     Super innocentem munera non accipies.
Pleaders should take much pains   to plead and help such;
Princes and prelates should   pay for their travail:
     A regibus & principibus erit merces eorum.
   But many justices and jurors   would do more for fees
Than *pro Dei pietate*   believe thou none other.
But he that spendeth his speech   and speaketh for the poor
That is innocent and needy   and no man oppresseth,
Comforteth them in that case   without coveting gifts,
And sheweth law for our Lord's love   as it hath learned,
Shall no devil at his death-day   daunt him with fear
That his soul is not safe   as witness the psalms:
     Domine, quis habitabit in tabernaculo tuo, etc.
   But to buy water, wind, wit   or fire, the fourth—
These four the Father of Heaven   made for his fold in common;
And these be Truth's treasures   true folk to help,
And shall never wax nor wane   without God himself.
   Those that pence of poor men   for their pleading take
Find their pardon full small   at their parting hence,
When they draw on to die   and indulgences would have.
Ye legists and lawyers   hold this for the truth,
That if that I lie   Matthew is to blame,
For he bade me write this   and this proverb told:
     Quodcumque vultis ut faciant vobis homines, facite eis.
   All living labourers   that live by their hands
And take the just wages   they honestly earn,
And live in love and in law   for their lowly hearts
Have the same absolution   that was sent to Piers.
   Beggars and bidders   are not in the bull,
Unless the occasion be honest   that makes them to beg.
He that beggeth or cadgeth   unless he have need
Is as false as the fiend   and defraudeth the needy;
He beguileth the giver   all against his will
For if he wist he were not needy . he would give to another

That were more needy than he   so the neediest would be helped.
Cato teacheth men thus   and the Clerk of the Stories;
Cui des, videto   is Cato's teaching
And in the stories he teacheth   to bestow thine alms well:
    Sit elemosina tua in manu tua, donec studes cui des.
  But Gregory was a good man   and bade give to all
That asketh for his love   that giveth to us all:
Non eligas cui miserearis, ne forte praetereas illum qui meretur accipere.
Quia incertum est pro quo Deo magis placeas.
  For wit ye never who is worthy   but God wot who hath need.
In him that taketh is the treachery   if treason there be;
For he that giveth, parteth   and prepareth him to rest,
But he that beggeth, borroweth   and bringeth himself in debt.
For beggars borrow evermore   and their bail is God
To repay those that give to them   with interest added:
Quare non dedisti pecuniam meam ad mensam,
Ut ego veniens cum usuris exegissem illam?
  Therefore beg not, ye beggars   unless ye've great need.
For whoso must buy him bread   the Book beareth witness,
Hath enough that hath bread enough   though he have naught else.
    Satis dives est, qui non indiget pane.
  Find habit and solace   in reading saints' lines;
The Book banneth begging   and blameth them thus:
    Junior fui, et jam senui: et non vidi justum derelictum, nec semen ejus
      quaerens panem.
  For ye live not in love   and hold to no law.
Many of you wed not   the women you go with,
But like whinnying beasts   mount them and tread them,
And so bring forth children   that bastards men call.
If the back or some bone   is broken in youth,
Ye will exploit that child   for evermore after.
There is more misshaped people   among all these beggars
Than of other manner of men   that on this mould move.
And they that live thus their life   may well loathe the time
That ever he was born   when he shall hence fare.
  But old men and hoary   without help or strength,
And all women with child   that can work no more,
The blind and bedridden   and broken in limb,
That bear mischief meekly   as lepers and others,
Have as plenary a pardon   as the plowman himself;
For love of their lowly hearts   our Lord hath them granted

Their penance and purgatory   here on this earth.

   'Piers,' quoth a priest then   'thy pardon must I read,

For I will construe each clause   and tell it in English.'

   And Piers at his prayer   the pardon unfoldeth,

And I behind both   beheld all the bull.

All in two lines it lay   and not a leaf more,

And was written right thus   in witness of Truth:

> *Et qui bona egerunt, ibunt in vitam aeternam; qui vero mala, in ignem aeternum.*

   'Peter!' quoth the priest then   'I can no pardon find

But "Do well and have well   and God shall have thy soul;

But do evil and have evil   and after thy death-day

The Devil have thy soul   hope thou none other."'

   And Piers in vexation   tore it in twain,

And said: '*Si ambulavero in medio umbrae mortis non timebo mala: quoniam tu mecum es.*

   'I shall cease from my sowing   and swink not so hard,

Nor about my belly-joy   so busy be more.

Of prayers and of penance   shall my plow be hereafter,

And I'll weep when I should sleep   though my wheat-bread fail.

The prophet his bread ate   in penance and sorrow,

And by what psalter saith   so did many others;

Whoso loveth God loyally   can live upon little:

> *Fuerunt mihi lacrimae meae panes die ac nocte.*

   'And, unless Saint Luke lie   he shows by the birds

We should not be too busy   about the world's bliss.

Ne solliciti sitis   he saith in the gospel,

And sheweth us by examples   our own selves to guide.

The fowls in the fields   who feeds them in winter?

They've no garner to go to   God finds for them all.'

   'What!' quoth priest to Perkin   'Peter! as methinketh,

Thou art lettered a little   who learned thee thy book?'

   'Abstinence the abbess,' quoth Piers   'mine A B C taught me,

And Conscience came after   and taught me much more.'

   'Wert thou priest, Piers,' quoth he   'thou mightest preach where thou wouldest,

As a divine in divinity   with *dixit insipiens* for theme.'

   'Ignorant fool!' quoth Piers   'little lookest thou on the Bible,

And the saws of Solomon   seldom thou seest:

> *Ejice derisores et jurgia cum eis, ne crescant, etc.*'

   Thus the priest and Perkin   opposed one to the other.

Through their words I awoke   and looked about
And saw the sun in the south   set at that time,
Meatless and moneyless   on Malvern hills
And musing on this vision   I went on my way.
    Many times this vision   hath made me study
Of that I saw sleeping   if so it might be;
And also of Piers Plowman   full pensive in heart;
And what pardon he had   all the people to comfort,
And how the priest had impugned it   with just two words.
I've no savour in soothsaying   I see it oft fail;
And the canonists and Cato   counsel us not
To put faith in divining   for *somnia ne cures.*
But the book of the Bible   clearly bears witness
How Daniel divined   the dreams of a king,
That was Nebuchadnezzar   named by the clerks.
To whom Daniel said: 'Sir King   thy dream betokeneth
That unknown knights shall come   thy kingdom to cleave;
Amongst lower lords thy lands   shall be divided.'
And as Daniel divined   indeed it fell out,
The king lost his lordship   and lower men had it.
And Joseph dreamed marvellously   how the moon and sun
And the eleven stars of heaven   saluted him all.
Then Jacob judged   of Joseph's dream:
'*Beau fils,*' then quoth his father   'for our lack we shall,
I myself and my sons   seek you in our need.'
    As his father said it befell   in Pharaoh's time,
That Joseph was justice   Egypt to govern;
It befell as his father told   his friends there him sought.
And all this maketh me   on this dream to think:
And how the priest proved   no pardon like Do-well,
And deemed that good deeds   an indulgence surpassed,
And biennials and triennials [1]   and letters of bishops.
And how Do-well at Doomsday   is honourable held,
Surpassing the pardon   of Saint Peter's church.
    Now hath the pope power   to grant the people
Remission of penance   to pass into Heaven:
This is our belief   as lettered men teach us:
        Quodcumque ligaveris super terram, erit ligatum et in coelis, etc.
So I believe loyally   (the Lord forbid else!)
That pardon, penance, and prayers   cause to be saved
                    [1] See page 204.

Souls that have sinned   seven times deadly.
But to trust to indulgences   truly methinketh,
Is not so safe for the soul   as it is to do well.
    Therefore I advise all you   the rich on this earth
That on trust of your treasure   triennials can have,
Be ye never the bolder   to break the ten laws
And especially ye, masters   mayors, and judges,
Who for wise men are held   and have this world's wealth
To purchase your pardons   and the pope's bulls.
At the dreadful Doom when   the dead shall arise
And come all before Christ   their account to yield,
How thou leddest thy life   and here his laws kept,
And how thou didst day by day   the doom will declare:
Then a poke full of pardons   as provincials' letters,
Though found in the fraternity   of all the friars' orders
With doublefold indulgence   unless good deeds help you,
I put your patents and pardons   at one pea-pod's value!
Therefore I counsel Christians   to cry God mercy,
And Mary his mother   be our mediatress,
That God give us grace here   ere that we go hence
That we may work such works   while we are here
That after our death-day   Do-well will declare
At the day of Doom that   we did as he bade.

PASSUS VIII

THUS robed in russet   I roamed about
All a summer season   for to seek Do-well,
And inquired full oft   of folk that I met,
If any wight wist   where Do-well was at in,
And what man he might be   of many men I asked.

    Was never wight as I went   that could show me the way
Where this man dwelled   less nor more;
Till it befell on a Friday   two friars I met,
Masters of the Minors   men of great wit.[1]
I hailed them politely   as I had learned,
And prayed them, for charity   ere they passed further,
If they knew any country   or coasts, as they went,
Where that Do-well dwelleth   grant me to know.

    For they be men of this mould   that most widely walk,
And know countries, and courts   and poor men's cots,
And Do-well and Do-evil   where they dwell both.

    'Amongst us,' quoth the Minors   'that man is dwelling,
And ever hath, as I hope   and ever shall hereafter.'

    '*Contra*,' quoth I like a clerk   and began to dispute,
And told them truly, '*septies   in die cadit justus;*
Seven times, saith the Book   sinneth the righteous.
And whoso sinneth,' I said   'doth evil, as methinketh,
And Do-well and Do-evil   may not dwell together.
Ergo, he is not always   among you friars;
He is sometimes elsewhere   teaching the people.'

    'I shall tell thee, my son'   said the friar then,
'How seven times the upright   in a day sinneth;
By a picture,' quoth the friar   'I shall thee fair show.

    'Put a man in a boat   on a broad water,
The wind and the water   and the boat rocking
Make the man many a time   to fall and recover;
For stand he never so firm   he stumbleth if he move;
And yet is he safe and sound   and so it behoves him,
For if he did not rise quickly   and reach for the helm,

[1] See page 204.

66

The wind would with the water   the boat overthrow;
And then were his life lost   through his own neglect.
And thus it falleth,' quoth the friar   'to folk here on earth;
The water is likened to the world   that waneth and waxeth,
The goods of this earth are like   to the great waves,
That as winds and weather   toss about.
The boat is likened to our body   that brittle is by nature,
So through the fiend and the flesh   and the fickle world,
Sinneth the upright   a day, seven times.

'But deadly sin doth he not   for Do-well him keepeth,
And that Christ the champion   chief help against sin;
For he strengtheneth man to stand   and steareth man's soul,
And though thy body waver   as boat doth in water,
Ever is thy soul safe   unless thyself will
Do a deadly sin   and drown so thy soul;
God will suffer well thy sloth   if thyself liketh.
For he gave thee a new year's gift [1]   to care well for thyself,
And that is wit and free will   to every wight a portion,
To flying fowls   to fishes and to beasts.
But man hath most thereof   and most is to blame
Unless he work well therewith   as Do-well him teacheth.'

'I have no natural knowing,' quoth I   'to conceive all your words,
But if I may live and look   I shall go to learn better.'
'I commit thee to Christ,' quoth he   'that on the cross died.'
And I said, 'The same   save you from mischance,
And give you grace on this ground   good men to become.'

And thus I went widely   walking alone,
By a wild wilderness   and by a wood side.
Bliss of the birds   made me abide,
And under a linden in a glade   leaned I awhile,
To listen to the lays   the lovely fowls made.
Mirth of their mouths   made me there to sleep;
The most marvellous dream   met me then
That ever dreamed wight   in world as I ween.

A tall man, as methought   and like to myself,
Came and called me   by my own name.
'What art thou?' quoth I then   'that thou my name knowest?'
'That thou knowest well,' quoth he   'and no wight better.'

'Know I what thou art?'   'Thought,' said he then,
'I have attended thee these seven years   sawest thou me no sooner?'

---

[1] See page 204.

   'Art thou Thought?' quoth I then   'canst thou me show
Where that Do-well dwelleth   and let me know?'
   'Do-well and Do-better   and Do-best the third,' quoth he,
'Are three fair virtues   and be not far to find.
Whoso is true of his tongue   and of his two hands,
And through his labour or through his land   his livelihood winneth,
And is trusty of his tallying   taketh but his own,
And is not a drunkard nor disdainful   Do-well is with him.
   'Do-better doth right thus   but he doth much more;
He is as lowly as a lamb and gentle of speech,
And helpeth all men   as they are in need;
The bags and the purses   he hath burst them all
That the earl Avaricious   held, and his heirs;
And thus with Mammon's money   he hath made him friends,
And hath hurried into religion   and hath translated the Bible,
And preacheth to the people   St Paul's words.
     Libenter suffertis insipientes, cum sitis ipsi sapientes.
"And suffer the unwise   with you for to live."
And with glad will do them good   for so God you bids.
   'Do-best is above both   and beareth a bishop's crozier;
It is hooked at one end   to hale men from hell.
A spike is on that staff   to strike down the wicked
That watch for any wickedness   Do-well to vex.
And Do-well and Do-better   amongst them ordained
To crown one to be king   to rule them both;
But if Do-well or Do-better   act against Do-best,
Then shall the king come   and cast them in irons,
And unless Do-best plead for them   they to be there for ever.
   'Thus Do-well and Do-better   and Do-best the third,
Crowned one to be king   to watch over them all,
And to rule the Realm   by their three wits,
And none otherwise   but as they three assented.'
   I thanked Thought then   that he me thus taught;
'But yet satisfies me not thy saying   I long to learn
How Do-well, Do-better and Do-best   do amongst the people.'
   'But Wit can teach thee,' quoth Thought   'where those three dwell;
Else know I none that can   that now is alive.'
   Thought and I thus   three days we went,
Discussing Do-well   day after other,
And ere we were aware   with Wit did we meet.
He was long and lean   like to no other,

Was no pomp in his apparel   nor poverty neither,
Sober in his semblance   and of mild mien.
I dared move no matter   to make him dispute,
But I begged Thought then   to be intermediary,
And put forth some proposition   to test his wits,
What was Do-well from Do-better   and Do-best from them both.
 Then Thought at that time   said these words,
'Where Do-well, Do-better   and Do-best be in the land,
Here is Will would know   if Wit can teach him,
And whether he be man or no man   this man fain would discover,
And act as they three would have   this is his purpose.'

PASSUS IX

'Sir Do-well dwelleth,' quoth Wit   'not a day hence,
In a castle that Kind [1] made   of four kinds of things;
Of earth and air is it made   mingled together,
With wind and with water   certainly joined.
Nature hath closed therein   craftily withal,
A beloved that he loveth   as himself,
Anima [2] she is called   but Envy her hateth,
A proud pricker of France   *princeps hujus mundi,*
And would win her away   with wiles, if he might.
But Kind knoweth this well   and keepeth her the better,
And hath placed her with Sir Do-well   who is duke of these marches.
Do-better is her damsel   Sir Do-well's daughter,
To serve this lady truly   both early and late.
Do-best is above both   a bishop's peer;
What he bids must be done   he ruleth them all;
Anima that lady   is led by his teaching.
  'But the constable of that castle   who keepeth all the watch,
Is a wise knight withal   Sir Conscience he is called,
And hath five fair sons   by his first wife;
Sir See-well and Say-well   and Hear-well the kind,
Sir Work-well-with-thine-hand   an active man of strength,
And Sir Godfrey Go-well   great lords in truth.
These five are set   to save this lady *Anima*,
Till Kind come or send   to save her for ever.'
  'What kind of thing is Kind,' quoth I   'canst thou me tell?'
  'Kind,' quoth Wit 'is a being   of all kinds of things;
Father and former   of all that ever was made;
And that is the great God   that beginning had never,
Lord of life and of light   of joy and of pain.
Angels and all things   are at his will.
But man is him most like   in mark and in form;
For through the word that he spake   came forth beasts,
    Dixit, et facta sunt;
And made man likest   to himself, one,

And Eve of his rib-bone   without any mediary.
For he was sole of himself   and said *faciamus*,
As who saith, "more must be here   than my word one;
My might must help   now with my speech."
Right as a lord should make letters   and he lacked parchment,
Though he knew how to write never so well   if he had no pen,
The letters for all the lordship   I believe, were never made.
  'And so it seemeth by him   as the Bible telleth,
      There he said, *dixit, et facta sunt*;
He must work with his word   and his wit show.
And in this manner was man made   through might of God almighty,
With his word and workmanship   and with life to endure.
And thus God gave him a soul   of the Godhead of heaven,
And of his great grace   granted him bliss,
And that is life that aye shall last   to all his lineage after.
And that is the castle that Kind made   *Caro* it is called,
And is as much as to say   man with a soul;
And that he wrought with work   and with word both;
Through might of the majesty   man was made.
  'Conscience and all wits   closed be therein,
For love of the lady *Anima*   who Life is named;
Over all in man's body   she walketh and wandereth,
And in the heart is her home   and her chief rest.
But Conscience is in the head   and to the heart he looketh,
What *Anima* loves or loathes   he allows her at his will;
For after the grace of God   the greatest is Conscience.
  'Much woe to that man   that misruleth his Conscience,
And that be greedy gluttons   their god is their belly;
      Quorum deus venter est.
For they serve Satan   their soul shall he have;
That liveth sinful life here   their soul is like the devil.
And all that live good life   are like God almighty,
      Qui manet in caritate, in Deo manet, etc.
  'Alas! that drink shall undo   what God bought dear,
And makes God forsake them   that he shaped to his likeness;
      *Amen dico vobis, nescio vos; et alibi: et dimisi eos secundum desideria
      eorum.*
  'Simpletons that lack Conscience   I find that holy church
Should provide for them that fail   and fatherless children;
And widows that have naught wherewith   to win them their food,
Mad men, and maidens   that helpless were;

All these lack Conscience   and should be taught.
    'Of this matter I might   make a long tale,
And find many witnesses   amongst the four Doctors,
And that I lie not in that I teach thee   Luke beareth witness.
    'Godfather and godmother   that see their godchildren
In grief and misfortune   and may them comfort,
Shall have penance in purgatory   unless they them help.
For more is due to the little child   ere he the law knows,
Than naming of name   and he never the wiser!
Would no Christian creature   cry at the gate,
Nor lack bread nor soup   if prelates did as they should.
A Jew would not see a Jew   go begging for need,
For all the goods on this earth   if he amend it might.
    'Alas! that a Christian creature   shall be unkind to another,
Since Jews that we judge   Judas' fellows,
Each of them helpeth the other   in that that he needeth.
Why will not we Christians   of Christ's goods be as generous
As Jews, that be our teachers?   shame to us all!
The commons for their uncharity   I fear me, shall pay.
    'Bishops shall be blamed   for beggars' sake;
He is worse than Judas   that giveth a jester silver,
And biddeth the beggar go   for his torn clothes:

> *Proditor est prelatus cum Juda, qui patrimonium Christi minus distri-*
> *buit; et alibi:*

> *Pernitiosus dispensator est, qui res pauperum Christi inutiliter consumit.*

He doth not well that doth thus   nor dreadeth not God almighty,
Nor loveth not Solomon's sayings   that Wisdom taught;

> *Initium sapientiae, timor Domini:*

That dreadeth God, he doth well;   that dreadeth him for love,
And not for dread of punishment   doth in that the better;
He doth best, that withdraweth him   by day and by night
From wasting any speech   or any space of time;

> *Qui offendit in uno, in omnibus est reus.*

    'Squandering of time   as true as true!
Is most hated upon earth   by them that be in heaven,
And to waste speech   that germ is of grace,
And God's glee-man   and a game of heaven;
Would never the faithful Father   his fiddle were un-tuned,
Nor his gleeman a vagabond   a goer to taverns!
    'To all true upright men   that work desire,
Our Lord loveth them and lends   in calm or storm,

Grace to go to them   and gain their livelihood;
 Inquirentes autem dominum non minuentur omni bono.
'True wedded living folk   in this world is Do-well;
For they must work and earn   and the world sustain.
For of their kind they come   that confessors are called,
Kings and knights   caesars and serfs,
Maidens and martyrs   out of one man come.
The wife was made the way   for to help the work,
And thus was wedlock wrought   with a middle person;
First by the father's will   and the friends' council,
And then by assent of themselves   as they two might accord.
And thus was wedlock wrought   and God himself it made;
In earth its heaven is   himself was the witness.
 'But false folk faithless   thieves and liars,
Wasters and wretches   out of wedlock, I trow,
Conceived be in evil time   as Cain was by Eve.[1]
Of such sinful wretches   the psalter maketh mention,
 Concepit in dolore, et peperit iniquitatem, etc.:
And all that came of that Cain   came to evil end.
For God sent to Seth   and said by an angel,
"Thine issue with thine issue   I will that they be wedded,
And not thy kind with Cain's   coupled nor espoused."
 'Yet some, against the sending   of our Saviour of heaven,
Cain's kind and his kind   coupled together,
Till God was wrath for their works   and such a word said,
"That I made man   now it me repenteth";
 Poenitet me fecisse hominem.
And came to Noah anon   and bade not stay:
"Quickly go shape a ship   of planks and of boards.
Thyself and thy sons three   and then your wives,
Hurry you to that boat   and bideth ye therein,
Till forty days be fulfilled   that the flood have washed
Clean away the cursed blood   that Cain made.
Beasts that now be   shall blame the time,
That ever that cursed Cain   came on this earth;
All shall die for his deeds   by dales and by hills,
And the fowls that fly   forth with other beasts,
Except only   of each kind a couple,
That in thy shingled ship   shall be saved."
 'In this the child   for the grandsire's guilt,

[1] See page 204.

And all for their forefathers   they fared the worse.
The gospel is against this   in one degree, I find,

Filius non portabit iniquitatem patris, et pater non portabit iniquitatem filii, etc.

'But I find, if the father   be false and a rascal,
That somewhat the son   shall have the sire's splotches.
Graft on an elder   and if thine apple be sweet,
Much marvel methinketh   and more, of a rascal
That bringeth forth any child   unless he be the same,
And have a savour of the sire   seldom seest thou other;

Numquam colligimus de spinis uvas, nec de tribulis ficus.

And thus through cursed Cain   came care upon earth;
And all for they wrought wedlock   against God's will.
Therefore have they punishment for their marriages   that marry so their
    children;
For some, as I see now   truly to tell,
For covetousness of wealth   unnaturally be wedded.
As unhappy conception   cometh of such marriages,
As befell of the folk   that I before told.
For good should wed good   though they no goods have;
"I am *via et veritas*," saith Christ   "I may prosper all."
'It is an uncomely coupling   by Christ, as methinketh,
To give a young wench   to an old dotard,
Or wed any widow   for wealth of her goods,
That never shall child bear   except in her arms!
Many a pair since the pestilence   have plight them together;
The fruit that they bring forth   are foul words,
In jealousy joyless   and scolding in bed.
Have they no children but strife   and abusing each other.
'And though they betake them to Dunmow [1]   unless the devil help
To try for the flitch   fetch they it never;
And unless they both be forsworn   that bacon they lose.
'Therefore I council all Christians   covet not to be wed
For covetousness of wealth   nor of kindred rich.
But young men and maidens   match you together,
Widows and widowers   do the same.
For no lands, but for love   look ye to be wedded,
And then get ye the grace of God   and goods enough to live with.
'And every manner layman   that may not continue,
Wisely go wed   and beware him of sin;

[1] See page 204.

For lechery in desire   is a limed snare of hell.
Whilst thou art young   and thy weapon keen,
Content thee with wiving   if though wilt be exempt.
Dum sis vir fortis   ne des tua robora scortis,
Scribitur in portis   meretrix est janua mortis.
　'When ye have wived, beware   and act in due time;
Not as Adam and Eve   when Cain was engendered.
For unseasonably, truly   between man and woman,
Should no play in bed be   unless they both be clean
Both of life and of soul   and in perfect charity,
That same private deed   do no man should.
And if they lead thus their life   it pleaseth God almighty;
For he made wedlock first   and himself it said;
　　Bonum est ut unusquisque uxorem suam habeat, propter fornicationem.
　'And they that otherwise be got   for vagabonds be held,
As false folk, foundlings   cheaters and liars;
Ungracious in getting goods   or love of the people,
Wandering and wasting   what they may gain.
Against Do-well they do evil   and the devil serve,
And after their death-day   shall dwell with the same,
But God give them grace here   themselves to amend.
　'Do-well, my friend, is   to do as law teacheth;
To love thy friend and thy foe   believe me, that is Do-better.
To give and to cherish   both young and old,
To heal and to help   is Do-best of all.
And Do-well is to dread God   and Do-better to suffer,
And so cometh Do-best of both   and bringeth down the proud,
And that is wicked will   that many a work ruins,
And driveth away Do-well   through deadly sins.'

PASSUS X

THEN had Wit a wife   was called Dame Study,
That lean was of face   and of body both.
She was wondrously wrath   that Wit me thus taught,
And all staring Dame Study   sternly said,
'Well art thou wise,' quoth she to Wit   'any wisdom to tell
To flatterers or to fools   that frantic be of wit!'
And blamed him and scolded him   and bade him be still,
With such wise words   from teaching any sots;
And said '*noli mittere*, man   margery pearls [1]
Amongst hogs, that have   haws at will.
They do but drivel there-on   draff is dearer to them
Than all the precious stones   that in Paradise grow.
I say it of such,' quoth she   'that showeth by their works,
That they would rather land   and lordship on earth,
Of riches or rents   and rest at their will,
Than all the true sayings   that Solomon said ever.
    'Wisdom and wit now   is not worth a cress,
Unless it be carded with covetousness   as clothiers comb their wool.
Whoso can contrive deceits   and conspire wrongs,
And conduct a law-day   to hinder truth,
He that such crafts knows   to council is called;
They lead lords with lies   and belie truth.
    'Job the gentle   in his tales witnesseth,
That wicked men they wield   the wealth of this world,
And that they be lords of each a land   that out of law live;
      Quare impii vivunt? bene est omnibus, qui praevaricantur et inique agunt.
The psalter saith the same   of such that do ill,
      Ecce ipsi peccatores abundantes; in saeculo obtinuerunt divitias.
"Lo!" saith Holy Scripture   "these lords be rascals!"
Those to whom God most giveth   least goods they dealeth,
And most unkind to the commons   that most wealth wieldeth;
      Quae perfecisti, destruxerunt; justus autem quid fecit?
Ribalds for their ribaldry   may have of their goods,
And jesters and jugglers   and tellers of tales.

[1] See page 204.

'But he that hath holy writ   ever in his mouth,
And can tell of Tobit   and of the twelve apostles,
Or preach of the punishment   that Pilate wrought
On Jesus the gentle   that Jews tortured:
Little is he loved   that such a lesson showeth,
Or cherished for advancement   I call on God himself!
　'But those that fain them fools   and with falsehood live,
Against the law of our Lord   and lie in themselves,
Spit and spew   and speak foul words,
Drink and drivel   and make men gape,
Mimic and lie against them   that give them no gifts,
They know no more minstrelsy   nor music,
Than Mund the miller   of *multa fecit Deus*!
Nor were their vile ribaldry   have God my troth,
If never king nor knight   nor canon of Saint Paul's
Gave them for the new year   the gift of a groat!
But mirth and minstrelsy   amongst men is now
Lechery, lying   and vagabonds' tales;
Gluttony and great oaths   this mirth they loveth.
　'But if they chatter of Christ   these ignorant clerks
At meat in their pleasures   when minstrels be still,
Then telleth they of the Trinity   a tale or two,
And bring forth a bald reason   and take Bernard [1] to witness,
And put forth an assumption   to prove the truth.
Thus they drivel at their dais   the deity to know,
And gnaw God with their gorge   when their guts are full.
　'But the miserable may cry   and call at the gate,
Both a-hungered and a-thirst   and for chill a-quake;
Is none to receive near   his anguish to heal,
But shout at him as a hound   and bid him go thence.
Little loveth he that lord   that gave him all that bliss,
That thus shares with the poor man   a portion when he is in need.
Unless mercy were in common men   more than in rich,
Mendicants meat-less   might go to bed.
God is much in the mouth   of these great masters,
But amongst poor men   his mercy and his works;
And so saith the psalter   I have seen it oft,
　　Ecce audivimus eam in Ephrata, invenimus eam in campis silvae.
　'Clerks and other kinds of men   talk of God in plenty,
And have him much on their lips   but mean men at heart.
　　　　　　　　　[1] See page 204.

Friars and deceivers   have found such questions
To please with proud men   since the pestilence time,
And preach at Saint Paul's [1]   for pure envy of clerks,
So that folk are not confirmed in the faith   nor free of their goods,
Nor sorry for their sins   so is pride waxed
In religion and in all the realm   amongst rich and poor,
That prayers have no power   the pestilence to stay.
And yet the wretches of this world   is none warned by the other,
Nor for dread of the Death   withdrawn not their pride,
Nor be plenteous to the poor   as pure charity wills,
But in gayness and gluttony   devour their goods themselves,
And give not to the beggar   as the Book teacheth,

> *Frange esurienti panem tuum, etc.*

And the more he winneth and wields   wealth and riches,
And lordeth it in lands   the less goods he distributes.
   'Tobit telleth you not so   take heed, ye rich,
How the book Bible   of him beareth witness:

> *Si tibi sit copia, abundanter tribue; si autem exiguum, illud impertiri stude
>   libenter:*

Whoso hath much, expend it humanely   so meaneth Tobit,
And whoso little wieldeth   rule himself accordingly;
For we have no compact of our life   how long it shall last.
Such lessons lords should   love to hear,
And how they might the most of the poor   humanely succour.
   'Not to fare as a fiddler or a friar   for to seek feasts,
At home in other men's houses   and hating their own.
Wretched is the hall   each day in the week,
Where the lord nor the lady   liketh not to sit.
Now hath each rich man a rule   to eat by himself
In a private parlour   because of poor men,
Or in a chamber with a chimney   and leave the chief hall,
That was made for meals   men to eat in;
And all to spare from spilling   what spend shall another.
   'I have heard high men   eating at table,
Talk as they clerks were   of Christ and of his powers,
And lay faults upon the Father   that formed us all,
And carp against clerks   crabbed words;
"Why would our Saviour suffer   such a worm [2] into his paradise,
That beguiled the woman   and the man after,
Through whose wiles and words   they went to hell,

And all their seed for their sin   the same death suffered?
Here lieth your lore"   these lords begin to dispute,
"Of that ye clerks us teacheth   of Christ by the gospel;
    Filius non portabit iniquitatem patris, etc.
Why should we that now be   for the works of Adam
Perish and be destroyed?   reason warrants it never;
    Unusquisque portabit onus suum, etc."
    'Such motions they move   these masters in their vainglory,
And make men disbelieve   that muse much on their words;
Imaginative hereafter   shall answer to your purpose.
Augustine to such arguers   he telleth them this text,
    Non plus sapere quam oportet.
Wish never to know   why that God would
Suffer Satan   his seed to beguile,
But believe loyally   in the lore of holy church,
And pray him for pardon   and penance in thy life,
And in his great mercy   to amend you here.
For all that wish to know   the ways of God almighty,
I would his eye were in his arse   and his finger after,
That ever wisheth to know   why that God would
Suffer Satan   his seed to beguile,
Or Judas to the Jews   Jesu betray.
All was as thou would'st   Lord, worshipped be thou,
And all shall be as thou wishest   whatever we dispute!
    'And he that uses these mazes   to blind men's wits,
What is Do-well from Do-better   now deaf must he be,
(Since he wisheth to know   what they be both),
Unless he live in the life   that belongs to Do-well;
For I dare go bail   that Do-better will he never,
Though Do-best draw him   day after other.'
    And when that Wit was aware   what Dame Study told,
He became so confused   he could not look,
And as dumb as death   and withdrew him back;
And for no speaking I could after   nor kneeling to the ground,
I might get no grain   of his great wits,
But all laughing be bowed   and looked upon Study,
In sign that I should   beseech her of grace.
    And when I was aware of his will   to his wife began I bow,
And said, 'Your pardon, madame   your man shall I become,
As long as I live   both late and soon,
For to work your will   the while my life lasteth,

With that ye teach me of your kindness   to know what is Do-well.'
    'For thy meekness, man,' quoth she   'and for thy mild speech,
I shall bring thee to my cousin   that Clergy is called.
He hath wedded a wife   within these six months,
Is kin to the seven arts [1]   Scripture is her name.
They two, as I hope   after my teaching,
Shall guide thee to Do-well   I dare it undertake.'
    Then was I also joyful   as bird on fair morning,
And gladder than the gleeman   that gold has been given,
And asked her the highway   where that Clergy dwelt,
'And tell me some token,' quoth I   'for time is that I went.'
    'Ask the highway,' quoth she   'hence of Suffer-
Both-well-and woe   if that thou wilt learn,
And ride forth by Riches   but rest thou not therein,
For if thou couplest thee therewith   to Clergy comest thou never.
And also the lickerish land   that Lechery is called,
Leave him on thy left hand   a large mile or more,
Till thou come to a court   Keep-well-thy-tongue
From-lies-and-vicious-speech   and-lickerish-drinks.
    'Then shalt thou see Sobriety   and Simplicity-of-speech,
That each wight be willing   his wit thee to show,
And thus shalt thou come to Clergy   that knows many things.
Say to him this sign   I set him to school,
And that I greet well his wife   for I wrote her many books,
And set her to Wisdom   and to the psalter to gloss.
    'Logic I taught her   and many other laws,
And all the measures in music   I made her to know.
Plato the poet   I put him first to books,
Aristotle and others more   to argue I taught.
Grammar for children   I caused first to be written,
And beat them with a birch   unless they would learn.
Of all kinds of crafts   I contrived tools,
Of carpentry, of carvers   and masons with compasses,
And taught them level and line   though I look dull.
    'But Theology hath troubled me   ten score times,
The more I muse therein   the mistier it seemeth,
And the deeper I search   the darker me it thinketh;
It is no science forsooth   to be too subtle in;
A full idle thing it were   if it were not for love.
But because it puts Love first   I love it the better;

[1] See page 204.

For there that Love is leader   never lacked grace.
Look thou love loyally   if thou wouldst please Do-well;
For Do-better and Do-best   be of Love's kin.
In another science it saith   I saw it in Cato,
Qui simulat verbis, nec corde est fidus amicus,
Tu quoque fac simile, sic ars deluditur arte.
Whoso speaks fair as flatterers do   let each do the same,
And so shalt thou false folk   and faithless beguile,
This is Cato's saying   to clerks that he teacheth,
But Theology teacheth not so   whoso taketh heed,
He instructs us the contrary   against Cato's words;
For he bids us be as brethren   and pray for our enemies,
And love them that lie to us   and give to them when they need,
And do good against evil   God himself it commands,
    Dum tempus habemus, operemur bonum ad omnes, maxime autem ad
        domesticos fidei.
'Paul preached to the people   that perfection loved,
To do good for God's love   and give to men that asked,
And especially to such   that follow our faith.
And all that speak ill or lie to us   our Lord teacheth us to love,
And not to grieve them that grieve us   God himself has forbidden it,
    Mihi vindictam, et ego retribuam.
Therefore look thou love   as long as thou livest,
For there is no science under the sun   so sovereign for the soul.
    'But astronomy is a hard thing   and evil for to know,
Geometry and divination   are guileful of speech;
Whoso thinketh to work with those two   thriveth full late.
For sorcery is the sovereign book   that to these sciences belongeth.
And there are tricks in coffers   of many men's making,
Experiments in alchemy   the people to deceive,
If thou think on Do-well   deal therewith never.
All these sciences I myself   devised and ordained,
And founded them first   folk to deceive.
Tell Clergy these tokens   and Scripture after,
To counsel thee kindly   to know what is Do-well.'
    I said, 'Great thanks, madame'   and meekly saluted her,
And went quickly away   without more delay.
And till I came to Clergy   I knew no stop;
And saluted the good man   as Study me taught,
And afterwards the wife   and paid them both reverence,
And told them the tokens   that me taught were.

G 57¹

Was never man on this earth   since God made the world,
Fairer received   nor more at ease among friends,
Than myself truly   soon as he knew
That I was of Wit's house   and with his wife Dame Study.
I told him truly   that sent was I thither,
Do-well and Do-better   and Do-best to learn.
  'Do-well is a common life,' quoth Clergy   'on Holy Church to believe,
With all the articles of the faith   that should be known.
And that is to believe loyally   both the learned and unlearned,
On the great God   that beginning had never,
And on the true Son   that saved mankind
From the deadly death   and the devil's power,
Through the help of the Holy Ghost   the which Spirit is of both;
Three real persons   but not in plural number,
For all is but one God   and each is God himself;
    Deus Pater, Deus Filius, Deus Spiritus Sanctus;
God the Father, God the Son   God the Holy Ghost of both,
Maker of mankind   and of beasts both.
  'Austin [1] the old   hereof he made books,
And himself applied   to confirm us in faith.
Who was his authority?   all the four evangelists;
And Christ called himself so   the evangelists beareth witness:
    Ego in Patre et Pater in me est; et, qui videt me, videt et Patrem meum.
All the clerks under Christ   can not this explain,
But thus they should believe   the unlearned that wish to Do-well.
For had never man fine wit   the faith to dispute,
No man had any merit   could it all be proved:
    Fides non habet meritum, ubi humana ratio praebet experimentum.
  'Then it is Do-better to suffer   for thy soul's health,
All that the Book bids   by Holy Church's teaching;
And that is—"man, with thy might   for mercy's sake,
Look thou do the deed   that thy word declareth;
Such as thou seemest at sight   be, in the trial, found;
    Appare quod es, vel esto quod appares:
And let nobody be   by thy bearing beguiled,
But be such in thy soul   as thou seemest without."
  'Then is Do-best to be bold   to blame the guilty,
When thou seest thyself   as in soul clean;
But blame thou nobody   if thou be blameworthy:
Si culpare velis   culpabilis esse cavebis,

    [1] See page 205.

Dogma tuum sordet   cum te tua culpa remordet.
God in the gospel   grimly reproveth
All that blame anyone   and faults have themselves:

> *Quid consideras festucam in oculo fratris tui, trabem in oculo tuo non vides?*

Why movest thou thy wrath   for a mote in thy brother's eye,
Since a beam in thine own   blindeth thyself?

> *Ejice primum trabem de oculo tuo, etc.,*

Which stops thee from seeing   less or more.
   'I counsel every blind buzzard   to remedy himself;
For abbots and for priors   and for all manner of prelates,
As parsons and parish priests   that preach should and teach,
All manner of men   to amend with their might;
This text was told you   to be warned, ere ye taught,
That ye were such as ye spoke of   with which to save others.
For God's word would not be lost   for that worketh ever,
If it availed not the people   it might avail yourselves.
   'But it seemeth now truly   to the world's sight,
That God's word worketh not   on learned or unlearned,
Except in such a manner as Mark   meaneth in the gospel,

> *Dum caecus ducit caecum, ambo in foveam cadunt.*

Unlearned men may compare you thus   that the beam lieth in your eyes,
And the mote is fallen   by your fault,
Into all manner of men   through cursed priests.
The Bible beareth witness   that all the folk of Israel
Bitterly paid for the guilt   of two bad priests,
Hophni and Phineas;   for their avarice,
Archa dei [1] came to grief   and Eli broke his neck.
   'Therefore, ye correctors, grasp this   and correct first yourselves,
And then may ye safely say   as David made the psalter:

> *Existimasti inique quod ero tui similis: arguam te, et statuam contra faciem tuam.*

   'And then shall lay clerks be abashed   to blame you or to grieve,
And carp not as they carp now   and call you dumb dogs,

> *Canes non valentes latrare,*

And dread to anger you by any word   your work to hinder,
And be readier at your prayer   than for a pound of gold;
And all for your holiness   have ye this at heart.
Amongst true religious   this rule should be held;
Gregory the great clerk   and the good pope

[1] See page 205.

Of religion the rule   rehearseth in his "Morals,"
And saith it by illustration   what they should do thereafter,
"When fishes lack the flood   or the fresh water,
They die for drought   when they stay dry;
Right so," quoth Gregory   "religion wandereth,
Perisheth and stinketh   and stealeth lords' alms,
That out of convent and cloister   coveteth to live."
For if heaven be on this earth   and ease to any soul,
It is in cloister or in learning   by many proofs I find;
For in cloister cometh no man   to chide nor to fight,
But all is courtesy there and books   to read and to learn.
    'In school there is scorn   unless a clerk will learn,
And great love and liking   for each of them loveth the other.
But now is Religion a rider   a roamer of the streets,
A conductor of law-days   and a buyer of land,
A pricker on a palfrey   from manor to manor,
A heap of hounds at his arse   as he a lord were.
And unless his page kneel   that shall his cup bring,
He lowereth on him and asketh him   who taught him courtesy?
Little use for lords   to give land away from their heirs
To religious, who have no care   though it rain on their altars!
    'In many places where parsons be   by themselves at ease,
Of the poor have they no pity   and that is their charity;
But they hold themselves as lords   their land reacheth so far.
    'But there shall come a king   and confess you of religion,
And beat you, as the Bible telleth   for breaking of your rule,
And amend nuns   monks and canons,
And put them to their penance   *ad pristinum statum ire*;
And barons and earls beat them   through *beatus vir*'s teaching,
And their children make claims   and blame you terribly:
    Hi in curribus et hi in equis; ipsi obligati sunt, etc.,
    'And then friars in the refectory   shall find a key
Of Constantine's [1] coffers   in which is the wealth
That Gregory's god-children   have spent so ill.
And then shall the abbot of Abingdon   and all his issue for ever
Have a knock from a king   and incurable the wound.
    'That this is true, seek ye   that often study the Bible:
    Quomodo cessavit exactor, quievit tributum; contrivit Dominus baculum impiorum,
      et virgam dominantium caedentium plaga insanabili, etc.

                [1] See page 205.

But ere that king come   Cain shall awake.
But Do-well shall smite him down   and destroy his might.'
'Then is Do-well and Do-better,' quoth I   '*dominus* and knighthood.'
  'I will not be scornful,' quoth Scripture   'unless scribes lie;
Kinghood nor knighthood   by naught I can abide,
Helpeth not to heavenward   one hair's length,
Nor riches right not   nor pomp of lords.
Paul preacheth it impossible   rich men to have heaven,
Solomon saith also   that silver is worst to love;
 Nihil iniquius quam amare peccuniam.
And Cato teacheth us to covet it   not but as governed by need,
Diligere denarium, sed parce dilige formam.
And patriarchs and prophets   and poets both
Write to instruct us   to long for no riches,
And they praise poverty with patience;   the apostles bear witness,
That they have inheritance in heaven   and by true right,
Where rich men no right may claim   but of mercy and grace.'
  '*Contra*,' quoth I, 'by Christ   that I can disprove,
And prove it by Peter   and by Paul both,
That the baptized be safe   be he rich or poor.'
  'That is *in extremis*,' quoth Scripture   'amongst Saracens and Jews;
They must be saved so   and that is our belief,
That an un-Christian in that case   may christen a heathen,
And for his true belief   when his life fails,
Have the heritage of heaven   as any Christian man.
But Christians without more   may not come to heaven,
For Christ for Christian men died   and confirmed the law,
That whoso would and wisheth   with Christ to arise,
 Si cum Christo surrexistis, etc.,
He should love and believe   and the law fulfil.
That is—"love thy lord God   most dearly above all,
And after, all Christian creatures   in common, each man the other";
And thus they should love   that look to be saved.
And unless we do thus indeed   ere the day of doom,
It shall oppress us full bitterly   the silver that we hoard,
And our clothes that moth-eaten have become   and seen beggars go naked,
Or delight in wine and wild fowl   and know any in need.
  'For every Christian creature   should be kind to another,
And then the heathen to help   in hope of amendment.
God commandeth both high and low   that no man hurt other,
And saith, "slay not what resembles   mine own likeness,

Unless I send thee some token";   and saith, *non necabis,*
That is, slay not, but suffer   and all for the best.
  'For, *Mihi vindictam, et ego retribuam.*
"For I shall punish them in purgatory   or in the pit of hell,
Each man for his misdeeds   save mercy it hinders."'
  'This is a long lesson,' quoth I   'and little am I the wiser;
Where Do-well is, or Do-better   darkly ye show;
Many tales ye tell   that Theology teacheth;
And that I, man, made was   and my name entered
In the book of life   long ere I were,
Or else unwritten for some wickedness   as holy writ witnesseth,
    Nemo ascendit ad caelum, nisi qui de caelo descendit.
  'I believe it well,' quoth I, 'by our Lord   and on no doctrine better.
For Solomon the sage   that Wisdom taught,
God gave him grace of wit   and all his goods after,
To rule the realm   and rich to make;
He judged well and wisely   as holy writ telleth.
Aristotle and he   who taught men better?
Masters that of God's mercy   teach men and preach,
Of their words they tell us   for wisest in their time,
And all holy church   holdeth them damned!
And if I should go by their works   to win me heaven,
That for their works and wit   now live in pain,
Then did I unwisely   whatsoever ye preach.
  'But of many wise, in faith   little wonder I have,
Though their spirit be ungracious   God for to please.
For many men on this earth   more set their hearts
On goods than on God   therefore them grace faileth,
To their great mischief   when they shall life end.
As Solomon did, and such other   that showed great wits;
But their works, as holy writ saith   was ever the contrary.
Therefore wise witted men   and well lettered clerks,
As they say themselves   seldom do thereafter,
    Super cathedram Moysi, etc.,
  'But I think it be of many   as was in Noah's time,
When he shaped his ship   of planks and boards;
Was never wight saved that wrought thereon   nor other workman either,
But birds and beasts   and the blessed Noah,
And his wife with his sons   and also their wives;
Of wrights that it wrought   was none of them saved.
God grant it fare not so with folk   that the faith teach

Of holy church, that harbour is   and God's house to save,
And shield us from shame therein   as Noah's ship did beasts;
And men that made it   amid the flood drowned.
The *culorum* of this clause   pastors is to mean,
That be carpenters, holy church to make   for Christ's own beasts,

    Homines et jumenta salvabis, Domine, etc.

At doomsday the deluge be   of death and fire at once;
Therefore I counsel you clerks   of holy church the wrights,
Do your work as ye see written   lest ye be worth naught therein.

  'On Good Friday I find   a felon was saved,
That had lived all his life   with falsehood and theft;
And for he acknowledged on the cross   and to Christ confessed him,
He was saved before   Saint John the Baptist,
And either Adam or Isaiah   or any of the prophets,
That had lain with Lucifer   many long years.
A robber was ransomed   rather than them all,
Without any penance of purgatory   to perpetual bliss.

  'Then Mary Magdalen   what woman did worse?
Or who worse than David   that Uriah's death conspired?
Or Paul the apostle   that no pity had,
Many Christians   to kill to death?
And now be these as sovereigns   with saints in heaven,
Those that wrought most wickedly   in the world when they were.
And those that wisely spoke   and wrote many books
Of wit and wisdom   with damned souls live.
What Solomon saith, I trow be true   and certain of us all,

    Sunt justi atque sapientes; et opera eorum in manu Dei sunt, etc.;

  'They are wise and well-living   but their works be hid
In the hands of almighty God   and he knows the truth
Whether for love a man be valued there   and his true deeds,
Or else for his evil will   and envy of heart,
According as he lived   for by evil men know the good;
And whereby know men which is white   if all things black were,
And who was a good man   unless there were some rogue?
Therefore live we still with evil men   I think few be good.
For *quand oportet vient en place   il n'y a que pati,*
And he that can all amend   have mercy on us all!
For truest word that ever God said   was when he said, *nemo bonus.*

  'Clergy of Christ's mouth   commended was little,
For he said to Saint Peter   and to such as he loved,

    Dum steteritis ante reges et praesides, etc.;

"Though ye come before kings   and clerks of the law,
Be not abashed   for I shall be in your mouths,
And give you wit at will   and skill to refute
Them all that against you   about Christendom dispute."
    'David is an example   he spake amongst kings,
And might no king overcome him   in skill of speech.
But wit nor wisdom   won never the mastery,
When man was at mischief   without the more grace.
    'The doughtiest doctor   and interpreter of the Trinity,
Was Augustine the old   and highest of the four,
He said thus in a sermon   I saw it written once,
          Ecce ipsi idiotae rapiunt caelum, ubi nos sapientes in inferno mergimur:
And it means to English man   neither more nor less,
"Are none sooner ravished   from the right belief
Than are these clever clerks   that know many books;
Nor none sooner saved   nor firmer of belief,
Than plowmen and herdsmen   and poor common labourers."
Cobblers and shepherds   such ignorant fellows
Pierce with a *pater noster*   the palace of heaven,
And pass purgatory penance-less   at their parting hence,
Into the bliss of paradise   for their pure faith,
That imperfectly here   knew and indeed lived.
Yea, men know clerks   that have cursed the time,
That ever they knew more   than *credo in Deum Patrem*;
And above all their *pater noster*   many a person hath wished.
    'I see examples myself   and so may many another,
That servants that serve lords   seldom fall in debt,
But those that keep the lords' property   clerks and reeves.
Right so unlearned men   and of little knowledge,
Seldom fall they so foul   and so far in sin,
As clerks of holy church   that keep Christ's treasure,
The which is man's soul to save   as God saith in the gospel:
          Ite vos in vineam meam.'

PASSUS XI

THEN Scripture poured scorn on me   and a reason gave,
And rated me in Latin   and light by me she set,
    And said, '*multi multa sciunt, et seipsos nesciunt.*'
Then wept I for woe   and wrath of her speech,
And in a drowsy wrath   went I to sleep.
A marvellous dream   met me then,
So I was ravished on the spot   and Fortune me fetched,
And into the land of Longing   alone she me brought,
And in a mirror called Middle-Earth   she made me to behold.
Then she said to me   'Here may'st thou see wonders,
And know what thou covetest   and come thereto, by good luck.'
    Then had Fortune following her   two fair damsels,
Concupiscentia-carnis   men called the elder maid,
And Covetousness-of-eyes   called was that other;
Pride-of-perfect-living   followed them both,
And bade me, for my favour   account Clergy lightly.
    Concupiscentia-carnis   clasped me around the neck,
And said, 'Thou art young and alive   and hast years enough,
For to live long   and ladies to love;
And in this mirror thou might see   joys full many,
That lead thee will to loving   all thy life time.'
    The second said the same   'I shall attend thy wish;
Till thou be a lord and have land   leave thee I will not,
While I shall follow thy fellowship   if Fortune it like.'
'He shall find me his friend'   quoth Fortune thereupon;
'The man that followed my will   lacked never bliss.'
    Then was there one called Age   that heavy was of cheer,
'Man,' quoth he, 'if I meet with thee   by Mary of heaven,
Thou shalt find Fortune thee fail   at thy most need,
And *Concupiscentia-carnis*   clean thee forsake.
Bitterly shalt thou curse then   both days and nights
Covetousness-of-eyes   that ever thou her knew,
And Pride-of-perfect-living   to much peril thee bring.'
    'Yea, reck thee not,' quoth Recklessness   stood forth in ragged clothes,
'Follow forth as Fortune wills   thou hast a long way till old age;
A man may stoop times enough   when he has gone bald.

89

"*Homo proponit*," quoth a poet   and Plato he is called,
"And *Deus disponit*," quoth he   "let God do his will."
If Truth will witness it be well done   Fortune to follow,
Concupiscentia-carnis   nor Covetousness-of-eyes
Shall not grieve thee greatly   nor beguile thee, unless thou will it.'
     'Yea, farewell, Philip sparrow!' quoth Childishness   and began to
                                        lead me on,
Till *Concupiscentia-carnis*   accorded with all my works.
     'Alas, indeed!' quoth Age   and Holiness both,
'That wit shall turn to wretchedness   for Will to have his liking!'
     Covetousness-of-eyes   comforted me anon after,
And followed me forty winters   and five more,
So that Do-well nor Do-better   of no value I thought;
I had no liking, believe me if you will   of them aught to know.
     Covetousness-of-eyes   came more often to mind
Than Do-well or Do-better   amongst all my deeds.
Covetousness-of-eyes   comforted me often,
And said, 'Have no conscience   how thou come by thy goods
Go confess thee to some friar   and show him thy sins.
For whilst Fortune is thy friend   friars will thee love,
And fetch thee to their fraternity   and for thee beseech
Their prior provincial   a pardon for to have,
And pray for thee, each of them   if thou be *pecuniosus*.'
     Sed poena pecuniaria non sufficit pro spiritualibus delictis.
     By the teaching of this wench I went   the words were so sweet,
Till I forgot youth   and hurried into age.
And then was Fortune my foe   for all her fair promises,
And Poverty pursued me   and brought me low,
And then found I the friars afraid   and flitting both,
Against our first bargain   for I said I would not
Be buried at their house   but at my parish church.
For I heard once   how Conscience it told,
That where a man was christened   by rights he should be buried,
Or where he was a parishioner   right there he should be interred.
And because I said thus to the friars   a fool they me held,
And loved me the less   for my true speech.
But yet I cried at my confessor   that held himself so learned,
'By my faith, friar,' quoth I   'ye behave like these wooers,
That wed no widows   except to wield their goods;
Right so, by the rood   recked ye never
Where my body were buried   so long as ye had my silver.

I have much wondered at you   and so hath many another,
Why your convent coveteth   to confess and to bury,
Rather than to baptize children   that be catechumens.
Baptizing and burying   both be full needful,
But much more meritorious   methinketh it is to baptize.
For a baptized man may   as masters tell,
Through contrition come   to the high heaven;
    Sola contritio delet peccatum.
But a child without baptism   may not so be saved;
    Nisi quis renatus fuerit ex aqua, etc.;
Look, ye lettered men   whether I lie or do not.'
And Loyalty looked on me   and I lowered after.
'Wherefore lowerest thou?' quoth Loyalty   and looked at me hard,
'If I durst,' quoth I, 'amongst men   this dream avow!'
'Yea, by Peter and by Paul,' quoth he   'and take them both to witness,
    Non oderis fratres secrete in corde tuo, sed publice argue illos.'
'They will declare also,' quoth I   'and by the gospel prove,
    Nolite judicare quemquam.'
  'And wherefore serveth law,' quoth Loyalty   'if no man reproved it,
Falsehood nor fraud?   for some purpose the apostle said,
    Non oderis fratrem.
And in the psalter also   saith David the prophet,
    Existimasti inique quod ero tui similis, etc.
It is *licitum* for laymen   to declare the truth,
If it pleaseth them   to each a law it granteth,
Except parsons and priests   and prelates of holy church,
It falleth not to those folk   any tales to tell,
Though the tale were true   if it touched on sin.[1]
A thing that all the world knows   wherefore shouldst thou spare
To counsel on with rhetoric   to rate deadly sin?
But be never the first   the fault to blame;
Though thou see evil, speak of it not first   but be sorry it was not
                              amended.

Nothing that is private   publish thou it never,
Neither for love laud it not   nor attack it not for envy;
    Parum lauda, vitupera parcius.'
  'He speaketh true, quoth Scripture then   and skipped on high and
                              preached;
But the matter that she dealt with   if unlearned men it knew,
The less, I believe   love it they would.

        [1] See page 205.

This was her theme and her text   I took full good heed;
'*Multi* to a feast   and to the meat were summoned,
And when the people were come in plenty   the porter unlocked the gate,
And plucked in *pauci* privately   and let the rest go hang!'
    All for pain of her text   trembled mine heart,
And into a doubt I fell   and with myself began to dispute,
Whether I were chosen or not chosen   on Holy Church I thought,
That received me at the font   as one of God's chosen;
For Christ called us all   to come if we willed,
Saracens and schismatics   and so he did the Jews,
    O vos omnes sitientes, venite, etc.;
And bade them suck for sin   safely at his breast,
And drink cure for evil   receive it whoso will.
    'Then may all Christians come,' quoth I   'and claim their entry
By the blood that he bought us with   and through baptism after,
    Qui crediderit et baptizatus fuerit, etc.
For though a Christian man coveted   his Christianity to reject,
To reject it with probity   no reason will allow.
    'For may no churl charter make   nor his goods sell
Without leave of his lord   no law will it grant.
But he may run into arrears   and roam then from home,
And as a renegade rascal   recklessly go about;
But Reason shall reckon with him   and rebuke him at the last,
And Conscience account with him   and cast him into debt,
And put him after in a prison   in purgatory to burn,
And for his debts reward him there   to the day of judgment,
Unless Contrition will come   and cry, by his life,
Mercy for his misdeeds   with mouth or with heart.'
    'That is true,' said Scripture   'can no sin stop
Mercy from amending all   if meekness goes with her,
For they be as our books tell   the highest of God's works,
    Misericordia ejus super omnia opera ejus.'
    'Yea, bah for books!' quoth one   was broken out of hell,
Called Trajan,[1] had been a true knight   as a pope bore witness,
How he was dead and damned   to dwell in pain,
As an unchristened creature;   —'clerks know the truth,
That all the clergy under Christ   could not snatch me from hell,
But only love and loyalty   and my rightful judgement.
Gregory knew this well   and wished well for my soul
Unbeliever, for the virtue   that he saw in my works.

    [1] See page 205.

And, after that he wept   and longed I be granted
Grace, without any bead-bidding   his boon was accepted,
And I saved, as ye may see   without singing of masses;
By love, and by learning   of my living in truth,
Brought me from bitter pain   when no praying might.'
    Lo, ye lords, what faithfulness did   for an emperor of Rome,
That was an unchristian creature   as clerks find in books.
Not through prayer of a pope   but for his pure truth
Was that infidel saved   as Saint Gregory beareth witness.
Well ought ye lords, that laws keep   this lesson to have in mind,
And on Trajan's truth to think   and give truth to the people.
    This matter is murky for many of you   but, men of holy church,
The *Legenda Sanctorum* you teacheth   better than I you tell!
But thus loyal love   and living in truth
Pulled out of pain   a pagan of Rome.
Blessed be truth   that so broke hell-gates,
And saved this infidel   from Satan and his power,
Where no clergy could   nor knowledge of laws.
Love and loyalty   is a true science;
For that is the Book blessed   of bliss and of joy:
God wrought it and wrote it   with his finger alone,
And gave it to Moses upon the mount   all men to teach.
    'Law without love,' quoth Trajan   'count it a bean,
Or any science under sun   the seven arts and all,
Unless they be learned in our Lord's love   lost is all the time'—
'For no cause to catch silver thereby   nor to be called master,
But all for love of our Lord   and the better to love the people.
For Saint John said it   and soth are his words,
        Qui non diligit, manet in morte—
Whoso loveth not, believe me   he liveth in death-dying—
And that all manner of men   enemies and friends,
Love each other   and give as to themselves.
Whoso giveth not, he loveth not   God knows the truth,
And commandeth each creature   to conform him to love,
And above all poor people   their enemies next.
For them that hate us   it is our merit to love,
And poor people to please   their prayers may us help.
For our joy and our health   Jesu Christ of heaven,
In a poor man's apparel   pursueth us ever,
And looketh on us in their likeness   and that with lovely face,
To know us by our kind heart   and casting of our eyes,

Whether we love the lords here   before our Lord of bliss;
And exciteth us by the evangelist   that, when we make feasts,
We should not ask our kin thereto   nor no rich men;
     "*Cum facitis convivia, nolite invitare amicos:*
But call the unhappy thereto   the bent, and the poor,
For your friends will feed you   and foster you, to repay
Your feasting and your fair gift   each friend repayeth so the other.
But for the poor I shall pay   and well requite their toil,
That giveth them meat or money   and loveth them for my sake."
For of the best be some rich   and some beggars and some poor.
For all are we Christ's creatures   and of his coffers rich,
And brethren as of one blood   as well beggars as earls.
For on Calvary of Christ's blood   Christendom first sprang,
And brethren in blood we became there   by one body won,
As *quasi modo geniti*   and gentle men each one,
Nor beggar nor knave amongst us   unless it sin made;
     Qui facit peccatum, servus est peccati, etc.
   'In the old law   as holy scripture telleth,
Men's sons   men called us each one,
Of Adam's issue and Eve   ever till God-man died;
And after his resurrection   *Redemptor* was his name,
And we his brethren, through him bought   both rich and poor.
Therefore love we as true brethren shall   and each man laugh on the
                                          other,
And of that each man can spare   give aid where it is needed,
And every man help the other   for go hence shall we all;
     Alter alterius onera portate.
And be we not ungenerous with our goods   nor of our skill either,
For knows not man how nigh he is   to be taken from both.
Therefore blame no man another   though he more Latin knows,
Nor rebuke not foully   for is none without fault.
For whatever clerks prate   of Christianity or otherwise,
Christ to a common woman said   in public at a feast,
That *fides sua* should save her   and heal her of all sins.
   'Then is belief a true help   above logic or law;
For of logic or of law   in *Legenda Sanctorum*
Is little allowance made   unless belief them help.
For it is long ere logic   any lesson reveal,
And law is loth to love   unless he get silver,
Both logic and law   that loveth not to lie,
I counsel all Christians   cleave not thereon too closely.

For some words I find written   were of faith's teaching,
That saved sinful men   as Saint John beareth witness;

Eadem mensura qua mensi fueritis, remetietur vobis.

Therefore learn we the law of love   as our Lord taught,
And as Saint Gregory said   for man's soul's health,

Melius est scrutari scelera nostra, quam naturas rerum.

'Why I move this matter   is most for the poor,
For in their likeness our Lord   oft hath been known.
Witness in Pasch week   when he went to Emmaus;
Cleophas knew him not   that he Christ were,
For his poor apparel   and pilgrim's weeds,
Till he blessed and brake   the bread that they eat,
So by his works they wist   that he was Jesus;
But by clothing they knew him not   nor by speaking of tongue.

'And all was in example   to us sinful here,
That we should be humble   and courteous of speech,
And apparel us not over proudly   for pilgrims are we all;
And in the apparel of a poor man   and pilgrim's likeness
Many time God hath been met   among needy people,
When never man him saw   in company of the rich.

'Saint John and other saints   were seen in poor clothing,
And as poor pilgrims   begged men's charity.
Jesus Christ from a Jew's daughter was born   gentle woman though she
                                                                        were,
Was a pure poor maid   and to a poor man wedded.

'Martha about Mary Magdalen   a huge plaint made,
And to our Saviour himself   said these words,

*Domine, non est tibi curae quod soror mea reliquit me solam ministrare,
     etc.?*

And quickly God answered   and both their ways allowed,
Both Martha's and Mary's   as Matthew beareth witness,
But poverty God put first   and praised it the better;

Maria optimam partem elegit, quae non auferetur ab ea.

'And all the wise that ever were   by aught I can discover,
Praise poverty for best life   if patience go with it,
And both better and more blessed   by many times than riches.
Even though it be sour to suffer   there cometh sweet after;
As on a walnut without   is a bitter bark,
And after that bitter bark   (be the shell away),
Is a kernel of comfort   life to restore;
So it is, after poverty or penance   patiently taken.

For it maketh man to have mind of God   and a great will
To weep and to well pray   whereof groweth mercy,
Of which Christ is a kernel   to comfort the soul.
And much more peacefully he sleepeth   the man that is poor,
And less he dreadeth death   and in dark to be robbed,
Than he that is right rich   reason beareth witness;
Pauper ego ludo, dum tu dives meditaris.

   'Although Solomon said   as folk see in the Bible,
     Divitias nec paupertates, etc.,
A wiser than Solomon was   beareth witness and taught,
That perfect poverty was   no possession to have,
And life most pleasing to God   as Luke beareth witness,
     Si vis perfectus esse, vade et vende, etc.;
And means to men   that on this earth live,
Whoso will be pure perfect   must possession forsake,
Or sell it, as saith the Book   and the silver give
To beggars that wander and beg   and ask goods for God's love.
   'For failed never man meat   that mighty God served;
     Non vidi justum derelictum, nec semen ejus quaerens panem;
As David saith in the psalter   to such that be willing
To serve God in a godly way   nor grieveth him no penance,
     Nihil impossible volenti,
Nor lacketh never livelihood   linen nor wool,
     Inquirentes autem dominum non minuentur omni bono.
If priests were perfect   they would no silver take
For masses nor for matins   and not their meat of usurers,
Nor neither their kirtle nor coat   though they for cold should die,
If they their duty did   as David saith in the psalter,
     Judica me, Deus, et discerne causam meam.
Spera-in-deo speaketh of priests   that have no spending-silver,
That if they travail truly   and trust in God almighty,
They should lack no livelihood   neither woollen nor linen.
And the title that ye take your orders by   telleth ye are in authority;
Then needeth not you to take silver   for masses that ye sing.
For he that gave you your title   should give you your wages,
Or the bishop that blesseth you   if that ye be worthy.
   'For never king nor knight   but he had money to spend,
As became a knight   or provided him for his strength;
It is an unhappy knight   and of a caitif king's making,
That hath no land nor lineage rich   nor good fame of his deeds.
The same I say for sooth   of all such priests,

That have neither learning nor kin   but a tonsure one,
And a title, a tale of naught   for his livelihood, meaning mischief,
He hath more hope, I believe   of gaining through his tonsure
A cure of souls, than through learning   or—"fame for clean conduct."
I have wondered why   and wherefore the bishop
Maketh such priests   that unlearned men betray.

'A charter is challengeable   before a chief justice;
If false Latin be in the writing   the law it impugneth,
Or writing between the lines   or parts over-skipped;
The man that makes such charters   for a gawk is held.
So it is a gawk, by God   that in his gospel faileth,
Or in mass or in matins   maketh any fault,

> *Qui offendit in uno, in omnibus est reus, etc.*

And also in the psalter   saith David to over-skippers,

> *Psallite deo nostro, psallite; quoniam rex terrae Deus Israel; psallite sapienter.*

The bishop shall be blamed   before God, as I believe,
That tonsures such of God's servants   that can not *sapienter*
Sing nor psalms read   nor say a mass of the day.
But never neither is blameless   the bishop nor the chaplain,
For either of them is indicted   and that by "*ignorantia
Non excusat episcopos   nec* ignorant priests."

'This concern with unlearned priests   hath made me stray from poverty,
The which I praise, where patience is   more perfect than riches.'
And much more in dreaming thus   with me did one dispute,
And in sleeping I saw all this   and then came Kind,
And named me by my name   and bade me take heed,
And through the wonders of this world   wisdom take.
And on a mountain that Middle-Earth is called   as me then thought,
I was led forth   by examples to know,
Through each creature and Kind   my Creator to love.
I saw the sun and the sea   and the sand after,
And where that birds and beasts   by their mates they went,
Wild worms in woods   and wonderful birds,
With flecked feathers   and of many colours.
Man and his mate   I might both behold;
Poverty and plenty   both peace and war,
Bliss and bale   both I saw at once,
And how men took rewards   and mercy refused.
Reason I saw truly   attending all beasts
In eating, in drinking   and in engendering of kind:

H 57¹

And after course of conception   none took heed of the other,
As when they had met in rutting-time   anon right thereafter,
Males drew them to males   in mornings by themselves,
And in evenings also   went males from females.
There was not cow nor such creature   that conceived had,
That would bellow after bulls   nor boar after sow;
Both horse and hounds   and all other beasts
Meddled not with their mates   that with foal were.

   Birds I beheld   that in bushes made nests;
Had never man wit   to make in the least.
I had wonder from whom   and where the magpie learned
To lay the twigs   in which she lieth and breedeth;
There is no wright as I think   could make a nest would please him;
If any mason made a model thereof   much wonder it were.

   And yet me marvelled more   how many other birds
Hid and covered   their eggs full secretly
In marshes and moors   that men should them not find,
And hid their eggs   when they therefrom went,
For fear of other birds   and for wild beasts.
And some met their mates   and on trees bred,
And brought forth their birds so   all above the ground;
And some birds at the bill   through breathing conceived;
And some engendered thus   I took note how peacocks bred.
Much marvelled me   what master they had,
And who taught them on trees   to build so high,
Where neither man nor beast   may their birds reach.

   And then I looked upon the sea   thence forth upon the stars,
Many wonders I saw   which I say not now.
I saw flowers in the wood   and their fair colours,
And how among the green grass   grew so many hues,
And some sour and some sweet   wonder me thought;
Of their kind and their colour   to speak it were too long.

   But what most moved me   and impressed my mind,
Was that Reason regarded   and ruled all beasts,
Save man and his mate   many time and oft
No reason them followed   and then I rebuked
Reason, and right   to himself I said,
'I have wonder of thee,' quoth I   'that wise art held,
Why thou followest not man and his mate   that no mishap them attend?'

   And Reason rated me   and said, 'Reck thee never,
Why I allow or do not allow   thyself hast naught do with it;

Amend thou it, if thou might   for my time is to abide.
Patience is a sovereign virtue   and a swift vengeance.
Who is more long-suffering than God?' quoth he   'No man, as I believe!
He might amend in a minute's time   all that amiss standeth,
But he suffers it for some man's good   and so is it better for us.
    'Holy writ,' quoth that wight   'teacheth men patience;
        Propter Deum subjecti estote omni creaturae.
Frenchmen and free men   train thus their children,
Belle vertue est suffrance   mal dire est petit veniance,
Bien dire et bien soufrir   fait lui suffrant a bien venir.
Therefore I counsel,' quoth Reason   'rule thy tongue better,
And ere thou blame any man   look if thou be praiseworthy!
For is no creature under Christ   can form himself;
And if a man might make   himself good among the people,
Each life would be blameless   believe thou none other!
Nor shalt thou find but few   willing for to hear
Of their faults foul   before them rehearsed.
    'The wise and the clever   wrote thus in the Bible,
        De re quae te non molestat, noli certare.
For be a man fair or foul   it falleth not for to blame
The shape nor the form   that God shaped himself;
For all that he did was well done   as holy writ witnesseth,
        Et vidit Deus cuncta quae fecerat, et erant valde bona;
And bade every creature   in his kind increase,
All for mirth for man   that must woe suffer
In temptation of the flesh   and of the fiend both.
For man was made of such matter   he may not well avoid
That sometimes he is bid   to follow his kind;
Cato accordeth therewith   *nemo sine crimine vivit.*'
    Then caught I colour anon   and came to be ashamed,
And awoke therewith   woe was me then
That I in dreams might not   more have known.
And then spoke I to myself   and blamed that time:
'Now I know what Do-well is,' quoth I   'by dear God, as methinketh!'
And as I cast up mine eyes   one looked on me, and asked
Of me, what thing it were?   'Indeed, sir,' I said,
'To see much and suffer more   truly,' quoth I, 'is Do-well!'
    'Haddest thou been patient,' he said   'sleeping though thou were,
Thou shouldest have known what Clergy knows   and conceived more
                                    through Reason;
For Reason would have rehearsed thee   right as Clergy said,

But for thine intermeddling   here art thou forsook;
    Philosophus esses, si tacuisses.
Adam, while he spake not   had paradise at will,
But when he chattered about meat   and meddled to know
The wisdom and the knowledge of God   he was put from bliss;
And right so did Reason by thee   thou with rude speech
Blamed, and praised things   that belonged not to be done;
Then had he no wish   for to teach thee more.
   'Pride and Presumption   perchance, will thee call,
So that Clergy thy company   cares not to follow.
Shall never challenging nor chiding   chasten a man so soon
As shall Shame, and humble him   and shape him to amend.
For let a drunken dolt   in a ditch fall,
Let him lie, look not on him   till it pleases him to rise;
For though Reason rebuked him then   recketh he never,
Of Clergy nor of his council   he counteth not a rush;
To blame or for to beat him then   it were but pure sin.
But when Need pulleth him up   for doubt lest he die,
And Shame scrapes his clothes   and his shins washeth,
Then knows the drunken dolt   wherefore he is to blame.'
   'Ye say sooth,' quoth I   'I have seen it often,
There smites no thing so smart   nor smelleth so sour,
As Shame, where he showeth himself   for every man him shuns!
Why ye show me thus,' quoth I   'was for I rebuked Reason.'
   'Truly,' quoth he, 'that is so'   and prepared him to walk:
And I arose up right with that   and followed him after,
And prayed him of his courtesy   to tell me his name.

PASSUS XII

'I AM Imaginative,' quoth he   'idle was I never,
Though I sit by myself   in sickness or in health.
I have followed thee in faith   this five and forty winters,
And many times have moved thee   to think on thine end,
And how many old years are gone   and so few to come,
And of thy wild wantonness   when thou young were,
To amend it in thy middle age   lest strength thee failed
In thine old age   when hard it is to bear
Poverty or penance   or prayers make;
 Si non in prima vigilia, nec in secunda, etc.
Amend thee while thou might   thou hast been warned oft
With attacks of pestilences   with poverty and with troubles;
And with these bitter rods   God beateth his dear children,
 Quem diligo, castigo.
And David in the psalter saith   of such that loveth Jesus,
 Virga tua et baculus tuus, ipsa me consolata sunt, etc.
Although thou strike me with thy staff   with stick or with rod,
It is but joy as for me   to amend my soul.
And thou meddlest thee with verse-making   and mightest go say
          thy psalter,
And pray for them that giveth thee bread   for there are books
           enough
To tell men what Do-well is   Do-better, and Do-best both,
And preachers to prove what it is   of many a pair of friars.'
 I saw well he told me true   and, somewhat me to excuse,
Said, 'Cato comforted his son   clerk though he were,
To solace him sometimes   as I do when I make verse;
Interpone tuis interdum gaudia curis, etc.
And of holy men I heard,' quoth I   'how they at times
Played, the more perfect to be   in many places.
But if there were any wight   that would me tell
What were Do-well and Do-better   and Do-best finally,
Would I never do work   but go to holy church,
And there say my beads   except when I eat or sleep.'

'Paul in his epistle,' quoth he   'proveth what is Do-well;
Fides, spes, caritas; et major horum, etc.
Faith, hope, and charity   and all be good,
And save men sundry times   but none so soon as charity.
For he doth well without doubt   that doth as loyalty teacheth;
That is, if thou be man married   thy mate thou love,
And live forth as law wills   while ye live both.
  'Right so, if thou be a religious   run thou never further
To Rome nor to Roquemadour [1]   but as thy rule teacheth;
And hold thee under obedience   that highway is to heaven.
  'And if thou be maiden as to marriage   and may well continue so,
Seek thou never saint afar   for soul's health.
For what made Lucifer   to lose the high heaven,
Or Solomon his wisdom   or Sampson his strength?
Job the Jew his joy   dearly he it bought,
Aristotle and others more   Hippocrates, and Virgil;
Alexander that all won   miserably ended.
Wealth and their own wit   was cumbrance to them all.
Felicia's [2] fairness   brought her all to shame;
And Rosamund right so   unhappily used herself,
The beauty of her body   in badness she dispensed.
Of many such I may read   of men and of women,
That wise words would show   and do the contrary,
Sunt homines nequam bene de virtute loquentes.
  'And the rich right so   gather and save,
And then men that they most hate   spend it at the last;
And, for they permit and see   so many needy folks,
And love them not as our Lord bid   they lose their souls;
    Date et dabitur vobis, etc.
So wealth and their own wit   cumbreth full many;
Woe is him that them wieldeth   unless he well dispenses them;
    Scientes et non facientes variis flagellis vapulabunt;
Wisdom, saith the Book   swelleth a man's soul,
    Sapientia inflat, etc.;
And riches right so   unless the roots be sound;
But grace is a herb thereof   those ills to abate.
But grace groweth not   but amongst the lowly;
Patience and poverty   the place is there it groweth,
And in true-living men   and in the life-holy,

[1] See page 205.   [2] See page 205.

And through the gift of the Holy Ghost   as the gospel telleth,
> *Spiritus ubi vult spirat, etc.*

Clergy and Kind Wit [1]   cometh of seeing and teaching,
As the Book beareth witness   to men that can read,
> *Quod scimus, loquimur; quod vidimus, testamur.*

Of *quod scimus,* cometh Clergy   learning of heaven,
And of *quod vidimus* cometh Kind Wit   and of seeing of divers people.
But grace is a gift of God   and of great love springeth;
Knew never clerk how it cometh forth   nor Kind Wit the ways,
> *Nescit aliquis unde venit, aut quo vadit, etc.*

But yet Clergy is to be commended   and Kind Wit both,
And especially Clergy, for Christ's love   that of Clergy is root.
For Moses witnesseth that God wrote   for to teach the people,
In the old law, as the Scripture telleth   that was the law of the Jews,
That the woman who was in adultery taken   were she rich or poor,
With stones men should her strike   and stone her to death.
A woman, as we find   was guilty of that deed,
But Christ of his courtesy   through Clergy her saved;
For through the characters that Christ wrote   the Jews knew themselves
Guiltier as before God   and greater in sin
Than the woman that there was   and went away for shame.
The Clergy that there was   succoured the woman.
Holy Church knoweth this   that Christ's writing saved;
So Clergy is comfort   to creatures that repent,
And to cursed men   mischief at their end
  'For God's body might not be   of bread, without Clergy,
The which body is both   health to the righteous,
And death and damnation   to them that die evil.
As Christ's characters both comforted and   culpable showed
The woman that the Jews brought   that Jesus intended to save;
> *Nolite judicare, et non judicabimini, etc.*

Right so God's body, brethren   unless it be worthily taken,
Damneth us at the day of doom   as the characters did the Jews.
Therefore I counsel thee for Christ's sake   Clergy that thou love,
For Kind Wit is of his kin   and near cousins both
To our Lord, believe me   therefore love them, I say;
For both be as mirrors   to amend our faults,
And leaders for unlearned men   and for the lettered both.
  'Therefore attack thou never logic   law, nor his customs,

---

[1] See page 205.

Nor contradict clerks   I counsel thee for ever.
For as a man may not see   that lacketh his eyes,
No more can a clerk   unless he learnt it first through books.
Although men made books   God was the master
And Holy Spirit the teacher   and said what men should write.
And right as sight serveth a man   to see the high street,
Right so leadeth letters   unlearned men to Reason.
And as a blind man in battle   beareth weapon to fight,
And hath no luck with his axe   his enemy to hit,
No more can a man of Kind Wit   unless clerks him teach,
Come for all his Kind Wit   to Christendom and be saved;
This is the coffer of Christ's treasure   and clerks keep the keys,
To unlock it at their liking   and to the unlearned people
Give mercy for their misdeeds   if men it will ask
Humbly and gently   and pray it of grace.
    '*Archa dei* in the old law   Levites it kept;
Had never unlearned man leave   to lay hand on that chest,
Only if he were priest or priest's son   patriarch or prophet.
    'Saul, for he sacrificed   sorrow him befell,
And his sons also   for that sin came to harm,
And many more other men   that were not Levites,
That with *archa dei* travelled   in reverence and in worship,
And laid hand thereon to lift it up   and lost their life after.
Therefore I counsel all creatures   no Clergy to despise,
Nor set little by their science   whatever they do themselves.
Take we their words for worth   for their witness be true,
And meddle we not much with them   to move any wrath,
Lest strife chafe us   to chop each man the other;
        Nolite tangere christos meos, etc.
    'For Clergy is keeper   under Christ of heaven;
Was there never a knight   but Clergy him made.
But Kind Wit cometh   of all kinds of seeing,
Of birds and of beasts   of tastes of truth, and of deceits.
    'Men before us   used to mark
The wonders that they saw   their sons for to teach,
And held it a high science   their ways to know.
But through their science truly   was never a soul saved.
Nor brought by their books   to bliss nor to joy;
For all their knowing of nature   comes but of diverse sights.
    'Patriarchs and prophets   reproved their science,
And said, their words and their wisdom   were but folly;

As to the Clergy of Christ   they counted it but a trifle;
  Sapientia hujus mundi, stultitia est apud Deum.
For the high Holy Ghost   heaven shall cleave asunder,
And love shall leap out after   into this low earth,
And cleanness shall seize it   and clerks shall it find;
  Pastores loquebantur ad invicem.
  'He speaketh there of rich men right naught   nor of right wise,
Nor of lords that were unlearned men   but of the highest learned men,
  Ibant magi ab oriente, etc.
If any friar were found there   I give you five shillings;
Nor in no begger's cot   was that child born,
But in a burgess's [1] place   of Bethlehem the best;
  Sed non erat locus ei in diversorio; et pauper non habet diversorium.
  'To shepherds and to poets   appeared that angel,
And bade them go to Bethlehem   God's birth to honour,
And sung a song of solace   *Gloria in excelsis Deo!*
Rich men snored then   and at their rest were,
When it shone on the shepherds   a declarer of bliss.
  'Clerks knew it well   and came with their presents,
And did their homage honourably   to him that was almighty,
Why I have told thee all this—   I took full good heed
How thou contradicted Clergy   with crabbed words,
"How that unlearned men more readily   than lettered were saved,
Than clerks or clever men   of Christian people."
  'And thou said sooth of some   but see in what manner:—
Take two strong men   and in Thames cast them,
And both naked as a needle   neither safer than the other,
The one hath knowledge   and can swim and dive,
The other is ignorant of that labour   learned never to swim;
Which thinkest thou of those two   in Thames is in most dread?
He that never dived   nor naught knows of swimming,
Or the swimmer that is safe   if so himself pleases,
Where his fellow floats forth   as the flood pleaseth,
And is in dread to drown   that never did swim?'
  'He that swim can not,' I said   'it seemeth to my wits.'
  'Right so,' quoth the man   'reason it showeth,
That he that knoweth Clergy   can sooner arise
Out of sin and be safe   though he sin oft,
If he likes and pleases   than ignorant person.
For if the clerk be wise   he knoweth what is sin,

---

[1] See page 205.

And how contrition without confession   comforteth the soul,
And thou seest in the psalter   in psalms one or two,
How contrition is commended   for it snatcheth away sin;

> *Beati quorum remissae sunt iniquitates, et quorum tecta sunt peccata,*
> *etc.*

And this comforteth each clerk   and saveth him from despair,
In which flood the fiend   tries a man hardest;
There the unlearned lieth still   and looketh for Lent,
And hath no contrition ere he come to shrift   and then can he little tell,
And as his master teacheth him   believeth and holdeth:
And that is according to parson or parish priest   and, perchance both
Unlearned to teach ignorant men   as Luke beareth witness,

> *Dum caecus ducit caecum, ambo in foveam cadunt.*

'Woe was for him marked   that must wade with the ignorant!
Well may the child bless   him that set him to books;
That living according to the writing   saved him life and soul!
Dominus pars hereditatis meae   is a merry verse,
That has taken from Tyburn   twenty strong thieves; [1]
Where untaught thieves be strung up   look how they be saved!
The thief that had grace of God   on Good Friday as thou sayest,
Was, for he yielded him a believer to Christ on the cross   and acknow-
                                                        ledged him guilty,
And grace asked of God   that to grant it is ready
To them that humbly pray it   and mean to amend themselves.
But though that thief had heaven   he had not high bliss,
As Saint John and other saints   that deserved had better.
Right as some man gives me meat more than enough   and sets me on the
                                                        floor,
I have meat more than enough   but not so much honour
As those that sit at side table   or with the lords of the hall.
But sit as a beggar table-less   by myself on the ground.
So it fareth for that felon   that on Good Friday was saved;
He sits neither with Saint John   Simon, nor Jude,
Nor with maidens nor with martyrs   confessors nor widows,
But by himself solitary   and served on the ground.
For he that is once a thief   is evermore in danger,
And at the law's pleasure   to live or to die;

> *De peccato propitiato, nolo esse sine metu.*

And for to serve a saint   and such a thief together,
It were neither reason nor right   to reward them both alike.

[1] See page 205.

'And right as Trajan the true knight   dwelt not so deep in hell,
That our Lord had him not lightly out   so believe I the thief be in heaven.
For he is in the lowest heaven   if our belief be true,
And well at ease he lolleth there   by the law of holy church,
    Quia reddit uniquique juxta opera sua, etc.
'And why that one thief on the cross   yielded himself believer
Rather than that other thief   though thou wouldst question,
All the clerks under Christ   could not give the reason;
    Quare placuit, quia voluit.
And so I sayest for thee   that seekest after the whys,
And argued with Reason   rebuking as it were,
And of the flowers in the wood   and of their fair hues,
Whereof they catch their colours   so clear and so bright,
And wishest of birds and of beasts   and of their breeding to know,
Why some be low down and some aloft   thy liking it were,
And of the stones and of the stars   thou studiest, as I believe,
However beast or bird   hath such strong wit;
Clergy nor Kind Wit   knew never the cause,
But Kind knoweth the cause himself   and no creature else.
He is the magpie's patron   and putteth it in her ear,
That where the thorn is thickest   to build and to breed;
And Kind taught the peacock   to breed in such a way,
And taught Adam   to know his private parts,
And taught him and Eve   to cover them with leaves.
'Unlearned men many times   masters they question,
Why Adam covered not first   his mouth that eat the apple,
Rather than his body low down   the unlearned ask thus the clerks;
Kind knoweth why he did so   but no clerk else.
But of birds and beasts   men of old time
Examples took and patterns   as telleth these poets,
And that the fairest fowl   foulest engendereth,
And feeblest fowl   that flieth or swimmeth;
And that is the peacock and the peahen   proud rich men they betoken
For the peacock, if men pursue him   can not fly high;
For the trailing of his tail   is he overtaken soon,
And his flesh is foul flesh   and his feet too,
And unlovely of voice   and hateful for to hear.
'Right so the rich   if he his riches hoard,
And giveth it not till his death-day   the tail of all sorrow.
Right as the quills of the peacock   pain him in flight,
So is possession pain   of pence and of nobles

To all that them holdeth   till their tail be plucked.
And though the rich repent then   and bewail the time,
That ever he gathered so greatly   and gave thereof so little,
Though he cry to Christ then   with keen will, I believe
His voice be in our Lord's ear   like a magpie's chattering.
And when his body shall come   in cave to be buried,
I believe it will pollute full foully   the earth all about,
And all the others where it lieth   are envenomed through his poison.
By the peacock's feet is understood   as I have learned in Avianus,[1]
Executors, false friends   that fulfil not his will
That was written, and they were witnesses   to do right as it laid down.
Thus the poet proves that the peacock   for his feathers is reverenced,
Right so is the rich   by reason of his goods.
    'The lark, that is a lesser bird   is more lovely of voice,
And well away of wing   swifter than the peacock,
And of flesh, by many times   fatter and sweeter.
To lowly-living men   the lark is compared;
Aristotle the great clerk   such tales he telleth;
Thus he likens in his logic   the least bird there is.
And whether he be saved or not saved   that truth knows no cleric,
Not of Socrates nor of Solomon   no writing can tell.
But God is so good, I hope   that since he gave them wits
To teach us ways therewith   (that teach us to be saved,
And the better for their books)   to pray we are beholden,
That God for his grace   give their souls rest;
For lettered men were ignorant yet   but for the learning of their books.'
    'All these clerks,' quoth I then   'that on Christ believe,
Say in their sermons   that neither Saracens nor Jews,
Nor no creature of Christ's likeness   without christening is saved.'
    '*Contra*,' quoth Imaginative then   and began to frown,
And said, '*Salvabitur vix justus in die judicii.
Ergo salvabitur*,' quoth he   and said no more Latin.
'Trajan was a true knight   and took never christening,
And he is safe, so saith the book   and his soul in heaven.
For there is baptism of water   and baptism in blood-shedding,
And through fire is baptism   and that is firm belief;
      Advenit ignis divinus, non comburens, sed illuminans, etc.
    'But truth that trespassed never   transgressed not against his law,
But liveth as his law teacheth   and believeth there be no better,
And if there were, he would amend   and in such will dieth,

------

[1] See page 205.

Would never true God   but recognized truth;
And whether it be or be not   the strength is great of truth,
And a hope hanging therein   to have reward for his truth.

> For, *Deus dicitur quasi dans vitam aeternam suis, hoc est, fidelibus; et alibi:*
> *Si ambulavero in medio umbrae mortis, etc.*

The gloss granteth upon that verse   a great reward for truth.
And wit and wisdom,' quoth that wight   'was at some time a treasure,
To keep with a commonwealth   no wealth was held better,
And much mirth and manhood'   and right with that he vanished.

PASSUS XIII

AND I awaked therewith   nearly out of my mind,
And as a fellow that free were   forth began I to walk
In manner of a mendicant   many a year after,
And of this dream many times   much thought I had.
First, how Fortune me failed   at my most need,
And how that Age menaced me   should we ever meet;
And how that friars followed   folk that were rich,
And folk that were poor   at little price they set,
And no corpse in their churchyard   nor in their church was buried,
Unless alive he bequeathed them aught   or should help pay their debts.
And how this covetousness overcame   clerks and priests,
And how that unlearned men be led   unless our Lord them help,
Through ignorant curates   to incurable pains.
And how that Imaginative   in dream me told,
Of Kind and of his cleverness   and how courteous to beasts,
And how loving he is to beasts   on land and on water;
Forsakes he no living thing   less nor more;
The creatures that creep   of Kind be engendered.
And then how Imaginative said   *vix justus salvabitur*,
And when he had said so   how suddenly he passed.
    I lay down long in this thought   and at last I slept,
And, as Christ willed, there came Conscience   to comfort me that time,
And bade me come to his court   with Clergy should I dine.
And as Conscience of Clergy spoke   I came the more readily,
And there saw a master   what man he was I knew not,
That low bowed   and courteously to Scripture.
Conscience knew him well   and welcomed him fair;
They washed and wiped   and to the dinner.
But Patience in the palace stood   in pilgrim's clothes,
And prayed meat for charity   for a poor hermit.
    Conscience called him in   and courteously said,
'Welcome, wight, go and wash   thou shalt sit soon.
    This master was made sit   as for the most worthy,
And then Clergy and Conscience   and Patience came after.

Patience and I   were put to be mates,
And sat by ourselves   at a side table.
  Conscience called for meat   and then came Scripture,
And served them thus soon   of sundry meats many,
Of Augustine, of Ambrose   of all the four evangelists;
  Edentes et bibentes quae apud eos sunt.
But this master nor his man   no ordinary flesh eat,
But they eat food of more cost   messes and soups;
Of that which men mis-won   they made them well at ease.
But their sauce was over sour   and unsavourly ground,
In a mortar, *post mortem*   of many bitter pains,
Unless they sing for those souls   and weep salt tears:
  Vos qui peccata hominum comeditis, nisi pro eis lacrimas et orationes
    effunderitis, ea quae in deliciis comeditis, in tormentis evometis.
Conscience full courteously then   commanded Scripture
Before Patience bread to bring   and me that was his mate.
He set a sour loaf before us   and said, '*Agite poenitentiam,*'
And then drew us drink   *diu perseverans.*
'As long,' quoth I, 'as I live   and my body endures!'
'Here is proper service,' quoth Patience   'there fareth no prince better';
And then he brought us forth a mess of other meat   of *miserere-mei-*
                                                                    Deus;
And he brought us of *beati-quorum*   of *beatus-vir*'s making,
Et-quorum-tecta-sunt   peccata in a dish
Of secret shrift, *dixi*   and *confitebor tibi*!
'Bring Patience some pittance'   quietly quoth Conscience;
And then had Patience a pittance   *pro-hac-orabit-ad-te-omnis-sanctus-in-*
                                                    tempore-opportuno;
And Conscience cheered us   and told us merry tales,
  Cor contritum et humiliatum, Deus, non despicies.
  Patience was proud   of that proper service,
And made him mirth with his meat   but I mourned ever,
For this doctor on the high dais   drank wine so fast;
  Vae vobis qui potentes estis ad bibendum vinum!
He ate many sundry meats   messes and puddings,
Tripes and wild boar   and eggs fried with fat.
Then said I to myself   so that Patience it heard,
'It is not four days since that this man   before the dean of St Paul's,
Preached of penances   that Paul the apostle suffered,
In fame et frigore   and blows of scourges;
  Ter caesus sum et a Judeis quinquies quadregenas, etc.

'But one word they skip over   at each time that they preach,
That Paul in his epistle   to all the people told;

    Periculum est in falsis fratribus.

Holy writ bids men beware   I will not write it here
In English, in case   it should be repeated too often,
And grieve therewith good men   but grammarians shall read;

    Unus quisque a fratre se custodiat, quia, ut dicitur, periculum est in falsis fratribus.

    'But I knew never man that as friar went   before men in English
Take it for their text   and tell it plainly.
They preach that penance   is profitable to the soul
And what mischief and pain   Christ for man suffered.
But this God's glutton,' quoth I   'with his great cheeks,
Hath no pity on us poor   he performeth evil;
That he preacheth he doeth not,'   to Patience I told,
And wished heartily   with will full eager,
That dishes and platters   before this same doctor,
Were molten lead in his maw   and Mahomet [1] inside him!
'I shall demand of this jerry   with his pot belly,
To tell me what penance is   of which he preached readily.'—
Patience perceived what I thought   and winked at me to be still,
And said, 'Thou shalt see thus soon   when he may no more,
He shall have a penance in his paunch   and puff at each word,
And then shall his guts grumble   and he shall gape after;
For now he hath drunken so deep   he will know soon,
And prove it by their Apocalypse   and by the passion of Saint Advisa,[2]
That neither bacon nor brawn   boiled meat nor messes
Is neither fish nor flesh   but food for a penitent.
And then shall he testify by the Trinity   and take his fellow to witness,
What he found in a frail   for a friar's living,
And unless the first line be lying   believe never again!
And then is the time to take up   and to ask this doctor
Of Do-well and of Do-better   and if Do-best be any penance.'—
    And I sat still, as Patience said   thus soon this doctor,
As ruddy as a rose   rubbed his cheeks,
Coughed and exclaimed   and Conscience him heard,
And told him of a Trinity   and towards us he looked.
'What is Do-well, sir doctor?' quoth I   'Is Do-well any penance?'
'Do-well?' quoth this doctor—   and took the cup and drank—
'Do no evil to thy fellow Christian   as lies in thy power.'

        [1] See page 206.   [2] See page 206.

'By this day, sir doctor,' quoth I　'then be ye not in Do-well;
For ye have harmed us two　in that ye eat the pudding,
Messes, and other meat　and we no morsel had!
And if ye fare so in your infirmary　it is strange methinketh,
Unless strife be where charity should be　if young children dared
complain!
I would exchange my penance with yours　for I am following Do-well!'
　Then Conscience courteously　a gesture he made,
And winked upon Patience　to pray me to be still,
And said himself, 'Sir doctor　if it be your will,
What is Do-well and Do-better?　ye thinkers know.'
　'Do-well,' quoth this doctor　'do as clerks teach,
And Do-better is he that teacheth　and travaileth to teach others,
And Do-best doth himself so　as he saith and preacheth:—
　　Qui facit et docuerit, magnus vocabitur in regno caelorum.'
　'Now thou, Clergy,' quoth Conscience　'say what is Do-well.'
'I have seven sons,' he said　'serve in a castle,
There the lord of life dwelleth　to teach them what is Do-well;
Till I see those seven　and myself accord with them,
I am unfitted,' quoth he　'to any wight to explain it.
For one Piers the Plowman　hath impugned us all,
And set all sciences at nought　save love alone,
And no text taketh　to maintain his cause,
But *dilige Deum* and *Domine, quis habitabit, etc.*
And he saith that Do-well and Do-better　are two absolutes,
Which absolutes, with faith　find out Do-best,
Which shall save man's soul　thus saith Piers the Plowman.'
　'I can naught hereon,' quoth Conscience　'but I know well Piers;
He will not against holy writ speak　I dare well undertake;
Then pass we over till Piers come　and prove this in deed.
Patience hath been in many places　and perchance knoweth
That no clerk can　as Christ beareth witness;
　　Patientes vincunt, etc.'
'At your request,' quoth Patience then　'if no man displeases;
Disce,' quoth he, '*doce　dilige inimicos.*
Disce, and Do-well　*doce*, and Do-better;
Dilige, and Do-best　thus taught me once
A beloved that I loved　Love was her name.
"With words and with works," quoth she　"and will of thine heart,
Thy soul love faithfully　all thy life-time;
And so thou learn thee to love　for the Lord's love of heaven,
I 57¹

Thine enemy in all ways   treat as thyself.
Cast coals on his head   and all kind speeches,
Both with works and with words   try his love to win;
And lay on him thus with love   till he laugh on thee;
Unless he bow to this beating   blind may he be!
But for to do thus with thy friend   folly it were,
For he that loveth thee truly   little of thine coveteth.
True love coveteth naught   no goods but speech,
With half a lamp-line [1] in Latin   *ex vi transitionis.*"
   'I bear about herein   fast bound, Do-well,
In a sign of the Saturday   that first set the calendar,
And all the wit of the Wednesday   of the next week after;
The fullness of the moon   is the might of both.
And herewith am I welcome   where I have it with me.' [2]
   'Undo it, let this doctor judge   if Do-well be therein;
For, by him that me made   might never poverty,
Pain, nor mischief   nor man with his tongue,
Cold, nor care   nor company of thieves,
Nor either heat, nor hail   nor no hell's spirit,
Nor either fire nor flood   nor fear of thine enemy
Trouble thee any time   if thou take it with thee;
     Caritas nihil timet.
And indeed, have God my soul!   if thou wilt it crave,
There is not either emperor nor empress   earl, king, nor baron,
Pope, nor patriarch   that pure reason shall not make
The master of all those men   through might of this riddle;
Not through witch-craft, but through it   (if thou wish it thyself)
Shall king and queen   and all the commons after
Give thee all that they may give   as for the best guardian,
And, as thou judgest, will they do   all their days after;
     Patientes vincunt, etc.'
   'It is but a "Dido,"' quoth this doctor   'a popular tale.
All the wit of this world   and mighty men's strength
Can not make a peace   between the pope and his enemies,
Nor between two Christian kings   can no wight peace make,
Profitable to either people'   and pushed the table from him,
And took Clergy and Conscience   to council, as it were,
So that Patience then must pass   for pilgrims know well how to lie.
   But Conscience spoke aloud   and courteously said,
'Friends, farewell'   and fair spake to Clergy,

      [1] See page 206.   [2] See page 206.

'For I will go with this man   if God give me grace,
And be pilgrim with Patience   till I have tried more men.'
    'What?' quoth Clergy to Conscience   'are ye covetous now
After new year's gifts or presents   or eager to read riddles?
I shall bring you a Bible   a book of the old law,
And teach you, if you like   the least point to know,
That Patience the pilgrim   perfectly knew never.'
    'Nay, by Christ,' quoth Conscience to Clergy   'God thee requite,
For all that Patience me proffers   proud am I little.
But the will of the wight   and the will of folk here
Hath moved my mind   to mourn for my sins.
The good will of a wight   was never bought to the full;
For there is no treasure comparable   to a true will.
Had not Magdalen more   for a box of salve,
Than Zacheus when he said   *dimidium bonorum meorum do pauperibus?*
And the poor widow   for a pair of mites,
Than all those that offered   into *gazophilacium*?'
    Thus courteously Conscience   first took leave of the friar,
And then softly he said   in Clergy's ear,
'I would rather, by our Lord   if I live should,
Have patience perfectly   than half thy pack of books!'
Clergy of Conscience   no leave would take,
But said full soberly   'Thou shalt see the time,
When thou art weary for walking   and glad of my counsel.'
    'That is sooth,' said Conscience   'so me God help!
If Patience be our fellow   and friend of us both,
There is no woe in this world   that we should not amend,
And conform kings to peace   and all people's lands,
Saracens and Syria   and so all the Jews
Turn into the true faith   and into one creed.'
    'That is true,' quoth Clergy   'I see what thou meanest,
I shall dwell as I do   my duty to show forth,
And train children   and other folk teach,
Till Patience have proved thee   and perfect thee made.'
    Conscience then with Patience passed forth   pilgrims as it were.
Then had Patience, as pilgrims have   in his pouch victuals,
Sobriety, and simple speech   and steadfast faith,
To comfort him and Conscience   if they come in a place
Where unkindness and covetousness are   hungry countries both.
    And as they went by the way   of Do-well they talked;
They met with a minstrel   as me then thought.

Patience approached him first   and prayed him he should tell
To Conscience, what craft he knew   and to what country he went.
  'I am a minstrel,' quoth that man   'my name is *Activa Vita*:
All idleness I hate   for Active is my name.
A confectioner, would ye know   and serve many lords,
And few robes I receive   or furred gowns.
Could I lie to make men laugh   then I should get
Either mantle or money   amongst lords' minstrels.
But as I can neither play tabor nor trumpet   nor tell no tales,
Pipe, nor fiddle   at feasts, nor harp,
Joke nor juggle   nor gently play,
Nor neither dance nor leap   nor sing with the gittern,
I have no good gifts   from these great lords,
For no bread that I bring   save a benison on the Sunday,
When the priest tells the people   their *pater noster* to pray
For Piers the Plowman   and those that his profit serve.
And that am I, Active   that idleness hates,
For all true toilers   and tillers of the earth;
From Michaelmas to Michaelmas   I supply them with wafers.
  'Beggars and bidders   of my bread crave,
Vagabonds and friars   and folk with tonsures.
I find bread for the pope   and provender for his palfrey,
And I have never of him   have God my truth,
Neither provender nor parsonage   yet of the pope's gift,
Save a pardon with a peace of lead   with two heads amidst! [1]
Had I a clerk that could write   I would send him a petition,
That he send me under his seal   a salve for the pestilence,
And that his blessing and his bulls   boils might destroy:
    In nomine meo daemonia ejicient, et super aegros manus imponent, et
        bene habebunt.
And then would I be ready to the people   pastry for to make,
And willing and busy   about bread and drink
For him and for all his   found I that his pardon
Might heal a man   as I believe it should.
For since he hath the power   that Peter himself had,
He hath the pot with the salve   sothly, as me thinketh:
    Argentum et aurum non est mihi; quod autem habeo, hoc tibi do
        nomine Domini, surge et ambula.
  'But if might of miracle fails him   it is because men be not worthy
To have the grace of God   and no guilt of the pope.
                              [1] See page 206.

For may no blessing do us good   unless we will amend,
No man's mass make peace   amongst Christian people,
Till pride be completely destroyed   and that through lack of bread.
   'For ere I have bread of meal   oft much I sweat.
And ere the commons have corn enough   many a cold morning;
So, ere my wafers be made   much woe I endure.
   'All London, I believe   liketh well my wafers,
And lower when they lack them—   it is not long ago,
There were miserable commons   when no cart came to town
With baked bread from Stratford [1]   then began beggars to weep,
And workmen afraid enough   this will be remembered long.
In the date of our drought   in a dry April,
A thousand and three hundred   twice thirty and ten,
My wafers then were scarce   when Chichester was mayor.'
   I took good notice, by Christ   and Conscience too,
Of Haukyn the active man   and how he was clothed.
He had a coat of Christendom   as holy church believeth,
But it was marred in many places   with many sundry patches,
Of pride here a patch, and there a patch   of rude speech,
Of scorning and of scoffing   and of discourteous bearing,
As in apparel and in comporting   proudly amongst the people,
Otherwise than he is   with heart or sight showing;
Willing that all men think   he is what he is not.
For which he boasteth and braggeth   with many bold oathes,
And unwilling to be reproved   by any man living,
And so singular by himself   in the sight of the people,
Was none such as himself   nor none so pope-holy, [2]
Habited as a hermit   an order all to himself,
Religion without rule   and reasonable obedience;
Attacking lettered men   and unlearned men both,
Praising true living   and a liar in soul;
In thought and observation   imagination and study,
As best for his body be   and have a bad name;
And meddles he everywhere   where he hath no business,
Wishing men to think   his wit were the best,
Or his crafty skill   or of clerks he the wisest,
Or strongest on steed   sturdiest under girdle,
And loveliest to look on   and truest in deeds,
And none so holy as he   nor of life cleaner,
Or fairest of features   of form and of stature,

   [1] See page 206.   [2] See page 206.

And most skilled of song   or cunning of hand,
And generous to give   and loss thereby to suffer;
And if he giveth aught poor men   tell what he dealt them;
Poor in possessions   in purse and in coffer,
And as lion to look on   and lordly of speech.
Boldest of beggers   a boaster that naught hath,
In town and in tavern   telling tales,
And saying things that he never saw   and for truth swearing it;
Of deeds that he never did   speaking and boasting,
And of works that he well did   to witness and say—
'Lo! if ye believe me not   or think that I lie,
Ask him or him   and he you can tell,
What I suffered and saw   and sometimes had,
And what I could do and knew   and what kin I come of.'
All he wishes that men knew   of his works and words,
Which might please the people   and praise himself:

> *Si hominibus placerem, Christi servus non essem;*
> *Et alibi: nemo potest duobus dominis servire.*

'By Christ,' quoth Conscience then   'thy best coat, Haukyn,
Hath many stains and spots   it must be washed.'
'Yea, whoso took heed,' quoth Haukyn   'behind and before,
What is on back and what on front   and by the two sides,
Men would find many creases   and many foul patches.'
And he turned about quickly   and then I took heed,
It was fouler many times   than it first seemed.
It was spotted with wrath   and wicked will,
With envy and evil speech   provoking to fight,
Lying and laughing   and chiding with tongue;
All that he knew wicked   of any wight, he tells it,
And blames men behind their back   and wishes them misfortune;
And what he knows of Will   tells it to Wat,
And the thing Wat heard   Will heard after,
And made of friends foes   through a false tongue,
'Either with might of mouth   or through man's strength
I avenge me many times   or else fret myself
Within, as a seamstress shears';—   wretched man and cursed!

> *Cujus maledictione os plenum est, et amaritudine; sub lingua ejus labor*
> *et dolor:*
> *Et alibi: filii hominum, dentes eorum arma et sagittae, et lingua eorum*
> *gladius acutus:—*

'There is no man that I love   lasts any time,

For tales that I tell   no man trusteth me,
And when I may not have the mastery   with melancholy I am seized,
So that I catch cramp   heart spasms sometimes,
Or an ague in such an anger   and sometimes a fever,
That holdeth me all a twelve month   till that I despise
Leechcraft of our Lord   and trust in a witch,
And say, that no clerk can cure me   nor Christ, as I believe,
As the cobbler of Southwark   or of Shoreditch Dame Emma! [1]
And say, that no God's word   did me never good,
But through a charm had I good luck   and my chief healing!'
  I looked more carefully   and then saw it was soiled
With liking of lechery   as by looking of his eye.
For each maid that he met   he made her a sign
Seeming to sin-ward   and sometimes began to taste
About the mouth, or beneath   beginneth to grope,
Till either's will waxeth keen   and to the work they go,
As well in fasting days and Fridays   and forbidden nights;
And as well in Lent as out of Lent   all times alike,
Such works with them   be never out of season;
Till they might no more   and then had merry tales,
And how that lechers love   laugh and jest,
And of their harlotry and whoredom   in their old age tell.
  Then Patience perceived   places of his coat
Were grimy through covetousness   and unnatural desiring;
More to goods than to God   the man his love gave,
And imagined how   he them might have
With false measures and means   and with false witness;
He gave for love of the interest   and loth to do right,
And waited to see which   way to beguile,
And mixed his merchandise   and made a good show;—
'The worst within was   clever I called it,
And if my neighbour had any hind   or any beast else,
More profitable than mine   many sleights I made,
How I might have it   all my wit I cast,
And if I had it not by other ways   at last I stole it,
Or secretly his purse shook   unpicked his locks,
Or by night or by day   about was I ever,
Through guile to gather   the goods that I have.
  'If I went to the plough   I pinched so narrowly,
That a foot of land or a furrow   steal I would,

[1] See page 206.

From my next neighbour   take of his earth;
And if I reaped, I would reach over   or gave them orders that reaped,
To seize to me with their sickles   what I sowed never.
   'And whoso borrowed of me   rued the time,
With presents privately   or payed some amount.
So, willy nilly   take I would;
And both to kith and kin   I was mean with what I had.
   'And whoso bargained for my goods   abuse I would,
Till he proffered to pay me   a penny or two
More than it was worth   and yet would I swear,
That it cost me much more   and swore many oaths.
   'On holy days at holy church   when I heard Mass,
Had I never will, knows God   genuinely to beseech
Mercy for my misdeeds   I mourned more
For loss of goods, believe me   than for my body's guilts;
Thus, if I had deadly sin done   I dreaded not that so sore,
As when I lent and believed it lost   or it was long ere it was payed.
So if I showed any kindness   my fellow Christian to help,
Upon a cruel covetousness   my heart began to suffer.
And if I sent over sea   my servants to Bruges,
Or into Prussia my prentice   my profit to look after,
To deal with money   and make exchanges,
Might never me comfort   in the mean time,
Neither Mass nor matins   nor no manner of sights,
Nor never penance performed   nor *pater noster* said,
My mind was more   on my goods, in the balance,
Than on the grace of God   and his great helps:
    Ubi thesaurus tuus, ibi et cor tuum.'
And also the glutton with great oaths   his garment had soiled,
And foully muddied it   with false speech;
When no need was   he took God's name in vain,
Swore thereby very oft   and all sweated his coat.
And more meat eat and drank   than nature could digest—
'I caught sickness sometimes   for my frequent surfeits;
And then I dreaded to die   in deadly sin'—
So that into despair he fell   and thought not to be saved,
The which is sloth so strong   that no skill can help it,
Nor no mercy heal   the man that so dieth.
   Which be the ways   that bringeth a man to sloth?
It happens when a man mourneth not for his misdeeds   nor maketh no
                                     sorrow,

But the penance that the priest enjoineth   performeth badly,
Doth no alms-deeds   dreads him of no sin,
Liveth against the faith   and no law holdeth;
Each day is holiday with him   or a high feast day;
And if aught will hear   it is a harlot's tongue.
When men speak of Christ   or of cleanness of soul,
He waxeth wroth and will naught hear   but words of mirth.
Penance and poor men   and the passion of saints
He hateth to hear thereof   and all that tell it.
These be the ways, beware   that bringeth a man to despair!
Ye lords and ladies   and legates of holy church,
That feed wise fools   flatterers and liars,
And have liking to listen to them   to make you laugh;
    Vae vobis qui ridetis, etc.:
And give them meat and goods   and poor men refuse,
In your death-dying   I dread me full sore,
Lest those three kinds of men   to much sorrow you bring:
    Consentientes et agentes pari poena punientur.
Patriarchs and prophets   and preachers of God's word
Save through their sermons   man's soul from hell;
Right so flatterers and fools   are the fiend's disciples,
To entice men through their tales   to sin and harlotry.
But clerks that know holy writ   should teach lords,
What David saith of such men   as the psalter telleth:
    Non habitabit in medio domus meae, qui facit superbiam et qui loquitur
      iniqua.
Should no jester have audience   in hall nor in chambers,
Where wise men are   God's word witnesseth;
Nor no vain man   amongst lords be allowed.
  Clerks and knights   welcome king's minstrels,
And for love of the lord   listen to them at feasts;
Much more, methinketh   rich men should
Have beggars before them   the which be God's minstrels,
As he saith himself   Saint John beareth witness:
    Qui vos spernit, me spernit.
Therefore I say to you rich   revels when ye make
For to solace your souls   such minstrels to have:
The poor, not a wise fool   sitting at the high table,
And a learned man, to teach thee   what our Lord suffered,
For to save thy soul   from Satan thine enemy,
And fiddle to thee, without flattering   of Good Friday the story;

And a blind man for a jester   or a bed-ridden woman,
To cry for a largesse before our Lord   your good fame to show!
These three kinds of minstrels   make a man to laugh,
And, at his death-dying   they give him great comfort,
That in his life listened to them   and loved them here.
These solace the soul   till he comes to
A well good hope, for he wrought so   amongst true saints.
But flatterers and fools   through their foul words,
Lead those that love them   to Lucifer's feast,
With *turpiloquio*, a lay of sorrow   and Lucifer's fiddle.
    Thus Haukyn the active man   had soiled his coat,
Till Conscience accused him thereof   in a courteous manner
Why he had not washed it   or cleaned it with a brush.

PASSUS XIV

'I HAVE but one whole garment,' quoth Haukyn   'I am the less to blame
Though it be soiled and seldom clean   I sleep therein at nights;
And also I have a housewife   servants and children—
    Uxorem duxi, et ideo non possum venire—
That will bespot it many a time   inspite of my checks!
It hath been washed in Lent   and out of Lent both,
With the soap of sickness   that seeketh out wondrous deep,
And with the loss of goods   loth for to offend
God or any good man   by aught that I could;
And was shriven by the priest   that gave me, for my sins,
As penance patience   and poor men to feed,
All for care of my Christianity   in cleanness to keep it.
And could I never, by Christ   keep it clean an hour,
That I soiled it not with looking   or some idle speech,
Or through deed or through word   or will of mine heart,
That I dirtied it not foul   from morning till eve.'
   'And I shall teach thee,' quoth Conscience   'of contrition to make,
That shall scrape thy coat   of all kinds of filth,
    Cordis contritio, etc.:—
Do-well shall wash it and wring it   through a wise confessor,
    Oris confessio, etc.:—
Do-better shall beat it and scour it   as bright as any scarlet,
And dye it with good will   and God's grace to amend thee,
And then send thee to satisfaction   for to sew it after,
    Satisfactio, Do-best.
Shall never fog besmirch it   nor moth after bite it,
Nor fiend nor false man   befoul it in thy life;
Shall no herald nor harper   have a fairer garment
Than Haukyn the active man   if thou do my teaching;
Nor no minstrel be valued more   amongst poor and rich,
Than Haukyn's wife the waferer   with his *activa vita*.'
   'And I shall provide the paste,' quoth Patience   'though here is no
                                  ploughing,
And flour to feed folk with   as best be for the soul,
Though never grain growed   nor grape upon vine.

123

For all that liveth and looketh   livelihood will I find,
And enough shall none lack   of things that they need.
We should not be too busy   about our livelihood,

> *Ne solliciti sitis, etc.: volucres coeli Deus pascit, etc.: patientes vincunt,*
>   *etc.'*

Then laughed Haukyn a little   and lightly began to swear,
'Whoso believeth you, by our Lord   I believe he be not blessed!'
'No,' quoth Patience patiently   and out of his pouch took
Food of great virtue   for all manner of beasts,
And said, 'Lo! here is livelihood enough   if our belief be true!
For lent never was life   but livelihood was given,
Whereof or wherefrom   or whereby to live.

'First the wild worm   under wet earth,
Fish to live in the flood   and the fire the cricket,
The curlew by means of the air   most cleanest flesh of birds,
And beasts by grass and by grain   and by green roots,
Meaning that all men   might the same way
Live through true belief   and love, as God witnesseth;

> *Quodcunque petieritis a patre in nomine meo, etc.; et alibi,*
> *Non in solo pane vivit homo, sed in omni verbo, quod procedit de ore Dei.'*

I looked what livelihood it was   that Patience so praised,
And it was a piece of the *pater noster   fiat voluntas tua.*

'Have, Haukyn!' quoth Patience   'and eat this when thee hungereth,
Or when thou art benumbed with cold   or pinest with thirst.
Shall not gyves thee grieve   nor great lords' wrath,
Prison nor punishment   for—*patientes vincunt.*
If thou be sober   of sight and of tongue,
In eating and in handling   and in all thy five wits,
Darest thou never care for corn   nor linen cloth nor woollen,
Nor for drink, nor death dread   but die when God liketh,
Through hunger or through heat   at his will be it;
For if thou livest after his law   the shorter life the better
Si quis amat Christum   mundum non diligit istum.
For through his breath beasts grow   and go abroad,

> *Dixit et facta sunt, etc.:*

Ergo through his breath must   men and beasts live,
As holy writ witnesseth   when men say grace,

> *Aperis tu manum tuam, et imples omne animal benedictione*

'It is found that forty winters   folk lived without tilling,
And out of the stone sprang the water   that folk and beasts drank.
And in Elijah's time   heaven was closed,

That no rain rained   thus read men in books,
That many winters men lived   and no food won by tilling.
Seven slept, as saith the book   seven hundred winters,
And lived without livelihood   and at last they woke,
And if men lived according to measure   should never more be fault
Amongst Christian creatures   if Christ's words be true.
But unkindness *caristia* maketh   amongst Christian people,
And over plenty maketh pride   amongst poor and rich;
But measure is so much worth   it cannot be too dear,
For the mischief and mischance   amongst men of Sodom
Waxed through plenty of bread   and of pure sloth;

> *Otiositas et abundantia panis peccatum turpissimum nutrivit.*

For they measured not   of that they eat and drank,
Did deadly sin   that the devil liked,
So vengeance fell upon them   for their vile sins;
They sunk into hell   those cities each one.
Therefore measure we us well   and make our faith our strong shield,
And through faith cometh contrition   conscience knows well,
Which driveth away deadly sin   and makes it venial.
And though a man may not speak   contrition may him save,
And bring his soul to bliss   if so that faith beareth witness,
That, whilst he lived, he believed   on the law of holy church;
Ergo contrition, faith, and conscience   is truly Do-well,
And surgeons for deadly sins   when shrift of mouth faileth.

'But shrift of mouth more worthy is   if man be inly contrite;
For shrift of mouth slayeth sin   be it never so deadly;
Per confessionem to a priest   *peccata occiduntur,*
Where contrition doth but drive it down   into a venial sin,
As David saith in the psalter   *et quorum tecta sunt peccata.*
But satisfaction seeketh out the root   and both slayeth and maketh void,
And, as it never had been   to naught bringeth deadly sin,
So it never after is seen, nor hurts   but seemeth a wound healed.'

'Where dwelleth Charity?' quoth Haukyn   'I knew never in my life
Man that with him spake   widely as I have travelled!'
'Where perfect truth and poverty of heart is   and patience of tongue,
There is Charity, the chief chamberlain   for God himself!'
'Is patient poverty,' quoth Haukyn   'more pleasing to our Master
Than riches rightfully won   and reasonably spent?'
'But *quis est ille*?' quoth Patience   'quick *laudabimus eum*!
Though men talk of riches   right to the world's end,

I knew never man that rich was　　that when he reckon should,
When it drew to his death-day　　did not dread him sore,
And that at reckoning in arrears fell　　rather than out of debt.
Where the poor dare plead　　and prove by pure reason,
To have allowance of his Lord　　by the law he it claimeth,
Joy that never joy had　　of righteous Judge he asketh,
And saith, "Lo! birds and beasts　　that no bliss knoweth,
And wild worms in woods　　through winters thou them grievest,
And makest them well nigh meek　　and mild for want,
And after thou sendest them summer　　which is their sovereign joy,
And bliss to all that be　　both wild and tame."
Then may beggars, as beasts　　for good wait,
That all their life have lived　　in suffering and want.
Unless God sent them some time　　some manner of joy,
Either here or elsewhere　　would it never be just;
For to bad fortune was he wrought　　that never was for joy created.
Angels that in hell now be　　had joy at some time,
And Dives on dainties lived　　and in *douce vie*;
Right so reason showeth　　that those men that were rich,
And their mates also lived　　their life in mirth.

'But God is of a wondrous will　　as natural wit shows,
To give many man his reward　　ere he it hath deserved.
Right so doeth God by some rich　　a pity me it thinketh,
For they have their hire here　　a heaven as it were,
And great pleasure in living　　without labour of body;
And when he dieth, be disallowed　　as David saith in the psalter,
　　　Dormierunt, et nihil invenerunt;
And in another place also　　*velut somnium surgentium,*
　　　Domine, in civitate tua, et ad nihilum rediges.

'Alas! that riches should deprive　　and rob man's soul
From the love of our Lord　　at his last end!
Labourers that have their hire in advance　　are evermore needy,
And seldom dieth he out of debt　　that dines ere he deserve it,
And till he have done his duty　　and his day's work.
For when a workman hath wrought　　then may men see the truth,
What he is worth for his work　　and what he hath deserved;
And naught take before　　for dread of disapproval.
So I say to you rich　　it beseemeth not that ye shall
Have heaven in your life here　　and heaven hereafter;
Right as a servant taketh his salary before　　and then would claim more,
As he that none had　　and hath his hire at the last.

It may not be, ye rich men   or Matthew on God lieth;
   Vae! deliciis ad delicias difficile est transire.
  'But if ye rich have pity   and reward well the poor,
And live as law teacheth   deal truly with all,
Christ of his courtesy   shall comfort you at the last,
And reward all with double riches   that pitiful hearts have.
And as a hind that had his hire   ere he began,
And when he hath done his work well   men give him more reward,
Giveth him a coat above his covenant   right so Christ giveth heaven
Both to rich and to not rich   that mercifully live;
And all that do their work well   have double hire for their labours,
Here forgiveness of their sins   and heaven's bliss hereafter.
  'But it is but seldom seen   as by holy saints' books,
That God rewarded double rest   to any rich wight.
For much mirth is amongst the rich   as to meat and clothing,
And much mirth in May is   amongst wild beasts,
And so long as summer lasts   the solace endureth.
But beggars about midsummer   breadless they sup,
And it is in winter for them worse   for wet-shod they go.
Athirst sore and ahungered   and foul rebuked,
And berated by rich men   so that pity it is to hear.
Now, Lord, send them summer   and some manner of joy,
Heaven after their hence-going   that here had such want!
For all mightest thou have made   none meaner than another,
And equally clever and wise   if thee well had liked.
And have pity on these rich men   that reward not thy prisoners;
Of the good that thou them givest   *ingrati* be many;
But, God, of thy goodness   give them grace to amend.
For may no famine be to them hard   drought, nor wet,
Nor neither heat nor hail   if they have their health,
Of that they wish and want   lacketh them not here.
  'But poor people, thy prisoners   Lord, in the pit of misfortune,
Comfort those creatures   that much care suffer
Through famine, through drought   all their days here,
Woe in winter time   for wanting of clothes,
And in summer time seldom   sup to the full;
Comfort thy sorrowful   Christ, in thy kingdom,
For how thou comfortest all creatures   clerks bear witness,
   Convertimini ad me, et salvi eritis:
  'Thus, *in genere* of his humanity   Jesus Christ spoke,
To robbers and to thieves   to rich and to poor.

Thou taughtest them in the Trinity   to take baptism,
And be clean through that christening   from all kinds of sins;
And if it happens through folly   to fall into sin after,
Confession, and acknowledgement   and craving thy mercy
Should amend us as many times   as man can desire.
But if the devil should plead against this   and punish us in conscience,
Christ would take the acquittal quickly   and to the evil one show it,

    Pateat, etc., per passionem Domini,

And repel so the devil   and prove us to be under his pledge.
But the parchment of this patent   of poverty be most,
And of pure patience   and perfect faith.
From pomp and from pride   the parchment departs,
And above all from all people   unless they be poor of heart.
Else is all idleness   all that ever we wrote,
Pater nosters and penance   and pilgrimages to Rome.
Unless our alms-giving and spending   spring of a true will,
All our labour is lost   lo! how men write
On the windows at the friars   vainly, if false be the foundation;
Therefore Christians should be rich in common   none covetous for
                                             himself.

   'For the seven sins that there be   assail us ever,
The fiend accompanies them all   and gives them help,
But with riches that villain   chiefly men beguileth.
For where that riches reign   subservience followeth,
And that is pleasant to pride   in poor and in rich.
And the rich is reverenced   by reason of his riches,
Where the poor is but behind   and perchance knows more
Of wit and of wisdom   that far away is better
Than riches or royalty   and the rather heard in heaven.
For the rich hath much to reckon   and right soft walketh,
The high way heavenwards   oft riches closeth,

    Ita impossible diviti, etc.,

There the poor presses before the rich   with a pack at his back,

    Opera enim illorum sequuntur illos.

Importunes, as beggars do   and boldly he demands,
For his poverty and his patience   a perpetual bliss;

    Beati pauperes, quoniam ipsorum est regnum caelorum.

   'And Pride in riches reigneth   rather than in poverty,
Sooner in the master than in the man   some dwelling he hath.
But in poverty where patience is   Pride hath no might,
Nor none of the seven sins   can stay there long,

Nor have power in poverty   if patience it follows.
For the poor is always quick   to please the rich,
And ready at his bidding   for his bread's sake;
And obedience and boasting   are ever at war,
And each hateth the other   in all manner of works.

'If Wrath wrestle with the poor   he hath the worse;
For if they both plead   the poor is but feeble,
And if he chide or quarrel   it turns out worst for him;
For lowly he looketh   and lowly is his speech,
That meat or money   of other men must ask.

'And if Gluttony grieve poverty   he gains the less,
For his pay will not reach   rich meats to buy;
And if his gluttony be to good ale   he goeth to cold bed,
And his head uncovered   uneasily awry;
For when he straineth him to stretch   the straw is his sheets;
So for his gluttony and his great sloth   he hath a grievous penance,
That is woe when he waketh   and weepeth for cold,
And sometimes for his sins   so he is never merry,
Without mourning amongst it   and mishap as well.

'And if Covetousness would catch the poor   they can not come
together,
And round the neck especially   neither embrace the other.
For men knoweth well that Covetousness   is of a keen will,
And hath hands and arms   of a long length,
And poverty is but a little thing   reaches not to his navel,
And good encounter was there never   between the long and the short.

'And though Avarice would anger the poor   he hath but little might,
For poverty hath but pouches   to put his goods in,
Where Avarice hath aumbries   and iron-bound coffers;
And which be easier to break open   less noise it maketh,
A beggar's bag   or an iron-bound coffer!

'Lechery loveth him not   for he giveth but little silver,
Nor doth he not dine delicately   nor drink wine oft.
A straw for the stews!   they would stand not, I trow,
Had they nothing but from poor men   their houses were un-tiled!

'And though Sloth pursue poverty   and serves not God well,
Mischance is his master   and maketh him to think,
That God is his greatest help   and no one else,
And his servant, as he saith   and of his train too.
And wherever he be   he beareth the sign of poverty,
And in that company our Saviour   saved all mankind.

K 57¹

Therefore all poor that patient are   may claim and ask
After their ending here   bliss of heaven's kingdom.
Much bolder may he ask   that here could have his will
In land and in lordship   and pleasures of the body,
And for God's love leaveth all   and liveth as a beggar;
And as a maid for man's love   her mother forsaketh,
Her father and all her friends   and follows her mate,
Much is such a maid to be loved   by him that such a one taketh,
More than a maiden is   that is married through brokerage,
As by assent of sundry parties   and silver as well,
More for covetousness of goods   than human love between both:—
So it fareth by each person   that possessions forsaketh,
And puts himself to be patient   and poverty weddeth,
The which is kin to God himself   and to his saints.'
'Have God my truth,' quoth Haukyn   'ye praise poverty hard;
What is poverty with patience,' quoth he   'properly in meaning?'
'*Paupertas*,' quoth Patience   '*est odibile bonum,*

> *Remotio curarum, possessio sine calumnia, donum Dei, sanitatis mater;*
> *Absque sollicitudine semita, sapientiae temperatrix, negotium sine damno;*
> *Incerta fortuna, absque sollicitudine felicitas.*'

'I cannot construe all this,' quoth Haukyn   'ye must teach me this in
                                               English.'
'In English,' quoth Patience, 'it is hard   well to expound it;
But somewhat I shall say it   so thou understand.
(1) Poverty is the first point   that Pride most hateth,
And it is good that by good skill   terrifies Pride.
Right as contrition is a comforting thing   conscience knows well,
And a sorrow for himself   and a solace to the soul,
So poverty indeed   penance, and joy,
Is to the body   pure spiritual health,

> *Ergo paupertas est odibile bonum,*

And contrition comfort   and *cura animarum.*
(2) Seldom sits poverty   the truth to declare,
Or as justice to judge men   enjoined is no poor man,
Nor to be a magistrate above men   nor minister under kings;
Seldom is any poor man put   to punish any people;

> *Remotio curarum.*

Ergo poverty and poor men   perform the commandment,

> *Nolite judicare quemquam.*   The third:—

(3) Seldom becomes any poor man rich   but of rightful heritage;

Winneth he naught with weights false   nor with unsealed measures,
Nor borroweth of his neighbours   except what he can pay back,
    Possessio sine calumnia.
(4) The fourth is a fortune   that makes the soul flourish
With sobriety from all sin   and also yet more;
It restrains the flesh   from follies full many,
And extra comfort   Christ's own gift,
    Donum Dei.
(5) The fifth is mother of health   a friend in all temptations,
And for the land ever a healer   a lover of all cleanness,
    Sanitatis mater.
(6) The sixth is a path of peace   yea, through the pass of Alton [1]
Poverty might pass   without peril of robbing,
For there that poverty passeth   peace followeth after,
And ever the less that he beareth   the braver he is of heart;
Therefore saith Seneca   *paupertas est absque sollicitudine semita.*
And a brave man of heart   amongst a gang of thieves;
    Cantabit pauper coram latrone viator.
(7) The seventh is a well of wisdom   and few words showeth,
For lords allow him little   nor listen to his reason,
He tempereth the tongue truth-ward   and no treasure coveteth;
    Sapientiae temperatrix.
(8) The eighth is a loyal labourer   and loth to take more
Than he may well deserve   in summer or in winter,
And if he trades, he feels no loss   if he charity gains;
    Negotium sine damno.
(9) The ninth is sweet to the soul   no sugar is sweeter;
For patience is bread   for poverty himself,
And sobriety sweet drink   and good doctor in sickness,
Thus taught me a lettered man   for our Lord's love,
Saint Augustine, a blessed life   without over concern,
For body and for soul   *absque sollicitudine felicitas.*
Now God, that all good giveth   grant his soul rest,
That thus first wrote to teach men   what poverty meant!'
    'Alas!' quoth Haukyn the active man then   'that, after my christening
I had not been dead and buried   for Do-well's sake!
So dangerous it is,' quoth Haukyn   'to live and to do sin.
Sin followeth us ever,' quoth he   and sorrowful waxed,
And wept water with his eyes   and bewailed the time,
That ever he did a deed   that dear God displeased;

[1] See page 206.

Swooned and sobbed   and sighed full oft,
That ever he had land or lordship   less or more,
Or mastery over any man   other than himself.
'I am not worthy, knows God,' quoth Haukyn   'to wear any clothes,
Neither shirt nor shoes   save for shame one,
To cover my body,' quoth he   and cried mercy fast,
And wept and wailed   and therewith I awoke.

PASSUS XV

BUT after my waking   it was wondrous long,
Ere I could truly   know what was Do-well.
And so my wit waxed and waned   till I a fool were,
And some blamed my life   approved it few,
And held me as a wretch   and loth to reverence
Lords or ladies   or any man else,
As persons in fur   with pendants of silver;
To serjeants nor to such   said not once,
'God save you, lords!'   nor bowed fair;
So that folk held me a fool   and in that folly I raved,
Till Reason had pity on me   and rocked me asleep,
Till I saw, as it sorcery were   a marvellous thing withal,
One without tongue and teeth   told me whither I should go,
And whereof I came and of what kind   I begged him at last,
If he were Christ's creature   for Christ's love to tell.

    'I am Christ's creature,' quoth he   'and by Christians in many a place,
In Christ's court known   and of his kin a part.

    'It is neither Peter the porter   nor Paul with his falchion,
That will forbid me the door   knock I never so late.
At midnight, at midday   my voice is known,
So that each creature of his court   welcometh me fair.'

    'What are ye called,' quoth I, 'in that court   amongst Christian
                                 people?'
'The whiles I quicken the body,' quoth he   'called am I *Anima*;
And when I will and would   *Animus* I am named;
And for that I think and know   called am I *Mens*;
And when I make moan to God   *Memoria* is my name;
And when I make judgements   and do as truth teacheth,
Then is *Ratio* my right name   Reason in English;
And when I feel what folk telleth   my first name is *Sensus*,
And that is wit and wisdom   the well of all crafts;
And when I challenge or challenge not   permit or refuse,
Then am I Conscience called   God's clerk and his notary;
And when I love loyally   our Lord and all others,
Then is Love my name   and in Latin *Amor*;

And when I fly from the flesh   and forsake the corpse,
Then am I spirit speechless   and *Spiritus* then I am called.
Austin and Isidore   each of them both
Named me thus by name   now thou may choose,
How thou desirest to call me   now thou knowest all my names.

> *Anima pro diversus actionibus diversa nomina sortitur: dum vivificat
> corpus, Anima est; dum vult, Animus est; dum scit, Mens est; dum
> recolit, Memoria est; dum judicat, Ratio est; dum sentit, Sensus
> est; dum amat, Amor est; dum negat vel consentit, Conscientia est;
> dum spirat, Spiritus est.'*

'Ye be as a bishop,' quoth I   jesting that time,
'For bishops blessed   they bear many names,
Praesul and *pontifex*   and *metropolitanus*,
And other names a heap   *episcopus* and *pastor.'*
'That is sooth,' said he   'now I see thy will!
Thou would'st know and understand   the cause of all their names,
And of mine, if thou mightest   methinketh by thy speech!'
'Yea, sir,' I said   'if so no man were grieved,
All the sciences under sun   all the subtle crafts
I would I knew and understood   by nature in my heart!'
'Then art thou imperfect,' quoth he   'and one of Pride's knights;
For such a lust and liking   Lucifer fell from heaven:

> *Ponam pedem meum in aquilone, et similis ero altissimo.*

It is against nature,' quoth he   'and all kind of reason,
That any creature should know all   except Christ alone.
Against such Solomon speaketh   and despiseth their wits,

> And saith, *sicut qui mel comedit multum, non est ei bonum: sic qui
> scrutator est majestatis, opprimitur a gloria.*

To English men this means   that may speak and hear,
The man that much honey eateth   his maw it cloyeth;
And the more that a man   of good matter heareth,
Unless he do thereafter   it doth him double harm:
Beatus est, saith Saint Bernard   *qui scripturas legit,
Et verba vertit in opera*   fully to his power.
Covetousness to understand   and to know science
Pulled out of paradise   Adam and Eve;

> *Scientiae appetitus hominem inmortalitatis gloria spoliavit.*

And right as honey is evil to digest   and cloyeth the maw,
Right so those that through reason   would the root know
Of God and of his great mights   his graces it hindereth.

[1] See page 206.

For in the liking lieth a pride   and a covetousness of the body,
Against Christ's counsel   and all clerks' teaching,
     'That is, *non plus sapere quam operiet sapere.*
Friars and many other masters   that to ignorant men preach,
Ye touch on matters immeasurable   to tell of the Trinity,
So that oft times the unlearned people   of their faith doubt.
Better if abandoned many   doctors such teaching,
And told men of the ten commandments   and touched on the seven sins,
And of the branches that burgeoneth from them   and bring men to hell,
And how that folk in follies   mispend their five wits,
As well friars as other folk   foolishly spend
In housing, in clothing   and high learning to show,
More for pomp than for pure charity   the people know the truth
That I lie not, lo!   for lords ye please,
And reverence the rich   the rather for their silver;
     Confundantur omnes qui adorant sculptilia; et alibi:
     Ut quid diligitis vanitatem, et quaeritis mendacium?
Go to the gloss of the verse   ye great clerks;
If I lie on you in my ignorant wit   lead me to burning!
For as it seemeth, ye forsake   no man's alms,
Of usurers, of whores   of avaricious chapmen,
And bow to these lords   that may lend you nobles,
Against your rule and religion   I take record by Jesus,
That said to his disciples   *ne sitis personarum acceptores.*
     'Of this matter I might   make a long book,
But of curates of Christian people   as clerks bear witness,
I shall tell it for truth's sake   take heed whoso liketh!
As holiness and honesty   out from holy church spread
Through loyal living men   that God's law teach,
Right so out from holy church   all evils spread,
Where imperfect priesthood is   preachers and teachers.
And see it by example   in summer time on trees,
Where some boughs be leaved   and some beareth none;
There is a mischief in the root   of such manner boughs.
Right so parsons and priests   and preachers of holy church,
That are root of the right faith   to rule the people;
But where the root is rotten   reason knows the truth,
Shall never flower nor fruit   nor fair leaf be green.
Therefore, would ye lettered leave   the lechery of clothing,
And be kind, as befits clerks   and courteous with Christ's goods,
True of your tongue   and of your tally both,

And hate to hear harlotry   and not to receive
Tithes of untrue thing   tilled or chaffered,
Then loth were unlearned men   unless they your lore followed,
And amend them that misdo   more for your examples,
Than for to preach and practise not   hypocrisy that seemeth.
For hypocrisy in Latin   is likened to a dunghill,
That was covered with snow   and snakes within;
Or to a wall that was white-limed   and was foul within.
Right so many priests   preachers and prelates,
Ye are blanched with *belles paroles*   and with clothes also,
But your works and your words thereunder   are full unlovely.

   '*Johannes Chrysostomus* [1]   of clerks speaketh and priests,

> *Sicut de templo omne bonum progreditur, sic de templo omne malum procedit.*
>
> *Si sacerdotium integrum fuerit, tota floret ecclesia; si autem corruptum fuerit, omnis fides marcida est.*
>
> *Si sacerdotium fuerit in peccatis, totus populus convertitur ad peccandum.*
>
> *Sicut cum videris arborem pallidam et marcidam, intelligis quod vitium habet in radice,*
>
> *Ita cum videris populum indisciplinatum et irreligiosum, sine dubio sacerdotium ejus non est sanum.*

   'If unlearned men wist   what this Latin meaneth,
And who was my authority   much wonder methinketh,
Unless many a priest bore   instead of their daggers and their brooches,
A set of beads [2] in their hand   and a book under their arm.
Sir John and Sir Geoffrey [3]   have a girdle of silver,
A dagger, or a knife   with studs guilded.
But a breviary that should be his plow   *placebo* to say,
Had he never a service to save silver by   saith it with evil will!
Alas! ye ignorant men   much lose ye by priests,
But a thing that wickedly is won   and with false sleights,
Was never wisdom of wise God   save wicked men it had;
The which are priests imperfect   and preachers after silver,
Executors and subdeans   summoners and their lovers.
This which with guile was got   ungraciously is spended;
So harlots and whores   are helped with such goods,
And God's folk for lack thereof   ruined and destroyed.

   'Curates of holy church   as clerks that be avaricious,
Lightly what they leave   rascals it have,
Or die intestate   and then the bishop entereth,

    [1] See page 206.   [2] See page 206.   [3] See page 206.

And maketh merry therewith   and his men both,
And say, "he was a niggard   that no goods might spare
To friend nor to stranger   the fiend have his soul!
For a wretched house he held   all his life time;
And what he spared and locked up   spend we with mirth."
For learned, for unlearned   that loth is to spend,
Thus go their goods   when the spirit is fled.
But for good men, God wot   great dole men make,
And bemoan good meat-givers   and in mind have,
In prayers and in penances   and in perfect charity.'
   'What is Charity?' quoth I then   'a childlike thing,' he said;
     '*Nisi efficiamini sicut parvuli, non intrabitis in regnum caelorum;*
Without childishness or folly   a free liberal will.'
   'Where should men find such a friend   with so free a heart?
I have lived in the land,' quoth I   'my name is Long Will,[1]
And found I never full charity   before nor behind!
Men be merciful   to mendicants and to poor,
And will lend where they believe   honestly to be payed.
   'But charity that Paul praiseth best   and most pleasant to our Saviour,
     As, *non inflatur, non est ambitiosa, non quaerit quae sua sunt,*
I saw never such a man   so me God help,
That would not ask after his own   and other whiles covet
Things that he needed not   and take if he might!
Clerks teach me that Christ   is in all places;
But I saw him never truly   but as myself in a mirror,
     Ita in aenigmate, tunc facie ad faciem.
And so I trow truly   by what men telleth of charity,
It is not champions' contest   nor trade, as I think.'
   'Charity,' quoth he, 'chaffereth not   -   nor challengeth, nor craveth.
As proud of a penny   as of a pound of gold,
And is as glad of a gown   of a gray wool
As of a tunic of Tharsian silk   or of choice scarlet.
He is glad with all the glad   and good to all wicked,
And believeth and loveth all   that our Lord made.
Curseth he no creature   nor can he bear wrath,
Nor no liking hath to lie   nor laugh men to scorn.
All that men saith, he holds it true   and in peace taketh,
And all manner of mischiefs   in mildness he suffereth;
Coveteth he no earthly good   but bliss of heaven's kingdom.'
   'Hath he any rents or riches   or any rich friends?'

---

[1] See page 206.

'Of rents nor of riches   recketh he never.
For a friend findeth him   that faileth him never at need;
Fiat-voluntas-tua   finds him evermore.
And if he suppeth, he eats but a sop   of *spera-in-Deo*.
He can portray well the *pater noster*   and paint it with *aves*,
And otherwhiles is his wont   to wend in pilgrimage,
Where poor men and prisoners lie   their pardon to have.
Though he bear them no bread   he beareth them sweeter livelihood,
Loveth them as our Lord biddeth   and looketh how they fare.
     'And when he is weary of that work   then will he sometimes
Labour in a laundry   well the length of a mile,
And go to youth   and eagerly address
Pride with all its appurtenances   and pack them together,
And soak them in his breast   and beat them clean,
And labour on them long   with *laboravi-in-gemitu-meo*,
And with warm water at his eyes   wash them after.
And then he singeth when he doth so   and sometimes saith weeping,
     Cor contritum et humiliatum, Deus, non despicies.'
     'By Christ, I would that I knew him,' quoth I   'no creature rather!'
'Without help of Piers Plowman,' quoth he   'his person seest thou never.'
'Do clerks know him,' quoth I   'that keep holy church?'
     'Clerks have no knowing,' quoth he   'but by works and by words.
But Piers the Plowman   perceiveth more deeper
What is the will and wherefore   that many wights suffer,
     Et vidit Deus cogitationes eorum.
For there are full proud-hearted men   patient of tongue,
And polite as of bearing   to burgesses and to lords,
And to poor people   have pepper in the nose,
And as a lion he looketh   where men blame their works.
     'For there are beggars and bidders   beadsmen as it were,
Looketh as lambs   and seem life-holy,
But it is more to have their meat   with such an easy manner,
Than for penance and perfectness   the poverty that such have.
Therefore by sight nor by clergy   know shalt thou him never,
Neither through words nor works   but through will alone.
And that knoweth no clerk   nor creature on earth,
But Piers the Plowman   *Petrus, id est, Christus.*
For he is not among rascals   nor vagabond hermits,
Nor among anchorites, where a box hangeth [1]   all such they deceive.
Fie on deceivers   and *in fautores suos*!

     [1] See page 206.

For charity is God's champion   and as a good child mild,
And the merriest of mouth   at meat where he sitteth.
The love that lieth in his heart   maketh him light of speech,
And is companionable and cheerful   as Christ himself bids,

  Nolite fieri sicut hypocritae, tristes, etc.

For I have seen him in silk   and sometimes in russet,
Both in grey and in fur   and in gilt armour,
And as gladly he gave   to people that needed.
Edmund and Edward   both were kings,[1]
And saints considered   when charity them followed.
I have seen charity also   sing and read,
Ride and run   in ragged weeds,
But bidding as beggars   beheld I him never.
But in rich robes   soonest he walketh,
Capped and annointed   and his crown shaved,
And cleanly clothed   in lawn and in silk of Tartary.
And in a friar's frock   he was found once,
But it is far agone   in Saint Francis' time;
In that sect since   too seldom hath he been known.
Rich men he recommendeth   and of their robes taketh,
That without guile   lead their lives,

  Beatus est dives, qui, etc.

In king's court he cometh oft   where the counsel is true,
But if covetousness be of the counsel   he will not come therein.
In court among jesters   he cometh but seldom,
For brawling and back-biting   and bearing of false witness.
In the consistory before the commissary   he cometh not full oft,
For their law lasteth over-long   unless they take silver;
And matrimony for money   make and unmake,
And what Conscience and Christ   have knit fast,
They undo it unworthily   those doctors of law.
Amongst archbishops and other bishops   and prelates of holy church,
To dwell among them   his wont was some time,
And Christ's patrimony to the poor   deal out in portions.
But Avarice hath the keys now   and keepeth for his kinsmen,
And for his executors and his servants   and some for their children.
  'But I blame no man   but Lord, amend us all,
And give us grace, good God   charity to follow!
For whoso might meet with him   such manners him pleaseth,
Neither he blameth nor curseth   boasteth, nor praiseth,

----

[1] See page 206.

Taketh, nor loseth   nor looketh stern;
Craveth, nor coveteth   nor crieth after more,
    In pace in idipsum dormiam, etc.
The most livelihood that he liveth by   is love of God's passion,
Neither he asketh. nor beggeth   nor borroweth to repay;
Misdoth he no man   nor with his mouth grieveth.

'Amongst Christian men   this mildness should last;
In all manner of trials   have this at heart—
That though they suffered all this   God suffered for us more,
In example we should do so   and take no vengeance
On our foes that do us falseness   that is our Father's will.
For well may every man know   if God had willed himself,
Should never Judas nor Jew   have Jesu put on rood,
Nor have martyred Peter nor Paul   nor in prison held.
But he suffered in example   that we should suffer also,
And said to such that suffer would   that *patientes vincunt.*

'*Verbi gratia,*' quoth he   'and true examples many,
In *Legenda Sanctorum*   the life of holy saints,
What penance and poverty   and passion they suffered,
In hunger, in heat   in all manner of trials.
Anthony and Giles [1]   and other holy fathers
Wonned in wilderness   amongst wild beasts;
Monks and mendicants   men by themselves,
In caves and in caverns   seldom speak together.
But neither Anthony nor Giles   nor hermit that time
Of lions nor of leopards   livelihood took,
But of fowls that fly   thus find men in books.
Except that Giles   after a hind cried,
And through the milk of that mild beast   the man was sustained:
And day by day had he her not   his hunger for to slake,
But seldom and sundry times   as saith the book and teacheth.

'Anthony some days   about noon-time,
Had a bird that brought him bread   that he lived by;
And though the man had a guest   God found for them both.

'Paul *primus heremita* [2]   had enclosed himself,
So that no man might him see   for moss and for leaves;
Fowls him fed   many winters withal,
Till he founded friars   of Austin's order.
Paul, after his preaching   baskets he made,
And won with his hands   what his belly needed.

[1] See page 207.   [2] See page 207.

Peter fished for his food   and his fellow Andrew;
Some they sold and some they cooked   and so they lived both.
And also Mary Magdalen   by roots lived and dews,
But most through devotion   and thought of God almighty.
I could not these seven days   say them all,
That lived thus for our Lord's love   many long years.
But there was not lion nor leopard   that on land went,
Neither bear, nor boar   nor other beast wild,
That fell not at their feet   and fawned with their tails.
And if they could have talked   by Christ, as I trow,
They would have fed that folk   before wild fowls.
For all the courtesy that beasts know   they showed that folk oft
In pleasing and in reverencing   where they on land went.
But God sent them food by fowls   and by no fierce beasts,
In meaning that meek things   mild things should feed;
As who saith, religious   righteous men should support,
And lawful men to life-holy men   livelihood bring.
And then would lords and ladies   be loth to offend,
And to take of their tenants   more than truth wills,
If they found that friars   would forsake their alms,
And tell them to bear it   whence it was borrowed.
For we be God's fowls   and abide always,
Till birds bring us   what we should live by.
For had ye soup and bread enough   and penny ale to drink,
And a dish there-midst   of some manner of sort,
Ye had right enough, ye religious   and so your rule me told:
> Nunquam, dicit Job, rugit onager cum herbam habuerit? aut mugiet bos
>   cum ante plenum praesepe steterit?
> Brutorum animalium natura te condemnat, qui cum eis pabulum com-
>   mune sufficiat; ex adipe prodiit iniquitas tua.

'If unlearned men knew this Latin   they would look to whom they give,
And considered before   five days or six,
Ere they amortized to monks   or canons their rents.
Alas! lords and ladies   ignorant counsel have ye
To give from your heirs   what your forefathers you left,[1]
And give to pray for you   to such as be rich,
And be founded and endowed even   to pray for others.
Who performeth this prophecy   of the people that now live,
> Dispersit, dedit pauperibus, etc.?

If any people perform that text   it is these poor friars!

[1] See page 207.

For what they beg around   in building they spend,
And on themselves some   and such as be their labourers,
And from them that have they take   and give them that have not.
    'But clerks and knights   and commoners that be rich,
Many of you fareth   as if I a forest had,
That were full of fair trees   and I considered and thought
How I might more therein   amongst them set.
Right so, ye rich   ye robbeth those that be rich,
To help them that help you   and give where no need is.
As whoso filled a cask   from a fresh river,
And went forth with that water   to wet with the Thames.
Right so, ye rich   ye robbeth and feedeth
Them that have as ye have   them ye make at ease.
    'But religious that rich be   should rather feast beggars
Than burgesses that rich be   as the book teacheth;

> *Quia sacrilegium est res pauperum non pauperibus dare.*
> *Item: peccatoribus dare, est daemonibus immolare.*
> *Item: monache, si indiges et accipis, potius das quam accipis;*
>   *si autem non eges, et accipis, rapis.*
> *Porro non indiget monachus, si habeat quod naturae sufficit.*

Therefore I counsel all Christians   to conform them to charity;
For charity without demanding   unchargeth the soul,
And many a prisoner from purgatory   through his prayers he delivereth.
But there is a fault in the folk   that the faith keep;
Wherefore folk are the feebler   and not firm of belief.
As in counterfeit is an evil alloy   and yet looketh it like sterling,
The mark of that money is good   but the metal is feeble;
So it fareth by some folk now   they have fair speech,
Crown and christening   the king's mark of heaven,
But the metal, that is man's soul   with sin is foul alloyed;
Both lettered and unlearned   be now alloyed with sin,
That no man loveth the other   nor our Lord, as it seemeth.
For through war and wicked works   and weathers unreasonable,
Weather-wise shipmen   and wise clerks also
Have no belief in the sky   nor the lore of philosophers.
    'Astronomers all days   in their art fail,
That whilom warned before   what should befall after.
Shipmen and shepherds   that with ship and sheep went,
Wist by the welkin   what should betide;
As of weathers and winds   they warned men oft.
Tillers that tilled the earth   told their masters,

By the seed that they sowed   what they sell might,
And what to lend and what to live by   the land was so true.
Now faileth the folk of the flood   and of the land both,
Shepherds and shipmen   and so do these tillers;
Neither they see nor know   one course before another.
Astronomers also   are at their wits' end;
Of that was calculated by the elements   the contrary they find.
Grammar, the ground of all   beguileth now children;
There is none of these new clerks   whoso taketh heed,
That can versify fair   nor formally write;
Nor not one among a hundred   that an author can construe,
Nor read a letter in any language   but in Latin or in English.
Go now to any degree   and unless Guile be master,
And Flatterer his fellow   under him to work,
Much wonder methinketh   amongst us all.
Doctors of decrees   and of divinity masters,
That should learn and know   all kinds of knowledge,
And answers to arguments   and also to a *quodlibet* [1]
(I dare not say it for shame)   if such were opposed,
They would fail in their philosophy   and in physic both.
Wherefore I am afeared   of folk of holy church,
Lest they skip over as others do   in offices and in hours; [2]
But if they skip over, as I hope not   our belief sufficeth;
As clerks at Corpus Christi feast   sing and read,
That *sola fides sufficit*   to save with unlearned people.
    'And so may Saracens be saved   scribes and Jews;
Alas then! that our law-givers   might live as they teach us,
And, for their living, that unlearned men   be more loth God to offend.
For Saracens have somewhat   similar to our belief,
For they love and believe   on one person Almighty;
And we, learned and ignorant   on one God believe.
But one Mahomet, a man   into mis-belief
Brought Saracens of Syria   and see in what manner.
This Mahomet was a Christian man   and because he might not be a
                                        pope, [3]
Into Syria he sought   and through his subtle wits
Tamed a dove   and day and night her fed;
The corn that she cropped   he cast it in his ear.
And if he among the people preached   or in places came,
Then would the dove come   to the clerk's ear,

[1] See page 207.   [2] See page 207.   [3] See page 207.

In meaning after meat   thus Mahomet her enchanted,
And made folk then fall on knees   for he swore in his preaching
That the dove that came so   came from God of heaven
As messenger to Mahomet   men for to teach
And thus through wiles of his wit   and a white dove,
Mahomet in mis-belief   men and women brought,
So that learned there and unlearned too   live in his laws,
And so our Saviour suffered   the Saracens thus beguiled,
Through a Christian clerk   accursed in his soul;
But for dread of the death   I dare not tell truth,
How English clerks a dove feed   that Covetousness is called,
And follow Mahomet's custom   so that no man useth truth.

   'Anchorites and hermits   and monks and friars
Resemble apostles   through their perfect living.
Would never the faithful father   that his ministers should
Of tyrants that plague true men   take any alms,
But do as Anthony did   Dominic and Francis,
Benet and Bernard   the which them first taught
To live by little and in low houses   by true men's alms,
Grace should grow and be green   through their good living,
And folk should find   that be in divers sickness,
The better for their praying   in body and in soul.
Their prayers and their penances   to peace should bring
All that be at strife   if beadsmen were true;

     Petite et accipietis, etc.

Salt saveth cattle   say the wives;

     Vos estis sal terrae, etc.

The heads of holy church   if they holy were,
Christ calleth them salt   for Christian souls;

     Et si sal evanuerit, in quo salietur.

But fresh flesh or fish   when it salt lacketh,
It is unsavoury, indeed   seethed or baked.
So is man's soul sothly   that seeth no good example
From them of holy church   that the high way should teach,
And be guide, and go before   as a good standard-bearer,
And encourage them that behind be   and give them good proof.

   'Eleven holy men   all the world turned
Into true belief   the more methinketh,
Should all manner of men   we have so many masters,
Priests and preachers   and a pope above,
Who God's salt should be   to save man's soul.

'All was heathenness some time   England and Wales,
Till Gregory sent clerks   to come here and preach.
Austin at Canterbury   christened the king,
And through miracles, as men may read   all that march he turned
To Christ and to Christendom   and cross to honour,
And baptized folk fast   and the faith taught
More through miracles   than through much preaching,
As well through his works   as with holy words,
And told them what baptism   and faith was in meaning.
    'Cloth that cometh from the weaving   is not comely to wear,
Till it is fulled under foot   or on fulling-stocks,
Washed well with water   and with teasles scratched,
Tucked, and tented   and put under tailor's hand.
And so it fareth by a child   that born is of womb,
Till it be christened in Christ's name   confirmed by the bishop,
It is heathen as to heavenward   and helpless in the soul.
    'Heathen means after heath   and untilled earth;
As in wild wilderness   waxeth wild beasts,
Rude and irrational   running without cruppers.
    'Ye mind well how Matthew saith   how a man made a feast;
He fed them with no venison   nor pheasants baked,
But fouls that went not from him   but followed his whistling;
    Ecce altilia mea et omnia parata sunt, etc.;
And with calves' flesh he fed   the fold that he loved.
The calf betokeneth cleanness   in them that keep laws.
For as the cow with her milk   the calf nourisheth to an ox,
So love and loyalty   true men sustaineth,
And maidens and mild men   mercy desire;
Right as the cow-calf   coveteth sweet milk,
So do righteous men   mercy and truth.
And by the hand-fed fowls   this folk understand,
That loth be to love   without teaching of examples.
Right as poultry in a courtyard   come to men's whistling,
In search of meat   follow men that whistle,
Right so uncouth men   that little reason know,
Love and believe   by lettered men's doings,
And by their words and their works   think and trow.
And, as those fowls to find   food after whistling,
So hope they to have   heaven through their whistling.
And by the man that made the feast   the majesty is signified;
That is, God of his grace   giveth all men bliss;
    L 571

With weathers and with wonders   he warneth us with a whistler,
Where that his will is   to worship us all,
And feed us and feast us   for evermore together.
    'But who be that excuseth   they are parsons and priests,
That heads of holy church be   that have their will here,
Without toil, the tithe wield   that true men work for,
They will be wroth that I write thus   but to witness I take
Both Matthew and Mark   and *memento Domini David*;
      Ecce audivimus eam in Ephrata, etc.
What pope or prelate now   performeth what Christ said,
      Ite in universum mundum et praedicate, etc.?
    'Alas! that men so long   on Mohamet should believe,
So many prelates to preach   as the pope maketh,
Of Nazareth, of Nineveh   of Nepthali, and Damascus,[1]
That they go not as Christ teacheth   since they wish for their titles,
To be pastors and preach   the passion of Jesus,
And as himself said   so to live and die;
      Bonus pastor animam suam ponit, etc.;
And said for salvation   of Saracens and others.
For Christians and unchristened   Christ said to preachers
      Ite vos in vineam meam.
And since that these Saracens   scribes, and Jews
Have a bit of our belief   the more, methinketh,
They would turn, whoso travail would   to teach them of the Trinity,
      Quaerite et invenietis, etc.
    'It is ruth to read   how righteous men lived,
How they defouled their flesh   forsook their own will,
Far from kith and from kin   evil-clothed went,
Badly bedded   no book but conscience,
Nor no riches but the rood   to rejoice them in;
      Absit nobis gloriari, nisi in cruce Domini nostri, etc.
    'And then was plenty and peace   amongst poor and rich;
And now is ruth to read   how the red noble
Is reverenced over rood   received for the worthier
Than Christ's cross, that overcame   death and deadly sin!
And now is war and woe   and whoso "why" asketh,
It is covetousness after that cross   the crown shows in gold.
Both rich and religious   that rood they honour,
That on groats is engraven   and on gold nobles.
For covetousness of that cross   men of holy church
             [1] See page 207.

Shall turn as Templars [1] did   the time approacheth fast.
Know ye not, wise men   how those men honoured
More treasure than truth?   I dare not tell the soth;
Reason and rightful judgement   those religious judge.
Right so, ye clerks   for your covetousness, ere long,
Shall they judge *dos ecclesiae*   and your pride depose;
    Deposuit potentes de sede, etc.
If knighthood and kind wit   and common conscience
Together love loyally   believe it well, ye bishops,
The lordship of lands   for ever shall ye lose,
And live as *Levitici*   as our Lord you teacheth,
    Per primitias et decimas.
  'When Constantine of courtesy   holy church endowed
With lands and subjects   lordships and rents,
An angel me heard   on high at Rome cry,
"*Dos ecclesiae* this day   hath drunk venom,
And those that have Peter's power   are poisoned all."
A medicine must be thereto   that may amend prelates,
That should pray for the peace   possession them hindereth,
Take their lands, ye lords   and let them live by tithes.
If possession be poison   and imperfect men make,
Good it were to discharge them   for holy church's sake,
And purge them of poison   ere more peril fall.
  'If priesthood were perfect   the people would amend,
That cross Christ's law   and Christendom despise.
For all paynims pray   and perfectly believe
On the holy great God   and his grace they ask,
And make their moan to Mahomet   their message to offer.
And thus in a faith liveth that folk   and by a false mediator,
And that is pity for righteous men   that in the realm live,
And a peril to the pope   and prelates that he maketh,
That bear bishop's names   of Bethlehem and Babylon;
When the high king of heaven   sent his son to earth,
Many miracles he wrought   man to convert;
In example that men should see   that by grave reason
Men might not be saved   but through mercy and grace,
And through penance and passion   and perfect belief;
And became man of a maid   and *metropolitanus*,[2]
And baptized and bishoped   with the blood of his heart
All that willed, and would   with their mind believe it,

       [1] See page 207.   [2] See page 207.

Many a saint since   hath suffered to die,
All for to confirm the faith   in many countries died,
In India and in Alexandria   in Armenia and Spain,
In doleful death died   for their faith's sake;
In salvation of the faith   Saint Thomas [1] was martyred,
Amongst unnatural Christians   for Christ's love he died,
And for the right of all this realm   and all realms Christian.
Holy church is honoured   highly through his dying,
He is a pattern to all bishops   and a bright mirror,
And sovereignly to such   that of Syria bear the name,
That hop about in England   to hallow men's alters,
And creep amongst curates   and confess against the law,

Nolite mittere falcem in messem alienam, etc.

Many man for Christ's love   was martyred in Rome
Ere any Christianity was known there   or any cross honoured.
'Every bishop that beareth cross   by that he is held,
Through his province to pass   and to his people to show him,
Tell them and teach them   on the Trinity to believe,
And feed them with spiritual food   and needy folk to help.
But Isaiah of you speaketh   and Hosea both,
That no man should be bishop   unless he has both,
Bodily food and spiritual food   and give where there is need;

In domo mea non est panis neque vestimentum, et ideo nolite constituere me regem.

Hosea saith for such   that sick be and feeble,

Inferte omnes decimas in horreum meum, ut sit cibus in domo mea.

But we Christian creatures   that on the cross believe,
Are firm as in the faith   God forbid else!
And have clerks to keep us therein   and them that shall come after us.
'And Jews live in true law   our Lord wrote it himself,
In stone, for it steadfast was   and stand should ever—
Dilige Deum et proximum   is perfect Jewish law—
And gave it to Moses to teach men   till Messiah come;
And on that law they live yet   and hold it the best.
'And yet knew they Christ   that Christianity taught,
For a perfect prophet   that many people saved
From strange ills   they say it oft,
Both of miracles and marvels   and how he men feasted
With two fishes and five loaves   five thousand people;
And by that eating men might well see   that Messiah he was.

[1] See page 207.

And when he raised up Lazarus   that laid was in grave,
And under stone dead and stank   with loud voice him called,
    Lazare, veni foras,
Dead he rose and moved   right before the Jews.
But they said and swore   with sorcery he wrought,
And studied to destroy him   and destroyed themselves;
And through his patience their power   to pure naught he brought;
    Patientes vincunt.
Daniel of their undoing   divined and said,
    Cum sanctus sanctorum veniat, cessabit unxio vestra.
'And yet believe those wretches   that he was *pseudo-propheta,*
And that his lore be lyings   and blame it all,
And hope that he be to come   that shall them relieve,
Moses again, or Messiah   their masters still prophecy.
'But Pharisees and Saracens   Scribes and Greeks
Are folk of one faith   the Father God they honour;
And since the Saracens   and also the Jews
Know the first clause of our belief   *Credo in Deum patrem omnipotentem,*
Prelates of Christian provinces   should prove, if they might,
Teach them by little and little   *et in Jesum Christum, filium,*
Till they can speak and spell   *et in Spiritum Sanctum,*
And render it and record it   with *remissionem peccatorum,*
    Carnis resurrectionem, et vitam aeternam.   Amen.'

'Now fair befall you!' quoth I then   'for your fair showing,
For Haukyn's love the active man   ever I shall you love;
But yet I am in doubt   what charity means.'
'It is a full excellent tree,' quoth he   'truly to tell.
Mercy is the root thereof   the middle trunk is pity.
The leaves be true words   the law of holy church,
The blossom be courteous speech   and benign looking;
Patience is called the pure tree   and poor simple of heart,
And so, through God and through good men   groweth the fruit charity.'
'I would travel,' quoth I, 'this tree to see   twenty hundred miles,
And for to have my fill of that fruit   forsake all other food.
Lord,' quoth I, 'does any wight know   whereabouts it groweth?'
    'It groweth in a garden,' quoth he   'that God made himself,
Amidst man's body   the root is of that trunk;
Heart is called the garden   that it groweth in,
And *Liberum Arbitrium*   hath the land to farm,
Under Piers the Plowman   to hoe it and to weed it.'
'Piers the Plowman!' quoth I then   and all for pure joy
That I heard named his name   soon I swooned after,
And lay long in a lone dream   and at last me thought,
That Piers the Plowman   all the place me showed,
And bade me gaze on the tree   on top and on root.
With three piles was it under-propped   I perceived it soon.
'Piers,' quoth I, 'I pray thee   why stand these piles here?'
    'Against winds, if thou would'st know,' quoth he   'to keep it from
                                    falling;
    *Cum ceciderit justus, non collidetur; quia Dominus supponit manum
        suam;*
And, in blossom time, nip the flowers   unless the piles help.
The World is a wicked wind   to them that seek truth,
Covetousness cometh of that wind   and creepeth among the leaves,
And nearly destroys the fruit   through many fair sights.
Then with the first pile I strike him down   that is, *potentia-Dei-Patris.*
The Flesh is a fell wind   and in flowering time
Through liking and lusts   so loud he begins to blow,

150

That it nourisheth foolish sights   and sometimes words,
And wicked works thereof   worms of sin,
And biteth the blossoms   right to the bare leaves.
Then take I to the second pile   *sapientia-Dei-Patris,*
That is, the passion and the power   of our prince Jesus,
Through prayers and through penances   and God's passion in mind,
I save it till I see it ripen   and somewhat fruited.
And then tries the Fiend   my fruit to destroy,
With all the wiles that he can   and shaketh the root,
And casteth among the crop   unfriendly neighbours,
Backbiters mischief-making   brawlers and quarrellers,
And layeth a ladder thereto   of lies are its rungs,
And fetcheth away my flowers sometimes   before both my eyes.
But *Liberum Arbitrium*   hinders him sometimes,
Who is lieutenant to look to it well   by leave of myself;

      Videatis qui peccat in Spiritum Sanctum, nunquam remittetur, etc.;
      Hoc est idem, qui peccat per liberum arbitrium non repugnat.

But when the Fiend and the Flesh   forth with the World
Threaten behind me   my fruit for to steal,
Then *Liberum Arbitrium*   seizes the third pile,
And striketh down the demon   purely through grace
And help of the Holy Ghost   and thus have I the mastery.'
  'Now fair fall you, Piers,' quoth I   'so fair you describe
The power of these posts   and their own might.
But I have thoughts in a multitude   of these three piles,
In what wood they were   and where that they grew;
For are they all alike long   none less than another,
And to my mind, as methinketh   from one source they grew,
And of one greatness   and green of grain they seem.'
  'That is true,' said Piers   'so it may befall;
I shall tell thee at once   what this tree is.
The ground where it groweth   Goodness is called,
And I have told thee what the tree is named   the Trinity it meaneth'—
And sternly he looked on me   and therefore I spared
To ask him any more thereof   and asked him full fair
To describe the fruit   that so fair hangeth.
'Here now hangeth,' quoth he   'if I needs must,
Matrimony I mention   a moist fruit withal.
Then continence is near the top   like a sweet grafted pear,
Then beareth the crop good fruit   and cleanest of all,
Maidenhood, angels' pears   and soonest will be ripe,

And sweet without swelling   sour is it never.'
I prayed Piers to pull down   an apple, if he would,
And suffer me to try   what savour it had.
And Piers threw up among the crop   and then it began to cry,
And he shook widowhood   and it wept after.
And matrimony was moved   it made a foul noise,
I was sorry when Piers rocked it   it lamented so ruefully.
For ever as they dropped down   the devil was ready,
And gathered them all together   both great and small,
Adam and Abraham   and Isaiah the prophet,
Sampson and Samuel   and Saint John the Baptist;
Bore them forth boldly   nobody stopped him,
And made of holy men his hoard   in *limbo inferni*,
Where is darkness and dread   and the devil master.
And Piers for pure anger   one pile he seized,
And hit after him   happen how it might,
Filius by the Father's will   and grace of *Spiritus Sanctus*,
To go rob that ruffian   and take the fruit from him.
   And then spoke *Spiritus Sanctus*   in Gabriel's mouth,
To a maid called Mary   a meek one withal,
'That one Jesus, a justice's son   must rest in her chamber,
Till *plenitudo temporis*   fully come were,
That Piers' fruit flowered   and came to be ripe.
And then should Jesus joust for that   by judgement of arms,
Which should take the fruit   the Fiend or himself.'
The maid mildly then   to the messenger consented,
And said courteously to him   'Lo me, his handmaiden
For to do his will   without any sin';
      Ecce ancilla Domini; fiat mihi secundum verbum tuum, etc.
And in the womb of that girl   was he forty weeks,
Till he grew a child through her flesh   and of fighting knew
To have fought with the Fiend   ere full time came.
And Piers the Plowman   perceived the fullness of time,
And taught him medicine   his life for to save,
So that though he were wounded by his enemy   to heal himself;
And he did try his surgery   on them that sick were,
Till he was a perfect practitioner   if any harm fell,
And he sought out the sick   and sinful both,
And healed sick and sinful   both blind and lame,
And common women converted   and to good turned;
      Non est sanis opus medicus, sed infirmis, etc.

Both lepers and the dumb   and those with bloody flux,
Oft he healed such   he held it no great skill,
Save when he healed Lazarus   that had lain in the grave,
Quatriduanus dead   alive did he walk.
But as he made that mastery   *moestus coepit esse,*
And wept water with his eyes   there saw it many.
Some that the sight saw   said at the time,
That he was giver of life   and lord of high heaven.
The Jews argued against it   and judged by laws,
And said he wrought through witchcraft   and with the devil's might,
>   *Daemonium habes, etc.*
'Then are ye churls,' quoth Jesus   'and your children both,
And Satan your saviour   yourselves now ye witness.
For I have saved yourselves,' saith Christ   'and your sons after,
Your bodies, your beasts   and blind men helped,
And fed you with fishes   and with five loaves,
And left over baskets full of broken meat   bear away whoso would';—
And he attacked the Jews manfully   and threatened to beat them,
And struck them with a cord   and cast down their stalls,
That in church bartered   or changed any money,
And said it in sight of them all   so that all heard,
'I shall overturn this temple   and throw it down,
And in three days after   build it anew,
And make it as much or more   in all ways,
As ever it was, and as large   wherefore I command you,
Of prayers and of perfectness   call this place;
>   *Domus mea domus orationis vocabitur.'*
Envy and evil will   was in the Jews;
They cast about and contrived   to kill him when they might,
Each day after another   their time they awaited.
Till it befell on a Friday   a little before Passover,
The Thursday before   when he made his maundy,
Sitting at supper   he said these words—
'I am sold through one of you   he shall the time rue
That ever he his saviour sold   for silver or aught else.'
    Judas quarrelled with that   but Jesus him told,
It was himself truely   and said '*tu dicis.*'
Then went he forth, that wicked man   and with the Jews met,
And told them a token   how to know Jesus,
And which token to this day   too much is used,
That is, kissing and fair countenance   and unkind will;

And so it was by Judas then that Jesus was betrayed.
'*Ave, rabi,*' quoth that wretch and right to him he went,
And kissed him, to be caught thereby and killed of the Jews.
Then Jesus to Judas and to the Jews said,
'Falseness I find in thy fair speech,
And guile in thy glad cheer and gall is in thy laughing.
Thou shalt be mirror to many men to deceive,
But the worst and thy wickedness shall fall upon thyselves;

> *Necesse est ut veniant scandala; vae homini illi per quem scandalum*
>   *venit!*

Though I by treason be taken at your own will,
Suffer my apostles in peace and in peace to go.'
On a Thursday in darkness thus was he taken
Through Judas and the Jews Jesus was his name;
That on the Friday following for mankind's sake
Jousted in Jerusalem a joy to us all.
On cross upon Calvary Christ gave battle,
Against death and the devil destroyed both their mights,
Died, and death undid and day of night made.
 And I awoke therewith and wiped my eyes,
And after Piers the Plowman pried and stared.
Eastwards and westwards I searched hard,
And went forth as an idiot in country to espy
After Piers the Plowman many a place I sought.
And then met I with a man on a mid-Lenten Sunday,
As hoar as a hawthorne and Abraham he was called.
I asked him first from whence he came,
And of what part he was and whither he was going.
 'I am Faith,' quoth that man 'it befits not to lie,
And of Abraham's house a herald at arms.
I seek after a person that I saw once,
A full bold bachelor I knew him by his blazon.'
'What beareth that man?' quoth I then 'so bliss thee betide!'
'Three persons in one none longer than another,
Of one size and might in measure and in length;
What one doth, all do and each doth by his one.
The first hath might and majesty maker of all things;
Pater is his own name a person by himself.
The second of that sire is truth, *Filius,*
Warden of those who wisdom have was ever without beginning.
The third is called Holy Ghost a person by himself,

The light of all that life hath   on land and in water,
Comforter of creatures   of him cometh all bliss.
So three belongeth to a lord   that lordship claimeth,
Might, and a mediator   to know his own might,
Of him and of his servant   and what they suffer both.
So God that beginning had never   when him good thought,
Sent forth his son   as for servant at that time,
To work here   till issue were sprung,
That is, children of charity   and holy church the mother.
Patriarchs and prophets   and apostles were the children,
And Christ and Christendom   and Christian holy church.
Meaning that man must   on one God believe,
And where he liked and loved   in three persons himself showed.
  'And that it may be so and soth   manhood it showeth,
Wedlock and widowhood   with virginity named,
In token of the Trinity   was taken out of one man.
Adam father of us all   Eve was of himself,
And the issue that they had   it was of them both,
And either is the other's joy   in three different persons,
And in heaven and here   one single name;
And thus is mankind or manhood   of matrimony sprung,
And it betokeneth the Trinity   and true belief.
Mighty is matrimony   that multiplieth the earth,
And betokeneth truely   tell if I dare,
Him that first formed all   the Father of heaven.
The Son, if I it dare say   resembleth well the widow,
        Deus meus, Deus meus, ut quid dereliquisti me?
That is, creator became creature   to know what was both;
As widow without wedlock   was never yet seen,
No more might God be man   unless he mother had;
So widow without wedlock   may not well stand,
Nor matrimony without wife   is not much to praise;
        Maledictus homo qui non reliquit semen in Israel, etc.
Thus in three persons   is perfectly manhood,
That is, man and his mate   and the mother's children,
And is naught but offspring of one generation   before Jesus Christ in
                                                        heaven,
So is the Father forth with the Son   and free will of both;
        Spiritus procedens a Patre et Filio;
Which is the Holy Ghost of all   and all is but one God.
Thus in a summer I him saw   as I sat in my porch;

I rose up and reverenced him   and right fair him greeted;
Three men to my sight   I made well at ease,
Washed their feet and wiped them   and afterwards they eat
Calves' flesh and a cake of bread   and knew what I thought;
Full true tokens between us are   to tell when me liketh.
First he tried me   if I loved better
Him, or Isaac mine heir   the which he told me to kill.
He knew my will by him   he will me it allow,
I am full certain in soul thereof   and my son both.
I circumcised my son   then for his sake;
Myself and my household   and all that male were
Bled blood for that lord's love   and hope to bless the time.
My trust and my faith   is firm in this belief;
For himself promised me   and my issue both
Land and lordship   and life without end;
To me and to mine issue   more yet he me granted,
Mercy for our misdeeds   as many times as we ask;
     Quam olim Abrahae promisisti, et semini ejus.
And then he sent to me to say   I should do sacrifice,
And do him worship with bread   and with wine both,
And called me the foundation of his faith   his folk for to save,
And defend them from the fiend   folk that on me believed.
Thus have I been his herald   here and in hell,
And comforted many a sorrowful   that for his coming wait.
And thus I seek him,' he said   'for I heard said lately
Of a man that baptised him   John the Baptist was his name,
That to patriarchs and prophets   and to other people in darkness
Said that he saw him   that should save us all;
     Ecce agnus Dei, etc.'
  I had wonder at his words   and of his wide clothes;
For in his bosom he bore a thing   that he blessed ever.
And I looked on his lap   a leper lay therein
Amongst patriarchs and prophets   playing together.
'What awaitest thou?' quoth he   'and what would'st thou have?'
'I would know,' quoth I then   'what is in your lap?'
'Lo!' quoth he, and let me see   'Lord, mercy!' I said,
'This is a present of much price   what prince shall it have?'
'It is a precious present,' quoth he   'but the fiend it hath claimed,
And me therewith,' quoth that man   'may no pledge redeem us,
Nor no man be our bail   nor bring us from this danger;
Out of the fiend's pound   no surety may us fetch,

Till he come that I speak of   Christ is his name,
That shall deliver us some day   out of the devil's power,
And better pledge for us lay   than we be all worthy,
That is, life for life   or lie thus ever
Lolling in my lap   till such a lord us fetch.'
    'Alas!' I said, 'that sin   so long shall stay
The might of God's mercy   that might us all amend!'
I wept for his words   with that I saw another
Rapidly run forth   the same way he went.
I asked him first   from whence he came,
And what he was called and whither he was going   and willingly he told.

PASSUS XVII

'I AM Spes,' quoth he, 'a scout and I spy after a knight,
That gave me a commandment upon the mount of Sinai,
To rule all realms with I bear the writ here.'
'Is it sealed?' I said 'may men see thy letters?'
'Nay,' he said, 'I seek him that hath the seal to keep;
And that is, cross and Christendom and Christ thereon to hang.
And when it is sealed so I know well the truth,
That Lucifer's lordship last shall no longer.'
'Let see thy letters,' quoth I 'that we might the law know.'
Then plucked he forth a patent a piece of hard rock,
Whereon were written two words on this wise glossed,

> *Dilige Deum et proximum tuum, etc.*

This was the text truly I took full good notice;
The gloss was gloriously written with a gilt pen,

> *In his duobus mandatis tota lex pendet et prophetia.*

'Be here all thy lord's laws?' quoth I 'Yea, believe me well,' he said,
'And whoso doth according to this writ I will undertake,
Shall never death him hurt nor death in soul grieve.
For though I say it myself I have saved with this charm
Of men and of women many score thousands.'
'He saith soth,' said the herald 'I have found it oft;
Lo here in my lap that believed on that charm,
Joshua and Judith and Judas Maccabeus,
Yea, and sixty thousand more besides that be not seen here.'
  'Your words are wonderful,' quoth I then 'which of you is truest,
And firmest to believe on for life and for soul?
Abraham saith that he saw holy the Trinity,
Three persons individually separate from each other,
And all three but one God thus Abraham me taught,
And hath saved that believed so and were sorry for their sins,
He cannot say how many and some are in his lap.
What needed it then a new law to begin,
Since the first sufficeth to salvation and to bliss?
And now cometh *Spes*, and speaketh who hath espied the law,
And telleth naught of the Trinity that gave him his letters,

"To believe and love   on one Lord almighty,
And then right as myself   love all other people."
The man that walketh with one staff   he seemeth in greater health
Than he that walketh with two staves   in sight of us all.
And right so, by the rood!   reason me showeth,
It is lighter for unlearned men   one lesson to know,
Than for to teach them two   and hard enough to learn the least!
It is full hard for any man   on Abraham to believe,
And well away worse yet   for to love a rascal!
It is lighter to believe   in three lovely persons
Than for to love and to believe   as well wretches as the true.
Go thy ways,' quoth I to *Spes*   'so me God help!
Those that learn thy law   will a little while follow it!'
    And as we went thus on the way   conversing together
Then saw we a Samaritan   sitting on a mule,
Riding full speedily   the same way we were going,
Coming from a country   that men called Jericho;
To a joust in Jerusalem   he hurried away fast.
Both the herald and Hope   and he met at once
Where a man was wounded   and by thieves attacked.
He could neither walk nor stand   nor stir foot nor hands,
Nor help himself truly   for half alive he seemed,
And as naked as a needle   and none to help near him.
    Faith had first sight of him   but he hurried on the other side,
And would not come near him   by nine lands' length.
    Hope came trotting after   that had so boasted,
How he with Moses' commandment   had many men helped;
But when he had sight of that man   aside he began to draw,
Fearfully, by this day! as duck   doth from a falcon.
    But so soon as the Samaritan   had sight of this man,
He alighted from his horse   and led him by his hand,
And to the wight he went   his wounds to behold,
And perceived by his pulse   he was in peril to die,
And unless he had succour quickly   rise should he never;
And hurried to his bottles   and both he broached;
With wine and with oil   his wounds he washed,
Anointed him and bound his head   and in his lap him laid,
And led him then on his horse   to *Lex Christi*, a grange,
Well six miles or seven   from the new market;
Harboured him at a hostelry   and to the host called,
And said, 'Here, keep this man   till I come the jousts,

And lo here is silver,' he said   'for salve for his wounds.'
And he gave him two pence   for upkeep as it were,
And said, 'What he spendeth more   I make thee good hereafter;
For I may not stay,' quoth that man   and horse he bestrides,
And hastened him Jerusalem-ward   the straight way to ride.

Faith followeth after fast   and sought to meet him,
And *Spes* quickly him sped   to succeed if he could,
To overtake him and talk to him   ere they to town came.
And when I saw this, I stayed not   but started to run,
And followed that Samaritan   that was so full of pity,
And asked him to be his page   'Gramercy,' he said,
'Thy friend and thy fellow,' quoth he   'thou findest me at need.
And I thanked him then   and after I him told,
How that Faith flew away   and *Spes* his fellow both,
For sight of the sorrowful man   that robbed was by thieves.
'Hold them excused,' quoth he   'their help may little avail;
May no medicine on earth   the man to health bring,
Neither Faith nor fine Hope   so festered be his wounds,
Without the blood of a child   born of a maid.
And be he bathed in that blood   baptised, as it were,
And then plastered with penance   and passion of that baby,
He should stand and walk   but stalwart will he be never,
Till he have eaten all the child   and his blood drunk.
For went never wight in this world   through that wilderness,
But he was robbed or rifled   rode he there or walked,
Save Faith, and his fellow   *Spes*, and myself,
And thyself now, and such   as follow our works.
For outlaws in the wood   and under banks lurk,
And can each man see   and good note take,
Who is behind and who in front   and who be on horse,
For they hold him hardier on horse   than he that is on foot.
For they saw me, that am Samaritan   follow Faith and his fellow
On my steed that is called *Caro*   (of mankind I took it),
He was fearful, that villain   and hid him *in inferno*.
But ere this day three days   I dare undertake,
That he is fettered, that felon   fast with chains,
And never after grieve a man   that goeth this same way;
        O mors, ero mors tua, etc.,
And then shall Faith be forester here   and in this wood walk,
And direct common men   that know not the country,
Which is the way that I went   and forth to Jerusalem.

And Hope the hostelry's man shall be   where the man lieth healing;
And all that feeble and faint be   that Faith cannot teach,
Hope shall lead them forth with love   as his letter telleth,
And welcome them and heal   through holy church's faith,
Till I have salve for all sick   and then I shall return,
And come again through this country   and comfort all sick
That crave it or covet it   and cry thereafter.
For the child was born in Bethlehem   that with his blood shall save
All that live in faith, and follow   his fellow's teaching.'
   'Ah! sweet sir!' I said then   'am I to believe,
As Faith and his fellow   informed me both?
In three persons separable   that endless were ever,
And all three but one God   thus Abraham me taught;—
And Hope afterwards   he bade me to love
One God with all my strength   and all men after,
Love them like myself   but our Lord above all.'
'According to Abraham,' quoth he   'that herald at arms,
Set fast thy faith   and firm believe.
And, as Hope told thee   I command thee love
Thy fellow Christians evermore   equally with thyself.
And if conscience speak against it   or kind wit either,
Or heretics with arguments   thine hand thou them show;
For God is like a hand   hear now and know it.
   'The Father was first, as a fist   with one finger folding,
Till he loved and pleased   to unloosen his finger,
And proffer it forth as with a palm   to what place it would.
The palm is purely the hand   and proffereth forth the fingers
To minister and to make   what the might of the hand willeth,
And betokeneth truly   tell whoso liketh,
The Holy Ghost of heaven   he is as the palm.
The fingers that free be   to fold and to serve,
Betokeneth sothly the Son   that sent was to earth,
That touched and tasted   at teaching of the palm
Saint Mary a maid   and mankind took upon him;
      Qui conceptus est de Spiritu Sancto, natus, etc.
The Father is then as a fist   with finger to touch,
      Quia omnia traham ad meipsum, etc.,
All that the palm perceiveth   profitable to feel.
Thus are they all but one   as it a hand were,
And three different sights   in one showing.
The palm, for he putteth forth fingers   and the fist both,
   M 57¹

Right so readily   reason it showeth,
How he that is Holy Ghost   Sire and Son witnesseth.
And as the hand holds hard   and all things fast
Through four fingers and a thumb   forth from the palm,
Right so the Father and the Son   and Saint Spirit the third
Hold all the wide world   within them three,
Both sky and the wind   water and earth,
Heaven and hell   and all that there is in.
Thus it is, needeth no man   to think otherwise,
That three things belong   in our Lord of heaven,
And are separately by themselves   but apart were never,
No more than my hand may   move without fingers.
And as my fist is a full hand   folded together,
So is the Father fully God   former and shaper,

    Tu fabricator omnium, etc.,

And all the might with him is   in making of things.
  'The fingers form a full hand   to portray or paint
Carving and compassing   as craft of the fingers;
Right so is the Son   the science of the Father,
And fully God, as is the Father   no feebler nor no stronger.
  'The palm is truly the hand   hath power by himself
Otherwise from the closed fist   or workmanship of fingers,
For the palm hath power   to move out all the joints,
And to unfold the folded fist   and the fingers' purpose.
So is the Holy Ghost God   neither greater nor less
Than is the Sire and the Son   and of the same might,
And all are they but one God   as is mine hand and my fingers,
Unfolded or folded   my fist and my palm,
All is but a hand   however I look at it.
  'But who is hurt in the hand   even in the midst,
He may hold right naught   reason it showeth;
For the fingers, that fold should   and the fist make,
For pain of the palm   power them faileth
To clutch or to grasp   to clip or to hold.
Were the middle of my hand   maimed or pierced,
I should hold right naught   of that I might reach to.
But though my thumb and my fingers   both were flayed,
And the middle of my hand   without ill ease,
In many kinds of ways   I might myself help,
Both move and mend   though all my fingers ached.
By this, methinketh   I see an evidence,

That whoso sinneth against the Holy Spirit   absolved will he be never,
Neither here nor elsewhere   as I heard tell,

    Qui peccat in Spiritum Sanctum, nunquam, etc.,

For he pricketh God as in the palm   that *peccat in Spiritum Sanctum.*
For God the Father is as a fist   the Son is as a finger,
The Holy Ghost of heaven   is, as it were, the palm.
So whoso sinneth against the Holy Spirit   it seemeth that he grieveth
God, where he grasps with   and would his grace quench.
    'And to a torch or a taper   the Trinity is likened;
As wax and a wick   are entwined together,
And then a fire flames   forth out of both;
And as wax and wick   and hot fire together
Foster forth a flame   and a fair light,
So doth the Sire and the Son   and also *Spiritus Sanctus*
Foster forth amongst folk   love and faith,
That all kinds of Christians   cleanseth of sins.
And as thou seest sometimes   suddenly a torch,
The blaze thereof blown out   yet burneth the wick,
Without flame or light   the match burns,
So is the Holy Ghost God   and grace without mercy
To all unkind creatures   that covet to destroy
Loyal love or life   that our Lord made.
And as glowing embers   glad not those workmen,
That work and watch   on winter nights,
So much as a torch or a candle   that caught hath fire and blazeth,
No more doth Sire nor Son   nor Saint Spirit together,
Grant grace   nor forgiveness of sins,
Till the Holy Ghost begin   to glow and to blaze.
So the Holy Ghost   gloweth but as an ember,
Till that faithful love   light on him and blow,
And then flameth he as fire   on Father and on *Filius,*
And melteth their might into mercy   as men may see in winter
Icicles in eaves   through heat of the sun,
Melt in a minute while   into mist and to water;
So grace of the Holy Ghost   the great might of the Trinity
Melteth into mercy   to the merciful, and to none other.
And as wax without more   on a warm coal
Will burn and blaze   be they together,
And solace them that would see   that sit in darkness,
So will the Father forgive   folk of mild hearts
That ruefully repent   and restitution make,

In as much as they may   amend and repay.
And if it suffice not for assets   that in such a will dieth,
Mercy for his meekness   will make good the remnant.
And as the wick and fire   will make a warm flame
For to mirth men with   that in murk sit,
So will Christ of his courtesy   if men cry him mercy,
Both forgive and forget   and pray for us
To the Father of heaven   forgiveness to have.
  'But strike fire from a flint   four hundred winters,
Unless thou have tow to take it with   tinder or twigs,
All thy labour is lost   and all thy long travail;
For may no fire flame make   fail it fuel.
So is the Holy Ghost God   and grace without mercy
To all unkind creatures   Christ himself witnesseth,
        Amen dico vobis, nescio vos, etc.
  'Be unkind to thy fellow Christians   and all that thou canst pray,
Give and do penance   day and night ever,
And purchase all the pardons   of Pampeluna and Rome,
And indulgences enough   and be *ingratus* to thy kind,
The Holy Ghost heareth thee not   nor help thee by reason;
For unkindness quencheth him   so he can not shine,
Nor burn nor blaze clear   for blowing of unkindness.
Paul the apostle   proveth whether I lie,
        Si linguis hominum loquar, etc.
Therefore beware, ye wise men   that with the world dealeth,
That rich be and reason know   rule well your soul.
Be not unkind, I counsel you   to your fellow Christians.
For many of you rich men   by my soul, men telleth,
Ye burn, but ye blaze not   that is a hidden beacon;
        Non omnis qui dicit Domine, Domine, intrabit, etc.
  '*Dives* died damned   for his unkindness
Of his meat and his money   to men that it needed.
Each rich man I warn   notice of him take,
And give your goods to that God   that Grace ariseth from.
For they that be unkind to their own   hope I none other,
But they dwell where Dives is   days without end.
Thus is unkindness the contrary   that quencheth, as it were,
The grace of the Holy Ghost   God's own kind.
For what kind doth, unkind undoes   as these cursed thieves,
Unkind Christian men   for covetousness and envy,
Slayeth a man for his property   with mouth or with hands.

For what the Holy Ghost hath to keep   those villains destroy,
The which is life and love   the light of man's body.
For every manner of good man   may be likened to a torch,
Or else to a taper   to reverence the Trinity;
And who murdereth a good man   methinketh, by my conscience,
He undoes the dearest light   that our Lord loveth.
    'But yet in many more manners   men offend the Holy Ghost;
But this is the worst way   that any wight might
Sin against the Saint Spirit   by assenting to destroy,
For covetousness of any kind of thing   what Christ dearly bought.
How might he ask mercy   or any mercy him help,
That wickedly and wilfully   would mercy destroy?
Innocence is next to God   and night and day it crieth,
"Vengeance, vengeance   forgiven be it never,
That killed us and shed our blood   un-made us, as it were;
        Vindica sanguinem justorum!"
Thus "vengeance, vengeance"   very charity asketh;
And since holy church and charity   charge this so strongly,
Believe I never that our Lord will love   what charity blames,
Nor have pity for any prayer   there that he maketh.'
    'I pose I had sinned so   and should now die,
And now am sorry, that so   the Saint Spirit I have offended,
Confess me, and cry his grace   God, that all made,
And mildly his mercy ask   might I not be saved?'
'Yes,' said the Samaritan   'so well thou might repent,
That righteousness through repentance   to pity might turn.
But it is but seldom seen   where truth beareth witness,
Any creature that is guilty   before a king's justice,
Be ransomed for his repentance   where all reason him damneth.
For where the injured prosecutes   the appeal is so huge,
That the king may do no mercy   till both men agree,
And both have justice   as holy writ telleth:
        Numquam dimittitur peccatum, donec restituatur ablatum.
Thus it fareth by such folk   that falsely all their lives
Evil live and cease not   till life them forsake;
Dread of despair   driveth away then grace,
So that mercy on their mind   may not then fall;
Good hope, that help should   to despair turneth—
Not of the powerlessness of God   that he is not able
To amend all that amiss is   and his mercy greater
Than all our wicked works   as holy writ telleth,
        Misericordia ejus super omnia opera ejus.

But, ere his righteousness to pity turn   some restitution behoveth;
His sorrow is satisfaction   for him that cannot pay.
  'Three things there be   that make a man by their strength
For to flee his own house   as holy writ showeth.
The one is a wicked wife   that will not be chastened;
Her partner flee-eth from her   for fear of her tongue.
And if his house be unroofed   and rain on his bed,
He seeketh and seeketh   till he sleep dry.
And when smoke and smother   smite in his eyes,
It doth him worse than his wife   or wet to sleep.
For smoke and smother   smite in his eyes,
Till he be blear-eyed or blind   and hoarse in the throat,
He coughs, and curses   that Christ give them sorrow
Who should bring in better wood   or blow till it burn.
  'These three that I tell of   be thus to understand;
The wife is our wicked flesh   that will not be chastened,
For nature cleaveth to him ever   to oppose the soul.
And though it fall, it finds reasons   that frailty made it;
And that is lightly forgiven   and forgotten both,
To man that mercy asketh   and amendment thinketh.
The rain that raineth   where we rest would,
Be sicknesses and sorrows   that we suffer oft,
As Paul the apostle   to the people taught,
    Virtus in infirmitate perficitur, etc.
And though that men make   much noise in their affliction,
And be impatient in their penance   pure reason knoweth,
That they have cause to complain   by nature of their sickness;
And lightly our Lord   at their lives' end,
Hath mercy on such men   that such evil suffer.
But the smoke and the smother   that smite our eyes,
That is covetousness and unkindness   that quencheth God's mercy.
For unkindness is the contrary   of all forms of reason;
For there is none sick nor sorry   nor so great wretch,
That he may not love, if him like   and give from his heart
Good will and good word   both wish and will
All manner of men   mercy and forgiveness,
And love them like himself   and his life amend.
I may no longer stay,' quoth he   and his horse he spurred,
And went away as the wind   and therewith I awoke.

PASSUS XVIII

LINEN-LESS [1] and wet-shod   went I forth after,
As a reckless fellow   that of no woe recks,
And went like a vagrant   all my life,
Till I waxed weary of the world   and wished to sleep again,
And leaned me about till Lent   and long time I slept;
And of Christ's passion and penance   that the people saved,
I rested and dreamed there, and snored fast   till *ramis palmarum*; [2]
Of children and of *gloria laus*   greatly me dreamed,
And how *hosanna* to the organ   old folk sang.
One like to the Samaritan   and somewhat to Piers Plowman,
Bare-foot on an ass's back   boot-less came riding,
Without spurs or spear   lively he looked,
As is the way with a knight   that cometh to be dubbed,
To get him gilt spurs   or shoes slashed.
Then was Faith in a window   and cried '*a! fili David!*'
As doth a herald at arms   when the adventurous come to joust.
Old Jews of Jerusalem   for joy they sang,
     Benedictus qui venit in nomine Domini.
    Then I asked of Faith   what all that affair meant,
And who should joust in Jerusalem   'Jesus,' he said,
'And fetch what the Fiend claimeth   Piers' fruit the Plowman.'
'Is Piers in this place?' quoth I   and he looked on me,
'This Jesus of his nobility   will joust in Piers' arms,
In his helm and in his hauberk   *humana natura*;
That Christ be not known here   for *consummatus Deus*,
In Piers' garment the Plowman   this pricker shall ride;
For no dint shall him hurt   as *in deitate Patris.*'
'Who shall joust with Jesus?' quoth I   'Jews or scribes?'
'Nay,' quoth He, 'the foul Fiend   and falsehood and death.
Death saith he will undo   and down bring
All that liveth or looketh   in land or in water.
Life saith that he lies   and laith his life to pledge,
That for all that death can do   within three days,
He will go and fetch from the Fiend   Piers' fruit the Plowman,

[1] See page 207.   [2] See page 207.

And lay it where him liketh   and Lucifer bind,
And beat and down bring   sorrow and death for ever:
    O mors, ero mors tua!'
    Then came *Pilatus* with much people   *sedens pro tribunali,*
To see how daughtily death should do   and judge the rights of both.
The Jews and the justices   against Jesus they were,
And all their court on him cried   *crucifige* sharp.
Then put forth a robber   before Pilate, and said,
'This Jesus at our Jews' temple   japed and despised,
To undo it on one day   and in three days after
Edify it anew   (here he stands that said it)
And yet make it as much   in all manner of points,
Both as long and as large   by height and by length.'
'*Crucifige*,' quoth a catchpole   'I warrant him a witch!'
'*Tolle, tolle!*' quoth another   and took of keen thorns,
And began of keen thorn   a garland to make,
And set it hard on his head   and said in malice,
'*Ave, rabi!*' quoth that rascal   and threw reeds at him,
Nailed him with three nails   naked on the rood,
And poison on a pole   they put up to his lips,
And bade him drink his death drink   his days were done.
'And if that thou powerful be   help now thyself,
If thou be Christ, and king's son   come down off the rood;
Then shall we believe that Life thee loveth   and will not let thee die!'
'*Consummatum est*,' quoth Christ   and began for to swoon
Piteously and pale   as a prisoner that dieth;
The lord of life and of light   then layed his eyes together.
The day for dread withdrew   and dark became the sun,
The veil shook and was cleft   and all the world quaked.
Dead men for that din   came out of deep graves,
And told why that tempest   so long time lasted.
'For a bitter battle'   the dead body said;
'Life and Death in this darkness   one undoes the other;
Shall no wight know truly   who shall have the mastery,
Ere Sunday about sun-rising'   and sank with that to earth.
Some said that he was God's son   that so fair died,
    Vere filius Dei erat iste, etc.
And some said he was a witch   'it is good that one try,
Whether he be dead or not dead   down ere he be taken.'
    Two thieves also   suffered death that time,
Upon a cross beside Christ   so was the common law.

A catchpole came forth   and cracked both their legs,
And their arms after   of each of those thieves.
But was no boy so bold   God's body to touch;
For he was knight and king's son   nature granted that time,
That no rascal was so hardy   to lay hand upon him.
But there came forth a knight   with a keen spear ground,
Called *Longinus*, as the story telleth   and long had lost his sight.
Before Pilate and the other people   in the place he stood;
Spite his many teeth   he was made that time
To take the spear in his hand   and joust with Jesus;
For all they were afraid   that waited on horse or stood,
To touch him or to handle him   or take him down off rood.
But this blind bachelor then   struck him through the heart;
The blood sprung down by the spear   and unbarred the knight's eyes.
Then fell the knight upon knees   and cried him mercy—
'Against my will it was, lord   to wound you so sore!'
He sighed and said   'sore it methinketh;
For the deed that I have done   I deliver me to your grace;
Have on me pity, righteous Jesus!'   and right with that he wept.
   Then began Faith fiercely   the false Jews to despise,
Called them caitives   accursed for ever,
For this foul villainy   'vengeance to you all!
To make the blind beat him bound   it was a knave's counsel.
Cursed caitiff   knighthood was it never
To ill treat a dead body   by day or by night.
The prize yet hath he gained   for all his great wound.
For your champion of chivalry   chief knight of you all,
Yields him defeated in the running   right to Jesus' will.
For be this darkness done   his death will be avenged,
And ye, lordlings, have lost   for Life shall have the mastery.
And your franchise, that free was   fallen in thraldom,
And ye, churls, and your children   succeed shall ye never,
Nor have lordship in land   nor no land till,
But all barren be   and usery use,
Which is a life that our Lord   in all laws curseth.
Now your good days are done   as Daniel prophesied,
When Christ came, of their kingdom   the crown should fall;
   Cum veniat sanctus sanctorum, cessabit unctio vestra.'
   What with fear of this marvel   and of the false Jews,
I withdrew me in that darkness   to *descendit ad inferna.*
And there I saw sothly   *secundum scripturas,*

Out of the west   a wench, as me thought,
Came walking in the way   to Hell-ward she looked.
Mercy was called that maid   a meek thing withal,
A full benign lady   and gentle of speech.
Her sister, as it seemed   came softly walking,
Even out of the east   and westward she looked.
A full comely creature   Truth she was called,
For the virtue that her followed   afraid was she never.
When these maidens met   Mercy and Truth,
Each asked the other   of this great wonder,
Of the din and of the darkness   and how the day began to dawn,
And what a light and a brightness   lay before Hell.
'I wonder at these happenings   in faith,' said Truth,
'And am seeking to discover   what this marvel meaneth.'
'Have no wonder,' quoth Mercy   'joy it betokeneth.
A maiden called Mary   and mother without knowledge
Of any human creature   conceived through speech
And grace of the Holy Ghost   waxed great with child;
Without stain   into this world she brought him;
And that my tale be true   I take God to witness.
Since this child was born   be thirty winters passed;
Who died and death suffered   this day about midday.
And that is cause of this eclipse   that closeth now the sun,
In meaning that man shall   from darkness be drawn,
The while this light and this brightness   shall Lucifer blind.
For patriarchs and prophets   have preached hereof often,
That man shall man save   through a maiden's help,
And what was lost through tree   tree shall it win,
And what death down brought   death shall relieve.'
'What thou tellest,' quoth Truth   'is but a tale of waltrot!
For Adam and Eve   and Abraham with others,
Patriarchs and prophets   that in pain lie,
Believe thou never that yon light   them aloft will bring,
Nor have them out of Hell   hold thy tongue, Mercy!
It is but a trifle that thou tellest   I, Truth, know the soth.
For that is once in Hell   out cometh he never;
Job the prophet, patriarch   reproveth thy sayings,
     Quia in inferno nulla est redemptio.'
Then Mercy full mildly   mouthed these words,
'Through experience,' quoth she   'I hope they shall be saved.
For venom undoes venom   and that I prove by reason.

For of all venoms   foulest is the scorpion,
May no medicine help   the place where he stingeth,
Till he be dead and placed thereon   the evil he destroyeth,
The first venom   through venom of himself.
So shall this death undo   I dare my life lay,
All that Death undid first   through the devil's enticing;
And right as through guile   man was beguiled,
So shall grace that began   make a good sleight;
    Ars ut artem falleret.'
    'Now stay we,' said Truth   'I see, as methinketh,
Out of the cold of the north   not full far hence,
Righteousness come running   rest we the while;
For she knows more than we   she was ere we both.'
'That is soth,' said Mercy   'and I see here by south,
Where Peace cometh playing   in patience clothed;
Love hath coveted her long   believe I none other
But he sent her some letter   what this light meaneth,
That is over Hell thus   she us shall tell.'
    When Peace, in patience clothed   approached near them twain,
Righteousness her reverenced   for her rich clothing,
And prayed Peace to tell her   to what place she went,
And in her gay garments   whom greet she thought?
'My will is to wend,' quoth she   'and welcome them all,
That many day I might not see   for murkyness of sin.
Adam and Eve   and others more in Hell,
Moses and many more   mercy shall have;
And I shall dance thereto   do thou so, sister!
For Jesus jousted well   joy beginneth to dawn;
    Ad vesperum demorabitur fletus, et ad matutinum laetitia.
Love, that is my lover   such letters me sent,
That Mercy, my sister, and I   mankind should save;
And that God hath forgiven   and granted me, Peace, and Mercy,
To be man's surety   for evermore after.
Lo! here the patent!' quoth Peace   'in pace in idipsum—
And that this deed shall endure   *dormiam et requiescam.*'
    'What, ravest thou?' quoth Righteousness   'or thou art right drunk!
Believest thou that yonder light   unlock might Hell,
And save man's soul?   sister, ween it never!
At the beginning, God   gave the judgement himself,
That Adam and Eve   and all that them followed
Should die down right   and dwell in pain after,

If that they touched a tree   and the fruit ate.
Adam afterwards   against his warning,
Ate of that fruit   and forsook, as it were,
The love of our Lord   and his lore both,
And followed what the fiend taught   and his fellow's will,
Against reason, I, Righteousness   record thus with truth,
That their punishment be perpetual   and no prayer them help.
Therefore let them chew as they chose   and chide we not, sisters,
For it is helpless harm   the bite that they took.'
     'And I shall prove,' quoth Peace   'their pain must have an end,
And woe into well   must wend at last;
For had they wist of no woe   well had they not known.
For no wight knows what well is   that never woe suffered,
Nor what is called hunger   that had never lack.
If no night were   no man, as I believe,
Would know clearly   what day means;
Would never right rich man   that liveth in rest and ease
Know what woe is   except for natural death.
So God that began all   of his good will
Became man of a maid   mankind to save,
And suffered himself to be sold   to see the sorrow of dying,
The which un-knitteth all care   and commencing is of rest.
For till *modicum* meet with us   I may it well avow,
Knows no wight, as I ween   what enough means.
     'Therefore God of his goodness   the first man Adam,
Set him in solace   and in sovereign mirth;
And then he suffered him sin   sorrow to feel,
To see what well was   truly to know it.
And after, God ventured himself   and took Adam's nature,
To know what he hath suffered   in three sundry places,
Both in Heaven, and in earth   and now to Hell he thinketh,
To know what all woe is   that knew of all joy.
So it shall fare with these folk   their folly and their sin,
Shall teach them what anguish is   and bliss without end.
Knows no wight what war is   where that peace reigneth,
Nor what is indeed well   till "well-away" him teach.'
     Then was there a wight   with two broad eyes,
Book was called the *beau-père* [1]   a bold man of speech.
'By God's body,' quoth this Book   'I will bear witness,
That when this child was born   there blazed a star,

[1] See page 207.

That all the wise of this world   in one thought accorded,
That such a child was born   in Bethlehem city,
That man's soul should save   and sin destroy.
And all the elements,' quoth the Book   'hereof bear witness,
That he was God that all wrought   the welkin first showed;
Those that were in heaven   took *stella cometa*,
And kindled her as a torch   to reverence his birth;
And light followed the Lord   into the low earth.
The water witnessed that he was God   for he went on it;
Peter the apostle   perceived his going,
And as he went on the water   well him knew, and said,
    Jube me venire ad te super aquas.
And lo! how the sun began to lock   her light in herself,
When she saw him suffer   who sun and sea made!
The earth for heaviness   that he would suffer,
Quaked as a live thing   and all crushed the rock!
Lo! Hell might not hold   but opened when God suffered,
And let out Simeon's sons   to see him hang on rood.
And now shall Lucifer believe it   though him loth think;
For *Gigas* the giant   with a weapon made
To break and to beat down   those that be against Jesus.
And I, Book, will be burnt   but Jesus rise to live,
In all the might of man   and his mother gladden,
And comfort all his kin   and out of care bring,
And all the Jews' joy   dissolve and disjoin;
And unless they reverence his rood   and his resurrection,
And believe on a new law   be lost life and soul.'
  'Abide we,' said Truth   'I hear and see both,
How a spirit speaketh to Hell   and bids unbar the gates;
    Attollite portas, etc.'
A voice loud in that light   to Lucifer crieth,
'Princes of this place   unbolt and unlock!
For here cometh with crown   that king is of glory.
Then sighed Satan   and said to them all,
'Such a light, against our leave   Lazarus it fetched away;
Care and confusion   is come to us all.
If this king come in   mankind will he fetch,
And lead it where he liketh   and easily me bind.
Patriarchs and prophets   have talked hereof long,
That such a lord and a light   should lead them all hence.'
  'Listen,' quoth Lucifer   'for I this lord know,

Both this lord and this light   it is long ago I knew him.
May no death him harm   nor no devil's cunning,
And where he will, is his way   but ware him of the perils;
If he reave me of my right   he robbeth me by mastery.
For by right and by reason   those people that be here
Body and soul be mine   both good and ill.
For himself said   that sire is of heaven,
If Adam eat the apple   all should die,
And dwell with us devils   this threat he made;
And he that truth is   said these words;
And since I have been in possession   seven hundred winters,
I believe that law will not   let him in the least.'
'That is soth,' said Satan   'but I me sore dread,
For thou gained them with guile   and his garden broke,
And in semblance of a serpent   sat on the apple-tree,
And egged them on to eat   Eve by herself,
And told her a tale   of treason were the words;
And so thou haddest them out   and hither at last.
It is not easily held   where guile is the root.'
'For God will not be beguiled'   quoth Goblin, 'nor tricked;
We have no true title to them   for through treason were they damned.
'Certes, I dread me,' quoth the Devil   'lest truth will them fetch.
This thirty winter, as I ween   hath he gone and preached;
I have assailed him with sin   and at some time asked
Whether he were God or God's son?   he gave me short answer.
And thus he walked forth   this two and thirty winter,
And when I saw it was so   sleeping, I went
To warn Pilate's wife   what sort of man was Jesus;
For Jews hated him   and have done him to death.
I would have lengthened his life   for I believed, if he died,
That his soul would suffer   no sin in his sight.
For the body, while it on bones went   about was ever
To save men from sin   if they themselves would.
And now I see where a soul   cometh hitherward sailing
With glory and with great light   God it is, I know well.
I advise we flee,' quoth he   'fast all hence;
For us were better not be   than abide his sight.
For thy lies, Lucifer   lost is all our prey.
First through thee we fell   from heaven so high;
Because we believed thy lies   we leapt out all with thee,
And now for thy last lie   lost we have Adam,

And all our lordship, I believe   on land and on water;
> *Nunc princeps hujus mundi ejicietur foras.*'
Again the light bade unlock   and Lucifer answered,
'What lord art thou?' quoth Lucifer   '*quis est iste?*'
'*Rex gloriae*'   the light soon said,
'And lord of might and of main   and all manner of virtues; *dominus
    virtutum;*
Dukes of this dim place   anon undo these gates,
That Christ may come in   the king's son of heaven.'
And with that breath Hell broke   and Belial's bars;
Inspite of wight or ward   wide open the gates.
Patriarchs and prophets   *populus in tenebris,*
Sang Saint John's song   '*ecce agnus Dei.*'
Lucifer might not look   so light him blinded;
And those that our Lord loved   into his light he took,
And said to Satan, 'lo! here   my soul to amend
For all sinful souls   to save those that be worthy.
Mine they be and of me   I may the better them claim.
Although reason record   and right of myself,
That if they eat the apple   all should die,
I promised them not here   Hell for ever.
For the deed that they did   thy deceit it made;
With guile thou them got   against all reason.
For in my palace, paradise   in person of an adder,
Falsely thou fetchest thence   thing that I loved.
Thus like a lizard   with a lady's visage,
Like a thief thou me robbest   the old law granteth,
That beguilers be beguiled   and that is good reason;
> *Dentem pro dente, et oculum pro oculo.*
Ergo, soul shall soul quit   and sin drive out sin,
And all that man hath misdone   I, man, will amend.
Member for member   by the old law made amends,
And life for life also   and by that law I claim it,
Adam and all his issue   at my will hereafter.
And what death in them undid   my death shall relieve,
And both quicken and purchase   what was destroyed through sin;
And that grace guile destroy   good faith it asketh.
So believe it not, Lucifer   that against the law I fetch them,
But by right and by reason   ransom here my lieges:
> *Non veni solvere legem, sed adimplere.*
Thou fetchest mine from my place   against all reason,

Falsely and feloniously   good faith me it taught,
To recover them through ransom   and by no reason else,
So what with guile thou got   through grace it is won.
Thou, Lucifer, in likeness   of a wicked adder,
Got by guile   those that God loved;
And I, in likeness of a man   that lord am of Heaven,
Graciously thy guile have requited   go guile against guile!
And as Adam and all   through a tree died,
Adam and all through a tree   shall turn again to life;
And guile is beguiled   and in his guile fallen:

    Et cecidit in foveam quam fecit.

Now beginneth thy guile   against thee to turn,
And my grace to grow   ever greater and wider.
The bitterness that thou hast brewed   enjoy it thyself,
That art doctor of death   drink what thou madest!

  'For I, that am lord of life   love is my drink,
And for that drink today   I died upon earth.
I fought so, I thirst yet   for man's soul's sake;
May no drink me moist   nor my thirst slake,
Till the vintage fall   in the vale of Jehoshaphat,
And I drink right ripe must   *resurrectio mortuorum*,
And then shall I come as a king   crowned with angels,
And have out of Hell   all men's souls.

  'Fiends and fiendkins   before me shall stand,
And be at my bidding   wheresoe'er me liketh.
And to be merciful to man   then my nature asketh;
For we be brethren of blood   but not in baptism all.
But all that be my whole bretheren   in blood and in baptism,
Shall not be damned to the death   that is without end;

    Tibi soli peccavi, etc.

It is not the custom on earth   to hang a felon
More than once   though he were a traitor.[1]
And if the king of that kingdom   come in that time,
Where the felon suffer should   death or otherwise,
Law wills, he give him life   if he looked on him.
And I, that am king of kings   shall come in such a time,
Where judgement to the death   damneth all wicked;
And if law wills I look on them   it lieth in my grace,
Whether they die or die not   for what they did ill.
Be it anything ransomed   the boldness of their sins,

                     [1] See page 207.

I may do mercy through righteousness   and all my words true.
And though holy writ wills that I be avenged   on them that did ill,
  Nullum malum impunitum, etc.
They shall be cleansed clearly   and washed of their sins
In my prison Purgatory   till *parce* is called,
And my mercy shall be showed   to many of my bretheren.
For blood may suffer blood   both hungry and a'cold,
But blood may not see blood   bleed, without pity.
  Audivi arcana verba, quae non licet homini loqui.
But my righteousness and right   shall rule all Hell,
And mercy all mankind   before me in Heaven.
For I were an unkind king   unless I my kindred helped,
And above all at such need   when help needs must come;
  Non intres in judicium cum servo tuo, Domine.
Thus by law,' quoth our Lord   'lead I will from hence
Those that me loved   and believed in my coming.
And for thy lying, Lucifer   that thou told to Eve,
Thou shalt abide it bitterly'   and bound him with chains.
Ashtoreth and all the rout   hid them in corners,
They dared not look on our Lord   the boldest of them all,
But let him lead forth what he liked   and allowed him what he pleased.
  Many hundreds of angels   harped and sung,
  Culpat caro, purgat caro; regnat Deus Dei caro.
Then piped Peace   of poesy a note,
'*Clarior est solito post maxima nebula Phoebus,*
Post inimicitias clarior est et amor.
After sharp showers,' quoth Peace   'most glorious is the sun;
Is no weather warmer   than after watery clouds.
Nor no love dearer   nor dearer friends,
Than after war and woe   when Love and Peace be masters.
Was never war in this world   nor wickedness so keen,
That Love, if he pleased   could not bring to laughter,
And Peace through patience   all perils stopped.'
'Truce,' quoth Truth   'thou tellest us soth, by Jesus!
Clip we in covenant   and each of us kiss the other!'
'And let no people,' quoth Peace   'perceive that we chid!
For impossible is no thing   to him that is almighty.'
'Thou sayest soth,' said Righteousness   and reverently her kissed,
Peace, and Peace her   *per saecula saeculorum.*
  Misericordia et veritas obviaverunt sibi; justitia et pax osculatae sunt.
Truth trumpeted then, and sang   '*Te Deum laudamus*';

N 57[1]

And then played Love the lute   in a loud note,
    Ecce quam bonum et jocundum, etc.
  Till the day dawned   these damsels danced,
That men rang in the resurrection   and right with that I waked,
And called Kit my wife   and Calot my daughter—
'Arise and reverence   God's resurrection,
And creep to the cross on knees   and kiss it for a jewel! [1]
For God's blessed body   it bore for our saving,
And it frighteneth the fiend   for such is the might,
May no grisly ghost   glide near its shadow!'

[1] See page 208.

PASSUS XIX

Thus I awoke and wrote   what I had dreamed,
And dressed me neatly   and went me to church,
To hear holy the Mass   and to be houseled after.
In midst of the Mass   when men went to the offering,
I fell again asleep   and suddenly I dreamed,
That Piers the Plowman   was painted all bloody,
And come in with a cross   before the common people,
And right like in all limbs   to our Lord Jesu;
And then called I Conscience   to teach me the truth.
'Is this Jesus the Jouster?' quoth I   'that Jews did to death?
Or it is Piers the Plowman   who painted him so red?'
Quoth Conscience, and kneeled then   'these are Piers' arms,
His colours and his coat armour   but he that cometh so bloody
Is Christ with his cross   conqueror of Christians.'
    'Why call ye him Christ?' quoth I   'since Jews call him Jesus?
Patriarchs and prophets   prophesied before,
That all kind of creatures   should kneel and bow,
Anon as men named   the name of God Jesus.
Ergo there is no name   like to the name of Jesus.
Nor none so needful to name   by night or by day.
For all dark devils   are adread to hear it,
And the sinful are solaced   and saved by that name,
And ye call him Christ   for what cause, tell me?
Is Christ more of might   and more worthy name
Than Jesu or Jesus   that all our joy came of?'
    'Thou knowest well,' quoth Conscience   'if thou canst reason,
That knight, king, conqueror   may be one person.
To be called a knight is fair   for men shall kneel to him;
To be called a king is fairer   for he may knights make;
But to be conqueror called   that cometh of special grace,
And of hardiness of heart   and of courtesy both,
To make lords of lads   in land that he winneth,
And free men foul thralls   that follow not his laws.
The Jews, that were gentlemen   Jesu they despised,

Both his lore and his law   now are they low churls.
As wide as the world is   liveth there none
But under tribute and tax   as tykes and churls.
And those that become Christians   by counsel of the Baptist,
Are franklins, free men   through baptism that they took,
And gentlemen with Jesu   for Jesus was baptised,
And upon Calvary on cross   crowned King of Jews.

'It becometh to a king   to keep and to defend,
And conqueror of conquest   his laws and his bounty.
And so did Jesus the Jews   he justified and taught them
The law of life   that last shall ever;
And defended from foul evils   fevers and fluxes,
And from fiends that in them were   and false belief.
Then was he Jesus of Jews   called gentle prophet,
And king of their kingdom   and crown bore of thorns.
And then conquered he on cross   as conqueror noble;
Might no death him undo   nor down bring,
So that he arose and reigned   and ravished hell.
And then was he conqueror called   of quick and of dead;
For he gave Adam and Eve   and others more bliss,
That long had lain before   as Lucifer's churls.

'And then he gave largely   all his loyal lieges
Places in paradise   at their going hence,
He may well be called conqueror   and that is the meaning of
                                        Christ.[1]
But the cause that he cometh thus   with cross of his passion,
Is to teach us therewith   that when we be tempted,
Therewith to fight and defend us   from falling into sin,
And see by his sorrow   that whoso loveth joy,
To penance and to poverty   he must put himself,
And much woe in this world   accept and suffer.

'But to speak more of Christ   and how he came to that name,
Truly for to speak   his first name was Jesus.
When he was born in Bethlehem   as the Book telleth,
And came to take manhood   kings and angels
Reverenced him fair   with riches of earth.
Angels out of heaven   came kneeling and sang,
    Gloria in excelsis Deo, etc.
Kings came after   kneeled, and offered
Myrrh and much gold   without thanks asking,
                    [1] See page 208.

Or any kind of gift   but acknowledging him sovereign
Both of sand, sun, and sea   and after they went
To their kings' country   by counsel of angels.
And then was that word fulfilled   the which thou speakest of;
    Omnia caelestia, terrestria, flectantur in hoc nomine Jesu.
For all the angels of heaven   at his birth kneeled,
And all the wisdom of the world   was in those three kings;
Reason and righteousness   and pity they offered;
Wherefore and why   wise men that time,
Masters and lettered men   *Magi* them called.
The one king came with reason   signified by incense.
The second king then   truly offered
Righteousness under red gold   reason's fellow.
Gold is likened to loyalty   that last shall ever,
And reason to rich gold   to right and to truth.
The third king then came   kneeling to Jesu,
And presented him with pity   appearing as myrrh;
For myrrh is mercy in meaning   and mild speech of tongue.
Three like honest things   were offered thus at once,
Through three kin kings   kneeling to Jesu.
But for all these precious presents   our Lord Prince Jesus
Was neither king nor conqueror   till he began to grow
In the manner of a man   and that by much skill;
As it becometh a conqueror   to know many skills,
And many wiles and wit   that will be a leader;
And so did Jesu in his days   whoso had time to tell it.
Some time he suffered   and some time he hid him;
And some time he fought fast   and fled other whiles.
And sometimes he gave good   and granted health both,
Life and limb   as he pleased, he wrought.
As right is in a conqueror   so began Jesu,
Till he had all them   that he bled for.
  'In his youth this Jesus   at Jews' feast
Water into wine turned   as holy writ telleth,
And there began God   of his grace to Do-well.
For wine is likened to law   and life of holiness;
And law lacked then   for men loved not their enemies.
And Christ counselleth thus   and commandeth both,
Both to learned and unlearned   to love our enemies.
So at feast first   as I before told,
Began God, of his grace   and goodness, to Do-well:

And then was he named and called   not holy Christ, but Jesu,
A child fine, full of wit   *filius Mariae*.
For before his mother Mary   made he that wonder,
That she first and foremost   firm should believe,
That he through grace was begot   and of no person else.
He wrought that by no wit   but through word one,
According to the kind he came of   there began he Do-well.
And when he was waxed more   in his mother's absence,
He made lame to leap   and gave light to blind,
And fed with two fishes   and with five loaves
Sore hungered folk   more than five thousand.
Thus he comforted the sorrowful   and won a greater name,
The which was Do-better   wherever that he went.
For deaf through his deeds to hear   and dumb to speak he made,
And all he healed and helped   that him of grace asked.
And then was he called in country   of the common people,
For the deeds that he did   *fili David, Jesus!*
For David was doughtiest   of deeds in his time,
The maidens then sang   *Saul interfecit mille, et David decem millia*;
Therefore the country where Jesu came   called him *fili David*,
And named him of Nazareth   and no man so worthy
To be caesar or king   of the kingdom of Juda,
Over Jews a justice   as Jesus was, they thought.
Whereof Caiphas had envy   and other of the Jews,
And for to do him to death   day and night they cast about;
Killed him on cross   at Calvary on Friday,
And then buried his body   and bid that men should
Keep it from night comers   with knights armed,
For no friends should him fetch   for prophets them told,
That that blessed body   from sepulchre should rise,
And go into Galilee   and gladden his apostles,
And his mother Mary   thus men before deemed.
The knights that kept it   confessed it themselves,
That angels and archangels   ere the day dawned,
Came kneeling to the corpse   and sang, "*Christus resurgens*"
Very man before them all   and forth with them he went.
The Jews prayed them peace   and besought the knights
To tell the commons that there came   a company of his apostles,
And bewitched them as they woke   and away stole it.
But Mary Magdalen   met him by the way,
Going towards Galilee   in godhead and manhood,

And alive and looking   and she aloud cried,
In each company where she came   "*Christus resurgens!*"
Thus came it out that Christ overcame   recovered and lived;
    Sic oportet Christum pati, et intrare, etc.;
For what women know   may not well be judged!
Peter perceived all this   and pursued after,
Both James and John   Jesu for to seek,
Thaddeus and ten more   with Thomas of India.[1]
And as all these wise wights   were together,
In a house all shut   and their door barred,
Christ came in, and all closed   both door and gates,
To Peter and to his apostles   and said "*pax vobis!*"
And took Thomas by the hand   and taught him to grope,
And feel with his fingers   his fleshly heart.
Thomas touched it   and with his tongue said,
    "*Deus meus et dominus meus.*
Thou art my lord, I believe   God, lord Jesu!
Thou died and death suffered   and judge shall us all,
And now art living and looking   and last shall ever!"
Christ spoke then   and courteously said,
"Thomas, because thou trowest this   and truly believest it,
Blessed thou be   and be shalt for ever.
And blessed they all be   in body and in soul,
That never shall see me in sight   as thou dost now,
And loyally believe all this   I love them and bless them;
    Beati qui non viderunt, et crediderunt, etc."
  'And when this deed was done   Do-best he taught,
And gave Piers power   and pardon he granted
To all manner of men   mercy and forgiveness,
And might to absolve   of all manner of sins,
Under covenant that they come   and recognition pay,
To Piers' pardon the Plowman   *redde quod debes.*
Thus hath Piers power   be his pardon payed,
To bind and to unbind   both here and elsewhere,
And absolve men from all sins   save of debt alone.
Anon after on high   up into heaven
He went, and dwells there   and will come at last,
And reward him right well   that *reddit quod debet*—
Payeth perfectly   as pure truth wills.
And what person payeth it not   to punish he thinketh,

    [1] See page 208.

And judge them at doomsday   both quick and dead;
The good to the Godhead   and to great joy,
And wicked to dwell   in woe without end.'
Thus Conscience of Christ   and of the cross spoke,
And counselled me to kneel thereto   and then came, methought,
One *Spiritus Paraclitus*   to Piers and to his fellows;
In likeness of a lightning   he alighted on them all,
And made them understand and know   all kinds of language.
I wondered what that was   and shook Conscience,
And was afeared of the light   for in fire's likeness
Spiritus Paraclitus   over-spread them all.

   Quoth Conscience, and kneeled   'this is Christ's messenger,
And cometh from the great God   and Grace is his name.
Know now,' quoth Conscience   'and if thou canst sing,
Welcome him and worship him   with " *Veni, Creator Spiritus*."'
Then sung I that song   and so did many hundred,
And cried with Conscience   'help us, God of grace!'
And then began Grace   to go with Piers Plowman,
And counselled him and Conscience   the commons to summon—
'For I will deal today   and divide grace,
To all kind of creatures   that have their five wits,
Treasure to live by   to their lives' end,
And a weapon to fight with   that will never fail.
For Antichrist and his own   all the world shall grieve,
And encumber thee, Conscience   unless Christ thee help.
And false prophets many   flatterers and liars
Shall come, and be masters   over kings and earls,
And Pride shall be pope   prince of holy church,
Covetousness and Unkindness   cardinals him to lead.
Therefore,' quoth Grace, 'ere I go   I will give you treasure,
And a weapon to fight with   when Antichrist you assaileth.'
And gave each man a grace   to guide himself with,
That idleness encumber him not   envy, nor pride,
       Divisiones gratiarum sunt, etc.
   Some he gave wit   with words to show,
Wit to win their livelihood with   as the world asketh,
As preachers and priests   and prentices of law,
They honestly to live   by labour of tongue,
And by wit to show others   as Grace them would teach.
And some he taught craft   and cunning of sight,
With selling and buying   their livelihood to win,

And some he taught to labour   a loyal life and a true,
And some he taught to till   to ditch and to thatch,
To win with it their livelihood   by lore of his teaching.
And some to divine and divide   numbers to know;
And some to compass craftily   and colours to make;
And some to see and to say   what should befall,
Both of well and of woe   tell it ere it fell,
As astronomers through astronomy   and philosophers wise.
And some to ride and recover   what unrightfully was won;
He taught them to win it again   through quickness of hands,
And fetch it from false men   with Folville's laws.[1]
And some he taught to live   in longing to be hence,
In poverty and in penitence   to pray for all Christians.
And all he taught to be loyal   and each craft love the other,
And forbade them all strife   that none is among them.
'Though some be cleaner than some   ye see well,' quoth Grace,
'That he that useth the fairest craft   to the foulest I could have put
                                                      him,
Think all,' quoth Grace   'that grace cometh as my gift;
Look that none blame other   but love all as bretheren.
And who that most masteries has   be mildest of bearing,
And crown Conscience king   and make Craft your steward,
And after Craft's counsel   clothe you and feed.
For I make Piers the Plowman   my proctor and my reeve,
And registrar to receive   *redde quod debes.*
My purveyor and my plowman   Piers shall be on earth,
And for to till truth   a team shall he have.'
    Grace gave Piers a team   four great oxen;
The one was Luke, a large beast   and a mild faced,
And Mark, and Matthew the third   mighty beasts both,
And joined to them one John   most gentle of all,
The prize ox of Piers' plow   passing all other.
    And Grace gave Piers   of his goodness, four horses,
All that his oxen plowed   they were to harrow after.
One was called Austin   and Ambrose another,
Gregory the great clerk   and Jerome the good;
These four, the faith to teach   follow Piers' team,
And harrowed in a hand's space   all holy scripture,
With two harrows that they had   an old and a new,
    Id est, vetus testamentum et novum.

[1] See page 208.

And Grace gave grain   the cardinal virtues,
And sowed them in man's soul   and then he told their names.
Spiritus prudentiae   the first seed was called,
And whoso ate that   imagine he should,
Ere he did any deed   devise well the end;
And taught men a ladle to buy   with a long handle,
That mean for to keep a crock   to save the fat on top.
    The second seed was called   *spiritus temperantiae*.
He that ate of that seed   had such a nature,
Should never meat nor much drink   make him to swell,
Nor should no scorner nor scold   our of reason him bring,
Nor winning, nor wealth   of worldly riches,
Waste words of idleness   nor wicked speech move;
Should no curious cloth   come on his back,
Nor no meat in his mouth   that Master John spiced.
    The third seed that Piers sowed   was *spiritus fortitudinis*.
And whoso ate of that seed   hardy was ever
To suffer all that God sent   sickness and miseries;
Might no falsehood nor liar   nor loss of worldly goods
Make for him any mourning   that he was not merry in soul,
And bold and abiding   revilings to suffer,
And playeth all with patience   *et parce mihi, Domine*,
And covered him under the counsel   of Cato the wise;
Esto forti animo, cum sis damnatus inique.
    The fourth seed that Piers sowed   was *spiritus justitiae*,
And he that ate of that seed   should be ever true
With God, and not afraid   save of guile alone.
For guile goeth so privily   that good faith at times
May not be espied   by *spiritus justitiae*.
Spiritus justitiae   spareth not to over-spill
Them that be guilty   and for to correct
The king, if he fall   into guilt or in trespass.
For counteth he no king's wrath   when he in court sitteth
To judge as a judge   adread was he never,
Neither of duke nor of death   that he administered not the law,
For present or for prayer   or any prince's letters;
He gives equity to all   according to his power.
    These four seeds Piers sowed   and then he did them harrow
With old law and new law   that love might grow
Among the four virtues   and vices destroy.
For commonly in countries   rest harrow and weeds

Foul the fruit in the field   where they grow together;
And so do vices   virtues worthy.
Quoth Piers, 'harrow all that have common wit   by counsel of these
                                       doctors,
And till according to their teaching   the cardinal virtues.'
'When thy grains,' quoth Grace   'begin for to ripen,
Build thee a house, Piers   to harbour in thy corn.'
'By God! Grace,' quoth Piers   'you must give timber,
And build that house   ere you hence wend.'
And Grace gave him the cross   with the crown of thorns,
That Christ upon Calvary   for mankind suffered on,
And of his baptism and blood   that he bled on rood
He made a kind of mortar   and Mercy it was called.
And therewith Grace began   to make a good foundation,
And wattled it and walled it   with his pains and his passion,
And of all holy writ   he made a roof after,
And called that house Unity   Holy Church in English.
And when this deed was done   Grace devised
A cart, called Christendom   to carry Piers' sheaves;
And gave him horses to his cart   Contrition and Confession,
And made Priesthood overseer   the while himself went
As wide as the world is   with Piers to till truth.
   Now is Piers to the plow   and Pride it espied,
And gathered him a great host   to grieve he thinketh
Conscience and all Christians   and cardinal virtues,
Blow them down and break them   and bite asunder the roots;
And sent forth Arrogance   his serjeant at arms,
And his spy Spill-love   one Speak-evil-secretly.
These two came to Conscience   and to Christian people,
And told them tidings   'that lay waste they should the seeds,
That Piers there had sown   the cardinal virtues;
And Piers' barn will be broken   and they that be in Unity
Shall come out, and Conscience   and your two horses,
Confession and Contrition   and your cart the Faith
Shall be coloured so quaintly   and covered under our sophistry,
That Conscience shall not   know by Contrition,
Nor by Confession   who is Christian or heathen,
Nor no manner of merchant   that with money dealeth,
Whether he win by honesty   or by wrong or by usury.
With such colours and cunning   cometh Pride armed,
With the lord that liveth after   the lust of the body,

To waste, on fine living   and on wicked keeping,
All the world in a while   through our wit,' quoth Pride.
    Quoth Conscience to all Christians then   'my counsel is to wend
Hastily into Unity   and hold we us there,
And pray we that a peace were   in Piers' barn the Plowman.
For truly I wot well   we be not of strength
To go against Pride   unless Grace be with us.'
And then came Kind Wit   Conscience to teach,
And cried and commanded   all Christian people,
For to delve a ditch   deep about Unity,
So that Holy Church stood on Unity   as it a pile were.
Conscience commanded then   all Christians to delve,
And make a great moat   that might be a strength,
To help Holy Church   and them that it keepeth.
Then all kinds of Christians   save common women,
Repented and refused sin   save they alone;
And false men, flatterers   usurers and thieves,
Liars and inquest mongers   that were forsworn oft,
Wittingly and wilfully   with the false held,
And for silver were forsworn   truly they knew it.
There was no Christian creature   that kind wit had,
Save shrews alone   such as I spake of,
That did not help a quantity   holiness to increase.
Some through bead bidding   and some through pilgrimage,
And others private penance   and some through alms giving.
And then welled water   for wicked works,
Bitterly running   out of men's eyes.
Cleanness of the commons   and clerks' clean living
Made Unity Holy Church   in holiness to stand.
'I care not,' quoth Conscience   'though Pride come now,
The lord of lust shall be stopped   all this Lent, I hope.
Come,' quoth Conscience   'ye Christians, and dine,
That have laboured loyally   all this Lent time.
Here is bread blessed   and God's body thereunder.
Grace through God's word   gave Piers power,
And might to make it   and men to eat it after,
In help of their health   once in a month,
Or as oft as they had need   those that had payed
To Piers' pardon the Plowman   *redde quod debes*.'
'How?' quoth all the commons   'thou counselled us to yield
All that we owe any wight   are we going to housel?'

'That is my counsel,' quoth Conscience   'and cardinal virtues,
That each man forgive other   and that wills the *pater noster*,
 Et dimitte nobis debita nostra, etc.,
And so to be absolved   and then be houseled.'
 'Yea, bah!' quoth a brewer   'I will not be ruled,
By Jesu! for all your jangling   with *spiritus justitiae*,
Nor according to Conscience, by Christ   while I can sell
Both dregs and draff   and draw it at a hole,
Thick ale and thin ale   for that is my nature,
And not hack after holiness   hold thy tongue, Conscience.
Of *spiritus justitiae*   thou speakest much idly!'
'Caitiff,' quoth Conscience   'cursed wretch!
Unblessed art thou, brewer   unless thee God help;
Unless thou live by lore   of *spiritus justitiae*,
The chief seed that Piers sowed   saved wilt thou be never.
Unless Conscience the commons feed   and cardinal virtues,
Believe it well they be lost   both life and soul.'
'Then is many man lost,'   quoth an ignorant vicar,
'I am a pastor of Holy Church   and came never in my time
Man to me, that me could tell   of cardinal virtues,
Or that accounted Conscience   at a cock's feather or a hen's!
I knew never cardinal   that came not from the pope,
And we clerks, when they come   for their provisions pay,
For their fur and their palfreys' meat   and pillagers that them follow.
The commons *clamat cotidie*   each man to other,
"The country is the curseder   that cardinals come in;
And where they lie and linger most   lechery there reigneth:"—
Therefore,' quoth this vicar   'by very God, I would
That no cardinal come   among the common people,
But in their holiness   hold them still
At Avignon, among the Jews   *cum sancto sanctus eris, etc.*,
Or in Rome, as their rule will   the relics to keep;
And thou, Conscience, in king's court   and should never come thence,
And Grace, that thou praisest so   guide of all clerks,
And Piers with his new plow   and also with his old,
Emperor of all the world   and that all men were Christian!
Imperfect is that pope   that all people should help,
And sends them that slay such   as he should save;
And well for Piers the Plowman   that pursueth God in doing,
Qui pluit super justos   et injustos at once,
And sends the sun to save   a cursed man's tilth,

As bright as to the best man   and to the best woman.
Right so Piers the Plowman   works to till
As well for a waster   and wenches of the stews,
As for himself and his servants   save that he is first served;
And travaileth and tilleth   for a traitor as hard
As for a true honest man   all times alike.
And worshipped be he that wrought all   both good and wicked,
And suffereth the sinful   till some time that they repent.
And God amend the pope   that pillages Holy Church,
And claimeth before the king   to be keeper over Christians,
Yet counteth not though Christians   be killed and robbed,
And finds folk to fight   and Christian blood to spill,
Against the old law and new   as Luke thereof witnesseth,

> *Non occides: mihi vindictam, etc.*

It seemeth, if so   he had his will,
That he recketh right naught   of all the remnant.
And Christ of his courtesy   the cardinals save,
And turn their minds to wisdom   and to weal of soul!
For the commons,' quoth this curate   'count full little
The counsel of Conscience   or cardinal virtues,
Unless they see by sight   something to win;
Of guile nor of lying   care they never a jot.
For *spiritus prudentiae*   among the people, is guile,
And all those fair virtues   as vices they seem;
Each man devises a sleight   sin for to hide,
And disguises it as a clever   and a clean living.'

Then laughed there a lord   and 'by this light,' said,
'I hold it right and reason   of my reeve to take
All that mine auditor   or else my steward
Counselleth me by their account   and my clerk's writing.
With *spiritus intellectus*   they seek the reeve's rolls,
And with *spiritus fortitudinis*   fetch it I will.'

And then came there a king   and of his crown said,
'I am king with crown   the commons to rule,
And Holy Church and clergy   from cursed men to defend.
And if me lacketh to live by   the law wills I take it,
Where I may soonest it have   for I am head of law;
For ye be but members   and I above all.
And since I am head of you all   I am health of you all,
And Holy Church's chief help   and chieftain of the commons.
And what I take of you two   I take it at teaching

Of *spiritus justitiae*   for I judge you all;
So I may boldly be houseled   for I borrow never,
Nor crave of my commons   but as my status asks.'
   'On condition,' quoth Conscience   'that thou canst defend
And rule thy realm in reason   right well, and in truth,
Take thou may in reason   as thy law asketh;
    Omnia tua sunt ad defendum, sed non ad depraedandum.'
The vicar had far to go home   and fair took his leave,
And I awakened therewith   and wrote as I had dreamed.

PASSUS XX

THEN as I went by the way   when I was thus awaked,
Heavy-cheered I journeyed   and sad in heart;
I knew not where to eat   nor at what place.
And it came nigh the noon   and with Need I met,
That affronted me foully   and deceiver me called.
'Could'st thou not excuse thee   as did the king and others,
That thou took for thy livelihood   for clothes and for sustenance,
As by teaching and by telling   of *spiritus temperantiae*,
And thou seized no more   than Need thee taught,
And need hath no law   nor never shall fall in debt?
For three things he taketh   his life for to save,
That is, meat, when men him denieth   as he no money wieldeth,
Nor none will be his surety   nor pledge hath none to lay.
And he takes in that case   and comes thereto by sleight,
He sinneth not truly   that so winneth his food.
And though he come so to clothes   and can have no better bargain,
Need right at once   takes him under surety.
And if he wishes to lap   the law of kind wills
That he drink at each ditch   ere he for thirst died.
So Need, at great need   may take him as for his own,
Without counsel of Conscience   or cardinal virtues,
As long as he follow and guard   *spiritus temperantiae*.
For is no virtue by far   like *spiritus temperantiae*,
Neither *spiritus justitiae*   nor *spiritus fortitudinis*.
For *spiritus fortitudinis*   fails full oft,
He shall do more than measure   many time and oft,
And beat men over bitterly   and some of them too little,
And grieves men greater   than good faith wishes.
And *spiritus justitiae*   shall judge, willy nilly,
After the king's counsel   and the commons' will.
And *spiritus prudentiae*   in many a point shall fail
In what he thinks will happen   if it were not for his wit.
Weening is no wisdom   nor wise imagination,
Homo proponit et Deus disponit   and governeth all good virtues.
But Need is next to him   for anon he makes men meek,

And as low as a lamb   for the lack of what they need.
Wise men forsook wealth   for they would be needy,
And dwelt in wilderness   and would not be rich.
And God all his great joy   in heaven he left,
And came and took manhood   and became needy.
So needy he was, as saith the Book   in many sundry places,
That he said in his sorrow   on the rood itself,[1]
"Both fox and fowl   may fly to hole and creep,
And the fish hath fin   to swim with to rest,
But need hath seized me   so that I must need abide,
And suffer sorrow's full sorrow   that shall to joy turn."
Therefore be not abashed   to beg and to be needy;
Since he that made all the world   was by will needy,
Nor never none so needy   nor poorer died.'
    When Need had corrected me thus   anon I fell asleep,
And dreamed full marvellously   that, in man's form,
Antichrist came then   and all the crop of truth
Turned it upside-down   and overturned the root,
And made falsehood spring and spread   and increased men's needs;
In each country where he came   he cut away truth,
And made guile grow there   as he a god were.
Friars followed that fiend   for he gave them copes,
And religious reverenced him   and rang their bells,
And all the convent forth came   to welcome that tyrant,
And all his as well as him   save only fools;
Which fools were well liefer   to die than to live
Longer, since loyalty   was so rebuked.
And a false fiend Antichrist   over all folk reigned;
And those who were mild men and holy   and no mischief feared,
Defied all falseness   and folk that it used;
And whatever king them supported   knowing them any while,
They cursed, and their counsellors   whether clerk or unlearned.
    Antichrist had thus soon   hundreds at his banner,
And Pride it bore   boldly about,
With a lord that liveth   after liking of body,
That came against Conscience   that keeper was and guide
Over Christian people   and cardinal virtues.
'I counsel,' quoth Conscience then   'come with me, ye fools,
Into Unity Holy Church   and hold we us there,
And cry we to Nature   that he come and defend us,

[1] See page 208.

Fools, from this fiend's limbs   for Piers' love the Plowman.
And cry we to all the commons   that they come to Unity,
And there abide and bicker   against Belial's children.'
     Nature Conscience then heard   and came out of the planets,
And sent forth his messengers   fevers and fluxes,
Coughs and spasms   cramps and toothaches,
Rheums and running sores   and dirty scabs,
Boils and swellings   and burning agues;
Frenzies and foul evils   foragers of Nature,
Had pricked and preyed upon   the polls of people,
That fully a legion   lost their lives soon.
There was—'harrow and help!   here cometh Nature,
With Death that is dreadful   to undo us all!'
The lord that lived after lust   then aloud cried
After Comfort, a knight   to come and bear his banner.
'Alarm! alarm!' quoth that lord   'each man for himself!'
And then encountered these men   ere minstrels might pipe,
And ere heralds at arms   had named the champions.
     Age the hoary   he was in the vanguard,
And bore the banner before Death   by right he it claimed.
Nature came after   with many keen sores,
As pox and pestilences   and many people destroyed;
So Nature through corruptions   killed full many.
Death came driving after   and all to dust pashed
Kings and knights   caesars and popes;
Learned nor ignorant   he let no man stand,
Those he hit evenly   never stirred after.
Many a lovely lady   and lovers of knights
Swooned and died   for sorrow of Death's blows.
     Conscience of his courtesy   to Nature besought
To cease and hold   and see whether they would
Leave Pride privily   and be perfect Christians.
And Nature ceased then   to see the people amend.
Fortune began to flatter then   those few that were alive,
And promised them long life   and Lechery he sent
Amongst all manner of men   wedded and unwedded,
And gathered a great host   all against Conscience.
This Lechery laid on   with a laughing cheer,
And with privy speech   and painted words,
And armed him with idleness   and with high bearing.
He bore a bow in his hand   and many bloody arrows,

Were feathered with fair promise   and many a false truth.
And with his low tales   he troubled full oft
Conscience and his company   of Holy Church the teachers.
  Then came Covetousness   and cast about how he might
Overcome Conscience   and cardinal virtues,
And armed him in avarice   and greedily lived.
His weapon was all wiles   to win and to hide;
With lyings and with deceits   he beguiled the people.
Simony sent him   to assail Conscience,
And he preached to the people   and prelates they made,
To hold with Antichrist   their temporal power to save;
And he came to the king's counsel   as a bold baron,
And kneeled to Conscience   in court before them all,
And made Good Faith flee   and False to abide,
And boldly bore down   with many a bright noble
Much of the wit and wisdom   of Westminster hall.
He jogged to a justice   and jousted in his ear,
And overturned all his truth   with 'take-this-recompense.'
And to the court of the arches hastily   he went anon after,
And turned civil law into simony   and then won over the official;
For a mantle of miniver   he made true matrimony
Depart ere death came   and divorces made.
  'Alas!' quoth Conscience, and cried then   'would Christ, of his
                                                      grace,
That Covetousness were Christian   that is so keen a fighter,
And bold and abiding   while his purse lasteth!'
And then laughed Life   and had his clothes decorated,
And armed him in haste   in worthless words,
And held Holiness a joke   and Kindness a waster,
And looked on Loyalty as a churl   and Liar a free man;
Conscience and counsel   he counted it folly.
Thus rallied Life   at a little fortune,
And pricked forth with Pride   praiseth he no virtue,
He careth not how Nature slew   and shall come at last,
And kill all earthly creatures   save Conscience alone.
Life leapt aside   and took him a lover,
'Health and I,' quoth he   'and highness of heart
Shall make thee dread not   either Death or Age,
And to forget sorrow   and care naught of sin.'
This Life liked   and his lover Fortune,
And they begot in their glory   a vagabond at last,

One that much woe wrought   Sloth was his name.
Sloth waxed wondrous fast   and soon was of age,
And wedded one Wanhope   a wench of the stews;
Her sire was a jury-man   that never swore truth,
One Thomas Two-tongue   attainted at each inquest.
This Sloth was wary in war   and a sling made,
And threw dread of despair   a dozen miles around.
For care Conscience then   cried upon Age,
And bade him try to fight   and frighten Wanhope.

    And Age took good hope   and hastily shifted himself,
And waved away Wanhope   and with Life he fighteth.
And Life fled for fear   to Physic for help,
And besought him for succour   and of salve had,
And gave him gold, good measure   that gladdened his heart
And they gave him in return   a glass hood.
Life believed that leech-craft   would stay Age,
And drive away Death   with medicines and drugs.

    And Age adventured against Life   and at last he hit
A physician with a furred hood   so that he fell into a palsy
And there died that doctor   ere three days after.
'Now I see,' said Life   'that surgery nor physic
May not a mite avail   to meddle against Age.'
And in hope of his health   good heart he took,
And rode so to Revel   a rich place and a merry;
The company of comfort   men called it sometimes.
And Age came anon after me   and over my head went,
And made me bald in front   and bare on the crown,
So hard he went over my head   it will be seen ever.
'Sir evil-taught Age,' quoth I   'ill ways go with thee!
Since when was the way   over men's heads?
Had'st thou been polite,' quoth I   'thou would'st have asked leave!'
'Yea! dear lazy-bones!' quoth he   and laid on me with age,
And hit me under the ear   hardly can I hear;
He buffeted me about the mouth   and beat out my teeth,
And fettered me in gout   I may not go at large.
And of the woe that I was in   my wife had pity,
And wished full well   that I were in heaven.
For the limb that she loved me for   and glad was to feel,
On nights indeed   when we naked were,
I might not in no manner   make it serve her will,
So Age and she truly   had it enfeebled.

And as I sat in this sorrow   I saw how Nature passed,
And Death drew nigh me   for dread I began to quake,
And cried to Nature   out of care me to bring.
'Lo! Age the hoary   hath me beset,
Avenge me, if your will be   for I would be hence.'
'If thou wilt be avenged   wend into Unity,
And hold thee there ever   till I send for thee,
And look thou learn some craft   ere thou come thence.'
'Counsel me, Nature,' quoth I   'what craft is best to learn?'
'Learn to love,' quoth Nature   'and leave all others.'
'How shall I come to goods so   to clothe me and to feed?'
'If thou love truly,' quoth he   'lack shall thee never
Meat nor worldly weeds   while thy life lasteth.'
And there, by counsel of Nature   I began to roam
Through Contrition and Confession   till I came to Unity;
And there was Conscience constable   Christians to save,
And it was besieged sothly   with seven great giants,
That with Antichrist held   hard against Conscience.
    Sloth with his sling   a hard assault he made,
Proud priests came with him   more than a thousand,
In cloaks and peaked shoes   and pissers' long knives,
Came against Conscience   with Covetousness they held.
'By Mary,' quoth a cursed priest   of the march of Ireland,
'I count no more Conscience   if so I catch silver,
Than I do to drink   a draught of good ale!'
And so said sixty   of the same country;
And shot against him with shot   many a sheaf of oaths;
And broad hooked arrows   God's hurt, and his nails,
And had almost Unity   and holiness down.
    Conscience cried, 'help   Clergy, or else I fall
Through imperfect priests   and prelates of holy church.'
Friars heard him cry   and came him to help,
But as they knew not well their craft   Conscience forsook them.
Need came then near   and Conscience he told
That they come for covetousness   to have cure of souls—
'And if they are poor, by chance   for patrimony them lacketh,
They will flatter, to fare well   folk that be rich;
And since they chose chill   and low poverty,
Let them chew as they chose   and charge them with no cure!
For oftener he lieth   that livelihood must beg,
Than he that laboureth for livelihood   and giveth to beggars.

And since friars forsook   earthly felicity,
Let them be as beggars   or live by angels' food!'
    Conscience at this counsel then   began to laugh,
And courteously comforted them   and called in all friars,
And said, 'sirs, sothly   welcome be ye all
To Unity and Holy Church   but one thing I you pray,
Hold you in Unity   and have no envy
Of learned or of unlearned   but live after your rule.
And I will be your bail   ye shall have bread and clothes,
And other necessities enough   you shall no thing lack,
If that ye leave logic   and learn for to love.
For love left they lordship   both land and school,
Friar Francis and Dominic   for love to be holy,
And if ye coveteth a cure   Kind will you teach,
That in measure God made   all manner of things,
And set them at a certain   and at a fixed number,
And named names new   and numbered the stars;
    Qui numerat multitudinem stellarum, et omnibus eis nomina, etc.
Kings and knights   that keep and defend,
Have officers under them   and each of them numbered;
And if they wage men to war   they write them in number,
Or will no money them pay   travail they never so sore.
All others in battle   be held robbers,
Thieves and plunderers   in each place cursed.
Monks and nuns   and all men of religion
Their order and their rule wills   to have a fixed number.
Of unlearned and of learned   the law wills and asketh
A fixed number for a certain order   save only among friars!
Therefore,' quoth Conscience, 'by Christ   kind wit me telleth,
It is wicked to pay you   ye grow out of number!
Heaven hath an even number   and hell is without number;
Therefore I would indeed   that ye were in the register,
And your number under notary's seal   and neither more nor less!'
    Envy heard this   and bade friars go to college,
And learn logic and law   and also the contemplative life,
And preach to men of Plato   and prove it by Seneca,
That all things under heaven   ought to be in common.
    And yet he lieth, as I believe   that to the ignorant so preacheth,
For God made to men a law   and Moses it taught,
    Non concupisces rem proximi tui.
And evil is this held   in parishes of England,

For parsons and parish priests   that should the people shrive,
Be pastors called   to know and to heal,
All that be their parishioners   penance to enjoin,
And they should be ashamed at their confession   but shame makes
them go,
And flee to the friars   as false folk do to Westminster,
That borrow and bear it thither   and then ask friends
Earnestly for forgiveness   or a further year's loan.
But while he is in Westminster   he will be ahead,
And make him merry   with other men's goods.
And so it fareth with many folk   that to the friars confesseth,
As jurymen and executors   they will give the friars
A portion to pray for them   and make themselves merry
With the residue and the remnant   for which other men laboured,
And leave the dead man in debt   to the day of doom.
   Envy therefore   hated Conscience,
And friars for philosophy   he founded them colleges
The while Covetousness and Unkindness   Conscience assailed.
In Unity Holy Church   Conscience held him,
And made Peace porter   to bar the gates
Against all tale tellers   and idle tattlers.
Hypocrisy and he   a hard battle they had.
Hypocrisy at the gate   hard began to fight,
And wounded very wickedly   many a wise teacher,
That with Conscience accorded   and with cardinal virtues.
Conscience called a leech   that could well shrive,
'Go salve those that sick be   and through sin wounded.'
Shift shaped a sharp salve   and made men do penance
For their misdeeds   that they wrought had,
So that Piers was payed   *redde quod debes*.
   Some liked not this leech   and letters they sent,
If any surgeon were in the town   that softer could plaster.
Sir Lief-to-live-in-lechery   lay there and groaned;
For fasting of a Friday   he behaved as he would die.
'There is a surgeon in this town   that soft can handle,
And more of physic knows by far   and fairer he plastereth;
One friar Flatterer   is physician and surgeon.'
Quoth Contrition to Conscience   'let him come to Unity,
For here is many a man   hurt through Hypocrisy.'
'We have no need,' quoth Conscience   'I know no better leech
Than parson or parish priest   confessor or bishop,

Save Piers the Plowman   that hath power over them all,
And indulgences may give   unless debt prevent it.
I will allow,' quoth Conscience   'since ye desire,
That friar Flatterer be fetched   and physic you sick.'
    The friar heard hereof   and hied fast
To a lord for a letter   leave to have to cure,
As if a curate he were   and came with his letters
Boldly to the bishop   and his brief had,
In countries where he came into   confessions to hear;
And came where Conscience was   and knocked at the gate.
Peace unbarred it   was porter of Unity,
And in haste asked   'what his will were?'
'In faith,' quoth this friar   'for profit and for health
Speak I would with Contrition   and therefore come I hither.
'He is sick,' said Peace   'and so are many others,
Hypocrisy hath hurt him   full hardly will they recover.'
'I am a surgeon,' said the man   'and salves can make;
Conscience knoweth me well   and what I can do too.'
'I pray thee,' quoth Peace then   'ere thou pass further,
What art thou called? I pray thee   hide not thy name.'
'Certes,' said this fellow   'sir *Penetrans-domos*.'
'Yea, go thy ways,' quoth Peace   'by God, for all thy physic,
Unless thou know some craft   thou comest not herein!
I knew such a one once   not eight winters past,
Came in thus coped   at a court where I dwelt,
And was my lord's leech   and my lady's both.
And at last this begging friar   when my lord was out,
He salved so our women   till some were with child!'
Mild-speech told Peace   open the gates—
'Let in the friar and his fellow   and make them fair cheer.
He may see and hear   so it may befall,
That Life through his lore   shall leave Covetousness,
And be afeared of Death   and withdraw him from Pride,
And accord with Conscience   and kiss each the other.'
    Thus through Mild-speech   entered the friar,
And came in to Conscience   and courteously him greeted.
'Thou art welcome,' quoth Conscience   'canst thou heal the sick?
Here is Contrition,' quoth Conscience   'my cousin, wounded;
Comfort him,' quoth Conscience   'and take care of his sores.
The plasters of the parson   and powders bite sore,
He lets them lie over long   and loth is to change them;

From Lent to Lent   he lets his plasters bite.'
'That is over long,' quoth this friar   'I believe I shall amend it';—
And goeth and graspeth Contrition   and gave him a plaster
Of 'a privy payment   and I shall pray for you,
For all that ye be held for   all my life time,
And make you my lady   in mass and in matins,
As friars of our fraternity   for a little silver.'
Thus he goeth and gathereth   and lieth where he shriveth,
Till Contrition had clean forgotten   to cry and to weep,
And lie awake for his wicked works   as he was wont to do.
For comfort of his confessor   Contrition he left,
That is sovereignest salve   for all kind of sins.
    Sloth saw that   and so did Pride,
And came with a keen will   Conscience to assail.
Conscience cried then   and bade Clergy help him,
And also Contrition   for to keep the gate.
'He lieth and dreameth,' said Peace   'and so do many others;
The friar with his physic   this folk hath enchanted,
And plastered them so pleasantly   they dread no sin.'
'By Christ,' quoth Conscience then   'I will become a pilgrim,
And walk as wide   as all the world lasteth,
To seek Piers the Plowman   that Pride will destroy,
And that friars may have provision   that for need flatter,
And oppose me, Conscience   now Kind me avenge,
And send me good fortune and health   till I have Piers the Plowman!'
And so he cried after grace   till I began to wake.

Explicit hic dialogus Petri Plowman.

NOTES

[Page 2.] *Friars.* The friars preachers: Dominicans (Black friars), Francis-cans (Grey friars or friars Minor), Carmelites (White friars), and the Augustini-ans (Austin friars). They were mendicant, peripatetic, pastoral, and preaching clergy with certain monastic obligations, and so to be distinguished from the monks, who are not essentially priests and whose activities do not normally extend beyond the monastery walls. Langland is by no means the only medieval writer to castigate the particular abuses which their way of life and uncontrolled numbers gave rise to.

[Page 2.] *Pardoner.* A pardoner was licensed by ecclesiastical authority to preach and collect money for a specified object (e.g. to build a church or a bridge), for contributing to which a pardon (see note to page 18) was attached. This name and office was abolished entirely by the Council of Trent in 1563.

[Page 3.] *Bachelors.* Bachelors, masters, and doctors signify priests with various degrees—such as B.A., M.A., Ph.D., as we still know them—obtained from a university. The normal education of a priest was gained at a university, and the division between learning and the priesthood was hardly, in theory, conceivable; so we find Langland using 'Clergy' to signify both simultaneously. The whole idea of secular knowledge as against an especial form of priestly education has grown to its modern proportions steadily since the Renaissance, the Reformation, the scientific movement, and the reactions they produced in the Christian church.

[Page 4.] The general moral of this ancient fable of 'belling the cat' is clear. In its special application here the rats are the burgesses and weighty commons, the mice the lesser folk, the cat King Edward III, the kitten his grandson, the future Richard II.

[Page 10.] *Natural knowing.* Langland has 'kind knowing,' and a treatise could be written on the use and meaning of the word 'kind' both in medieval literature and later. It always has a connection with that which is natural and proper to the person in question as such, to a person as a man, for instance, or to God as God. 'Kind' as a noun can mean nature just, or the God who is the life of nature. Here 'kind knowing' means an instinctive knowledge, proper to a man, of the first general principles of moral action; not conscience, but the principles conscience judges by.

[Page 13.] *Meed.* Meed is reward; not necessarily a bad thing, but often misused and hence becoming something like bribery or, in a more general sense, graft.

[Page 14.] *Summoners.* Officers who called persons before the ecclesiastical courts. Such a court was the *Arches*, which is still in existence. This court dealt with such things as deciding the validity of marriages, on which only the church could pronounce, and it appears to have been particularly open to blatant bribery and corruption.

[Page 17.] *Paulines.* Referred to in medieval writing both as friars and hermits.

[Page 18.] *Pardons.* Pardons, or indulgences, originated in the early days of Christianity as remissions of the sometimes very rigorous and public penances imposed on individuals for heinous offences. In the Middle Ages, and still, they are remissions of the temporal punishment due to those sins of which the guilt has been forgiven (normally by confession and absolution), granted by the Church and ratified by God. Because of the origin, the amount of remission is expressed in terms of time, i.e. a hundred days (originally a hundred days off your long public penance). The common medieval custom of granting indulgences in return for, say, alms-giving to some good cause, was obviously easily abused, and all such indulgences or pardons where revoked by Pope Pius V, in 1567.

[Page 25.] *Regum.* The Book of Kings.

[Page 26.] *Placebo.* A colloquial term for the Office of the Dead. 'David' in the next line means the psalms, which were commonly all ascribed to David. The psalms form a major part of the office, the daily prayer of the Church; and of course the passage is telling priests to say or sing the office as they should instead of spending their time in sport.

[Page 27.] This sort of prophecy, with its semi-magical incantation, was popular. They may or may not have been intended to be clear at the time; they certainly are not to us. This one refers to the conversion of the Jews, infidels and Mohammedans at some future date; 'the full of the moon' is the full moon of Easter, the time of our redemption.

[Page 31.] *Recordare.* A name, from the first word of the introit—the 'entering' psalm at the beginning of the Mass, which varies according to the day—from the Mass for avoidance of death and plague.

[Page 33.] *Pestilences.* A reference to the recurrent epidemics of the plague, the 'Black Death,' which decimated the population of England during the fourteenth century, causing, among other things, widespread social changes. The 'south-west wind' in the following line is usually identified with a great storm on 15th January 1362, and thus becomes a significant clue in attempts to date the poem.

[Page 33.] *Women's punishment.* This is probably the ducking-stool, the popular and uncomfortable punishment for a scold.

[Page 36.] *Diapenidion.* An emollient medicine.

[Page 36.] *Limiters and lectors.* A limiter was a friar with a limited district in which to beg. A lector is probably the holder of an academic degree, that is, a Lector in Sacred Theology.

[Page 37.] Here is no question of ordaining women. Many abbesses and prioresses of the Middle Ages exercised complete temporal jurisdiction and tried to stretch their spiritual authority to match it, especially by claiming to 'hear confessions.' These had to be restrained by church authorities.

[Page 39.] *Rood of Bromholm.* One of the many English shrines of popular pilgrimage. Walsingham is also mentioned, which is becoming a centre of pilgrimage again in the twentieth century with its increasing revival of medieval Catholic practices.

[Page 41.] '*New fair*' game. Explanations of this game seem hardly clearer than Langland's own description. It was obviously a game of barter, and was known to be highly popular.

[Page 43.] *Benedicite.* The first word of grace before meat.

[Page 44.] *Love-days.* In fact, law-days; days set apart for manorial courts, hence days of reconciliation and concord. The term 'love-days' is used commonly for any days chosen for settling disputes by arbitration.

[Page 45.] *Dismas.* The name popularly and traditionally given to the good thief on Calvary.

[Page 46.] *Suit.* That is, Christ's bodily flesh, the same suit and the same armorial device as worn by human beings.

[Page 47.] A list of the various 'trophies' brought home by pilgrims to show what shrines they had visited. Ampullas were small flasks containing oly water—they were stamped with a sign showing the shrine they came from; such signs were the shells of Galicia and the keys of Røme. The vernicle was also commonly worn by pilgrims; it is the image of the face of our Lord from the veil of St Veronica who, traditionally, wiped the face of our Lord when he was on his way to Calvary, an impression of his countenance being left, miraculously, on the veil she used.

[Page 49.] *Waferer.* A maker of small wafers of bread and cakes.

[Page 50.] *Bull.* A papal rescript or edict.

[Page 53.] *Memento.* A prayer for the named dead in the Mass, *memento* being the first word of that prayer.

[Page 54.] *Religion.* A term used for a religious order, now obsolete; 'a religious' is still used to denote a member of a religious order.

[Page 58.] *Collops.* Apparently slices of salt meat, though it is not clear how the eggs come in.

[Page 59.] Another prophecy, with the distinction of the unconscious truth of one of its fanciful touches. About fifty years later the Maid of Orleans—Joan of Arc—did have the mastery.

[Page 60.] A pardon *a poena et a culpa* is a plenary indulgence, i.e. a remission not of part but all the temporary punishment due to forgiven sin. (See note to page 18.)

[Page 64.] *Biennials and triennials.* The saying of Masses for the dead over a period of two or three years.

[Page 66.] *Wit.* This term seldom, if ever, bears the modern meaning. It signifies intelligence, cleverness, intellectuality, brain, according to the context.

[Page 67.] *New year's gift.* The meaning here is a free gift; there seems, however, to have been a regular system of gifts at the new year, given, for instance, to the king's officers, which were 'free' but not overlooked by the prudent man.

[Page 70.] *Kind.* The God of nature. (See note to page 10.)

[Page 70.] *Anima.* The soul.

[Page 73.] This refers to the legend of the time that Cain was conceived during the period of penitence and fasting imposed on Adam and Eve after their expulsion from Eden. It should be remembered, to understand Langland's thought, that it was common medieval practice and considered of great merit, for husbands and wives to refrain from intercourse during times of penitence and general fasting such as Lent, and especially if there was any particular reason for doing penance.

[Page 74.] The Dunmow flitch was apparently as well known in Langland's day as it is in ours, and perhaps regarded more seriously.

[Page 76.] *Margery pearls.* That is, simply pearls. 'Margery,' an anglicized version of the Greek for 'pearl,' is a bit of poetic tautology.

[Page 77.] *Bernard.* St Bernard of Clairvaux, 1091–1153, saint, philosopher, and theologian, famous in his own time, and throughout the Middle Ages.

[Page 78.] The custom of preaching in the open air at St Paul's Cross was carried on after the Reformation; Latimer, for instance, preached there. A preacher was sure there of a good public hearing and a certain fame, if not necessarily great influence.

[Page 78.] *Worm.* Snake or serpent; the word had a more general sense at the time than we give it.

[Page 80.] *The seven arts.* A reference to the system of education at the universities. 'Arts' has not our connotation, but is in distinction to the higher studies of philosophy and theology. The seven arts consisted of the trivium: grammar, logic, and rhetoric; and the quadrivium: music, arithmetic, geometry, and astronomy.

[Page 82.] *Austin.* St Augustine of Hippo, 354–430, one of the four great 'fathers' of the early Western church, the others being St Ambrose, St Gregory the Great, and St Jerome. The works of all of them would be looked to as weighty, if not final, authorities, but St Augustine has always had the greatest popular influence.

[Page 83.] *Archa dei.* The Ark of the Covenant.

[Page 84.] *Constantine.* The fourth-century Roman emperor, Constantine the Great, whose conversion to Christianity by bringing to the Church the power and the wealth of the Western empire had such a profound and not in all ways happy effect on its development.

[Page 91.] A reference to the privacy of the confessional.

[Page 92.] *Trajan.* The great Roman emperor, A.D. 98–117. The reference is to a popular story, which may be found in that delightful work Caxton's translation of the Golden Legend, that Pope Gregory the Great held the memory of Trajan in such esteem and love that he plied God with prayers until Trajan's soul was delivered from hell. The whole passage shows Langland considering the question that troubled the mind of the Middle Ages very much, that of the salvation of the righteous heathen, for whom no explicit place had been made in the Church's economy of redemption. Langland's conclusion is that it is possible, but that, typically, it is through their own good works rather than the prayers even of the most holy of the faithful.

[Page 102.] *Roquemadour.* A much-loved shrine of our Lady in the Dordogne, with a long history. Charlemagne, in the eighth century, is supposed to have visited it, and Roland, his knight, left his sword there as an offering on the altar of the chapel of St Michael.

[Page 102.] *Felicia.* Probably a reference to the romance of Guy of Warwick, in which she is Sir Guy's wife and behaves with such disdain and contempt towards her husband that he leaves her, to her disgrace, after forty days. Rosamund, in the next line, was the mistress of King Henry II. Her story is well known; Tennyson, for instance, treats of it in his play 'Becket.'

[Page 103.] *Kind Wit.* Two of the most difficult words in *Piers Plowman* together (see notes to page 10 and page 66). Here the interpretation is something like 'instinctive understanding' of the sort that comes from experience and study.

[Page 105.] This seems an odd gloss on the stable at Bethlehem of St Luke's gospel. It is possibly derived from the word *domum* used in St Matthew's account of the coming of the wise men from the east. If this was thought of as a house and that house identified as the inn, i.e. the best house of a small town, and our Lord was born in the stable of that inn, then the idea is possible; but it can hardly be said to be more than a strained explanation.

[Page 106.] A reference to the 'neck verse' which saved many a rogue from hanging. So close was the connection between learning and the clergy that the power of reading a verse from the Bible could be used as evidence of being in holy orders—not necessarily as a priest, but minor orders, deacon or subdeacon. The clergy were exempt from capital punishment, so it was a useful thing to be able to prove. This was most probably often merely a recognized convention, used to mitigate the extreme rigour of penalties for lesser crimes such as theft.

[Page 108.] *Avianus.* This term signifies simply a collection of fables. Avianus lived in the fourth century and wrote fables in Latin verse, but his name was used loosely to cover any writings of this nature.

[Page 112.] *Mahomet.* As a popularly considered infidel Mahomet's name was sometimes used as here to signify a devil; Langland elsewhere shows a somewhat more exact knowledge of Mohammedan beliefs.

[Page 112.] The apocalypse meant here is the Apocalypse of the Gluttons by Walter Mapes, a kind of parody of St John's Apocalypse. Saint Advisa was fed with fine white bread from heaven, the implication presumably being that such heavenly food is the only delicacy penitents should seek.

[Page 114.] *Lamp-line.* There seems to be no satisfactory explanation of this simple phrase. It *could* refer to a Latin inscription of some benevolent nature on the little lamps often kept burning before a shrine or statue (W. W. Skeat's suggestion), but there is nothing to say that it does.

[Page 114.] This riddle resembles the fanciful prophecies. It signifies generally baptism (the 'sign of the Saturday,' i.e. Holy Saturday before Easter Sunday on which day, traditionally, people were baptized into the Christian Church); repentance ('the wit of the Wednesday of the next week after,' i.e. the teaching of the epistle of the Wednesday after Easter); with Easter signified, as before, by 'The fullness of the moon.'

[Page 116.] The two heads are those of St Peter and St Paul on the seal (which in fact is the 'bull' itself) of a papal edict.

[Page 117.] *Stratford.* That is, the Stratford by London (Chaucer's Stratford-atte-Bowe) where lived many of the bakers who supplied London with bread.

[Page 117.] *Pope-holy.* 'Pious' as we tend to use that word to-day: superficially and perhaps hypocritically devout.

[Page 119.] Dame Emma of Shoreditch was presumably a well-known dabbler in the magic arts.

[Page 131.] *The pass of Alton.* At the time that part of Hampshire was heavily afforested, and this was a favourite spot for highway robbers and associated with them rather as Hampstead Heath was with highwaymen in the eighteenth century. The pass—passage or roadway—would be much used by travellers to and from Winchester, which was then an important city.

[Page 134.] This passage gives an account of the qualities or attributes of the soul (*Anima*) according to Catholic theology.

[Page 136.] *Johannes Chrysostomus.* John the 'Golden-mouthed.' The great saint and renowned preacher of the Eastern Church. He lived from about 344 to 407.

[Page 136.] *A set of beads.* Beads was common usage for what we now call the rosary; a 'set of beads' is a more extended way of saying it. 'Bidding one's beads' is saying the rosary.

[Page 136.] *Sir John and Sir Geoffrey.* The title 'sir' was used as one of respect, and often given, as here, to priests.

[Page 137.] *Long Will.* One of the small pieces of biographical information that can be gleaned from the text of the poem.

[Page 138.] That is, a box in which the charitable could put alms for the benefit of these anchorites, who were hermits in the sense of living alone in some sort of cell, but who had not retired to any 'wilderness' but on the contrary had their dwellings often in very public places.

[Page 139.] *Edmund and Edward.* St Edmund, King of East Anglia before the unification of the Anglo-Saxon states in England; martyred in 870. St Edward is the great king, Edward the Confessor, 1004–1066; he was patron of England before he was superseded by the chivalric but not entirely historical figure of St George.

[Page 140.] *Anthony, Giles.* St Anthony was one of the first hermits who lived in Egypt from, remarkably, 251 until 356. St Giles we would more accurately call a monk; he lived in Provence in the seventh and early eighth centuries, and was an extremely popular saint in the Middle Ages.

[Page 140.] *Paul, primus heremita.* Like St Anthony a hermit of Egypt, and celebrated as the first of them. Also like St Anthony the traditional dates of his life (230–342) suggests that the eremitical life was a peculiarly healthy one. The Paul mentioned almost immediately afterwards is of course the apostle.

[Page 141.] Langland refers here, as elsewhere, to the practice of leaving money for prayers to be said and Masses offered for the soul of the dead person. This, in view of the Catholic doctrine that the souls of the dead who have not gone straight to heaven can be helped in their state of expiation by the prayers of those still on earth, is reasonable. But in the Middle Ages the financial aspect of it, at least, had reached unreasonable proportions.

[Page 143.] *Quodlibet.* The method of thought, reasoning, and argument used by medieval philosophers and theologians, known as 'scholastic' and associated above all with St Thomas Aquinas, derived to a great extent from Aristotle. It was based on close reasoning, and question and answer. *Quodlibet* refers to a general question from anyone, which a master or doctor of divinity should be prepared to answer.

[Page 143.] *Offices and hours.* That is, the official daily prayer of the church, made up of psalms, prayers, lessons, and hymns; called 'hours' because appointed to be said or sung at set hours of the day.

[Page 143.] This account of Mahomet is Langland's version of a popular contemporary, and of course unfounded, story.

[Page 146.] This does not mean that these bishops actually had sees in these districts, although Langland is suggesting that if they were true Christians they should at least be preaching to the heathen there. These were a form of courtesy title given to certain prelates.

[Page 147.] *Templars.* A famous ecclesiastico-military order of a peculiarly medieval type which arose during the crusades. It became wealthy, although it cannot be said that its finances were mismanaged, and aroused the enmity especially of the powerful. After a great deal of intrigue and confusion it was suppressed by Pope Clement V in 1312.

[Page 147.] *Metropolitanus.* We would say 'archbishop,' here as it were archbishop of the whole world.

[Page 148.] *Saint Thomas.* St Thomas of Canterbury martyred in 1170 as an outcome of his struggle with King Henry II. His shrine in Canterbury Cathedral was one of the most popular in the Middle Ages. Already to Langland, as to many since, he is the symbol of the rights and well-being of the Church in face of the encroachment of the State.

[Page 167.] *Linen-less.* Langland has 'wolleward,' i.e. with wool next to the skin; he means without underlinen, so that his upper garment touched his skin.

[Page 167.] *Ramis palmarum.* Palm Sunday. *Ramis palmarum* and *gloria laus* are references to the entry of Christ into Jerusalem as described in St John's gospel, and also to the antiphons and hymn sung at the procession of palms before Mass on Palm Sunday.

[Page 172.] *Beau-père.* This name was sometimes given to a friar who was an authorized confessor. Here it probably signifies authority and benevolence.

[Page 176.] It may be wondered how such a thing was possible. The lines could be ironical; but more probably it is a reference to the custom of reprieving a criminal upon whom the penalty had been improperly carried out, especially if the king were near by and could be appealed to.

[Page 178.] A reference not simply to any performance of humble thanksgiving, but more specifically to the ceremony of creeping to the cross performed normally on Good Friday, in which worshippers process to a cross often genuflecting as they go, and kiss the foot of the cross.

[Page 180.] That of course is *not* the meaning of Christ—the meaning is 'anointed.' But Langland was not the only one, nor the first, to give it the signification of conqueror or king.

[Page 183.] *St Thomas of India.* There was a venerable tradition that the apostle Thomas preached the gospel in India.

[Page 185.] *Folville's laws.* This probably means something like 'lynch laws,' i.e. a form of popular justice which is not necessarily evil, and indeed serves a useful purpose in a community where the king's writ does not always run.

[Page 193.] Langland's words are a rather beautiful paraphrase and elaboration of something our Lord did say, but not of course on the cross.